Rural China Takes Off

D0194513

Rural China Takes Off

Institutional Foundations of Economic Reform

Jean C. Oi

UNIVERSITY OF CALIFORNIA PRESS
Berkeley · Los Angeles · London

University of California Press
Berkeley and Los Angeles, California

University of California Press, Ltd.
London, England

Library of Congress Cataloging-in-Publication Data

Oi, Jean Chun
    Rural China takes off: instutional foundations of
economic reform / Jean C. Oi.
        p.   cm.
    Includes bibliographic references and index.
    ISBN 0-520-20006-3 (alk. paper)
    1. Rural industries—China.   2. Rural
    development—China.   3. Entrepreneurship—
    China.   4. Local government—China.
    5. China—Economic conditions.   6. China—Politics
    and government—1976 -.   7. China—Rural
    conditions.   I. Title.
HC427.92.035   1999
330.951'058—dc21   98-26762
                                            CIP

Printed in the United States of America
9   8   7   6   5   4   3   2   1

The paper used in this publication meets the minimum
requirements of American National Standards for
Information Sciences—Permanence of Paper for
Printed Library Materials, ANSI Z39.48-1984.

Chapters 3 and 4 contain material previously
published in the following publications and revised
for this book:

"The Role of the Local State in China's Transitional
Economy," *China Quarterly*, December 1995,
no. 144, pp. 1132–1149.

"Fiscal Reform and the Economic Foundations of
Local State Corporatism in China," *World Politics*,
October 1992, vol. 45, no. 1, pp. 99–126.

"Cadre Networks, Information Diffusion, and
Market Production in Coastal China," World Bank,
Private Sector Development Department, Occasional
Paper No. 20, December 1995.

To Andrew

Contents

List of Illustrations and Tables xi

Acknowledgments xiii

Note on Measures and Transliteration xvii

1. Institutional Foundations of Chinese
   Economic Growth: An Introduction 1
   State and Development 3
   A Problem of Agency 6
   Property Rights and Economic Growth 10
   Local State Corporatism 11
   Institutional Reform, Incentives, and Change 14
   Précis of the Study 15
2. Reassigning Property Rights over Revenue:
   Incentives for Rural Industrialization 17
   Dividing Property Rights 18
   Decollectivization and the Loss of Income 19
   Fiscal Reform and Rights to the Residual 27
   Credible Commitment 47
   From Limited Indirect Extractions to Direct Taxation 52
   Fiscal Incentives for Local Development 56

3. Strategies of Development: Variation and Evolution
   in Rural Industry   58

   Intervening Incentives   59
   The Character of Rural Industrial Growth in the 1980s   61
   The Logic of Collectively Owned Enterprise Development   65
   Management and Ownership in the 1990s   80
   Changing Ownership Forms in Rural Industry   93

4. Local State Corporatism: The Organization
   of Rapid Economic Growth   95

   Maoist Legacy as the Foundation   95
   The Local Corporate State   99
   Adapting Maoist Institutions to Market Production   115
   Adapting Local State Corporatism to Private Enterprise   128
   The Evolution of Local State-Led Development   137

5. Principals and Agents: Central Regulation
   or Local Control   139

   Overlapping Lines of Authority   141
   The Corporate Nature of Local Regulation   152
   Local Appropriation of Central Controls   159

6. From Agents to Principals: Increasing
   Resource Endowments and Local Control   161

   Regulation of Extrabudgetary Funds   162
   Economic Retrenchment and a Test of Central Control   166
   The Erosion of Credit Controls   172
   Local Corporate Interests and Collusion   178
   Nonbank Sources of Capital   182
   The Limits of Central Control in a Changing
      Economic Context   189

7. The Political Basis for Economic Reform:
   Concluding Reflections   191

   The Security of Property Rights and Economic Growth   193
   The Political Consequences of Economic Reform   196
   Local State Corporatism and Central Control
      in a Transitional System   198
   Remaining Questions   199

Appendix A. Research and Documentation   205
  The Interview Sample   206
  The Interview Procedure   207
  Limitations   209

Appendix B. Changes in China's Fiscal System   211

Bibliography   219

Index   237

Illustrations and Tables

ILLUSTRATIONS

1. Agricultural investment as percentage of total investment,
   1952–1991   22
2. Central and local extrabudgetary revenues, 1982–1994   40
3. Tax revenue from agriculture and industry, 1952–1994   41
4. Extrabudgetary funds by source, 1981–1990   44
5. Rural enterprises by ownership type, 1978–1990   63
6. Average number of employees in rural enterprises
   by ownership type, 1978–1990   64
7. Rural enterprise output by ownership type, 1978–1990   65
8. Average peasant savings, 1979–1994   68

TABLES

1. Central-local revenue-sharing contracts in selected provinces
   and municipalities, 1992   32
2. Major within-budget taxes and extrabudgetary revenues,
   pre-1994   39
3. Changes in rural enterprises, 1985–1995   82
4. Three levels of the local corporate state   100
5. Economic duties of the local corporate state   105
6. Resources at the three levels of the local corporate state   110
7. Sources of funding for a North China county's
   finance bureau loans, 1984–1990   185

 8. A North China county's tax bureau loans, 1988–1991   185
 9. Interview locations, dates, and numbers   206
10. Revenue-sharing system, 1980   211
11. Revenue-sharing system, 1985   212
12. Evolution of China's financial management system,
    1949–1994   213
13. Division of tax categories, 1994   217

Acknowledgments

Many people and institutions deserve thanks for their help during the researching and writing of this book, but I can name only a few in this short acknowledgment. First, warm thanks go to my former colleagues at Harvard University, especially those at the Fairbank Center, where this book was begun, ideas tried out, and the initial draft completed. They provided not only perceptive comments but also a friendship and community that will always be treasured. Very special thanks go to Roderick MacFarquhar for his support and wise words over the years. The title "Rural China Takes Off" was his suggestion.

Many others have provided insightful comments and posed challenging questions. Joseph Fewsmith, Stanley Lubman, Michel Oksenberg, Gregory Ruf, Dorothy Solinger, and David Zweig provided detailed comments on earlier drafts of the manuscript. Thomas Bernstein and Jonathan Unger, reviewers of the original book manuscript for the University of California Press, provoked considerable rethinking and revision with their astute comments—although I doubt that they anticipated the changes those comments instigated. Steve Goldstein deserves credit for consuming hours with great discussions on the role of the state and development and for providing valuable bibliographic sources on transitional systems while he was on leave at the Fairbank Center. Kenneth Lieberthal's questions prompted me to rethink my arguments about the security of property rights of local governments over revenues. I also want to thank Lu Mai for insights into China's reform process and for help in preparing the table of changes in the fiscal system found in Appendix B of this book. Guo Xiaolin provided crucial information on the 1994 reforms. Thanks also go to Barrington Moore for comments on an early chapter of the manuscript and for insights into how to integrate the enjoyment of nature with the work of writing.

A number of institutions have provided assistance, among them the Hoover Institution at Stanford University. I thank Ramon Myers and the National Fellows program for a wonderful year. It was there that I first worked out the ideas that eventually became the basis of *local state corporatism* and became familiar with the work of Douglass North and others who are now my colleagues at Stanford: Barry Weingast, Terry Moe, and James March. That year also introduced me to Scott Rozelle, who helped convince me of the usefulness of the principal-agent model for understanding China. Thanks also to the Hong Kong University of Science and Technology and the efficient staff in the Division of Social Science. There I incorporated material on the many changes that took place in China's rural economy after I finished my initial draft of the manuscript. Henry Chan, Tony Chung, and Choi Shu Keung provided superb technical assistance with computers, statistical work, and graphics. Jean Xiong, the vice director of the Universities Service Centre and one of the world's most efficient and *youbanfa* researchers, brought crucial sources to my attention. Thanks also to a number of students at Harvard who worked cheerfully and efficiently for extended periods as research assistants during various stages of the project, among them Laura Dodge, Mark Henderson, David Lane, Dong Qiu, Daniel Silver, Wang Jiwei, and David Youd.

Those who have provided me with the most essential material for this book must remain anonymous: the organizations and individuals I interviewed in China. Details of the interviews are provided in Appendix A. To them goes sincere appreciation for sharing with me their strategies and problems as well as their successes. Special thanks are due to those who invited me into their homes and treated me to their warm hospitality. I also wish to thank the Chinese Academy of Social Sciences, the Liaoning Academy of Social Sciences, the Shandong Academy of Social Sciences, the Sichuan Academy of Social Sciences, and the Tianjin Academy of Social Sciences, as well as various central, provincial, and local governmental agencies for assistance in arranging my interviews.

I have been fortunate to receive funding from various organizations. The bulk of my funding was provided by the Committee on Scholarly Communication with China, with supplementary funds from Harvard

University. I thank Ashoka Mody and the World Bank for funding and China's State Council Development Research Center for assistance that allowed me to conduct research in coastal areas of China in 1994.

I would also like to recognize Sheila Levine, Laura Driussi, and Cindy Fulton and their staff at the University of California Press. They have been patient and accommodating in the production of this book. Photographer Jeffrey Aaronson provided me with the picture for the cover.

Tremendous thanks are also due to Nancy Hearst of Harvard's Fairbank Center Library. Not only did she provide a continuous supply of valuable sources, but she also cheerfully saw this book through from its rough early drafts and provided her usual incredible meticulous attention to the smallest details in proofing the final manuscript.

Finally, I owe an immeasureable amount of thanks to Andrew Walder, who I am happy to say is still my harshest critic and greatest supporter. Aside from his intellectual contributions, he played mother as well as father to our son when I went off on what must have seemed like endless weeks and months of fieldwork in China. Maybe worse, he then had to live through the many drafts of this manuscript. It is to him that I dedicate this book.

Note on Measures and Transliteration

1 mu = ¹/₁₅ hectare = ¹/₆ acre
1 yuan − approximately U.S. $0.12–$0.66*

All transliteration of Chinese terms is in the *pinyin* system of romanization of Mandarin (*putonghua*).

*The value of the yuan shifted from 1978 to 1998. The highest value was $0.66 in 1979. The lowest value was less than $0.12 in 1994.

CHAPTER I

Institutional Foundations of Chinese Economic Growth

An Introduction

At the core of China's "economic miracle" is a massive upsurge of rural industrialization. The decade of the 1980s saw the economy take off in vast areas of the Chinese countryside. By 1987 rural industry surpassed agriculture as the dominant source of total rural income.[1] Total output generated by rural enterprises rose almost ninefold from 1980 to 1987,[2] as output of rural enterprises grew more than 26 percent annually from 1978 to 1990.[3] These industries have yielded close to one-quarter of China's total exports.[4] Between 1978 and 1990, the percentage of the rural labor force engaged in village and township enterprises more than doubled,[5] and the 57 million new jobs created from 1978 to 1986 alone

---

1. *Zhongguo tongji nianjian, 1988,* p. 214.

2. In absolute amounts, gross value of output from rural industry rose from 49 billion yuan in 1980 to 474 billion yuan in 1987. In 1988 total output value rose another 36 percent, constituting well over 50 percent of total rural output and almost one-quarter of total national output. Frederick Crook, "Current Problems," p. 12. *Zhongguo xiangzhen qiye nianjian, 1978–1987,* p. 569, provides a useful statistical summary of the changes in collectively owned rural enterprises from 1978 to 1987.

3. Zhang Hongyu, "China's Land System Transformation and Adjustment of Agricultural Structure—Reviewing China's Rural Reform and Development Since 1978," *Liaowang Zhoukan* (overseas ed.), 25 November 1991, no. 47, pp. 16–17, translated in *FBIS-CHI-91-241,* 16 December 1991, pp. 52–54.

4. David Zweig, "Export-Led Growth," pp. 21–22; see also "Broad and Profound Impact of the Development of China's Township Enterprises," *Jingji daobao,* 20 October 1987, pp. 34–35, translated in *JPRS-CAR-87-061,* 31 December 1987, pp. 23–25.

5. It rose from 9.5 percent to 23.83 percent. Research Office of the State Council, "Town and Township Enterprises as a Motive Force in the Development of the National

equaled the total number of workers hired in all state-owned enterprises between 1952 and 1986.[6]

Such dramatic growth in any political system would be significant. What makes China's experience analytically noteworthy is that growth occurred without significant political change. While the late 1980s and early 1990s saw all communist governments fall from power in the Soviet Union and Eastern Europe, in China the Communist Party was in the midst of instituting economic reforms that have resulted in rapid and sustained growth. In contrast to its Leninist cousins, China refused to take bitter medicine to transform its economic system quickly with what has come to be known as the "big bang" approach.[7] Most notably, it firmly refused to privatize.[8] The private sector today is booming, but this is a product of the 1990s. China in the 1980s maintained state and collective ownership of enterprises and refused to free prices completely or abolish rationing. But it also reintroduced the market and embarked on reforms around the edges of the old system. Central planning was jettisoned only gradually, with some remnants still evident even today.

Most unexpected was the role that local communist officials played in the rural industrialization process. The rapid takeoff of China's rural industry was the result primarily of local government entrepreneurship. What lies behind this response of local cadres to reform initiatives? That is the central question posed by this book. This study seeks to illuminate how China's institutional changes—specifically, altering fiscal flows and property rights—prompted local officials in a socialist system to pursue

---

Economy," *Jingji yanjiu*, 20 May 1990, no. 5, pp. 39–46, translated in *JPRS-CAR-90-066*, 29 August 1990, pp. 34–42.

6. Huang Qingde, Wang Chengde, and He Daofeng, "The Relationship Between Agriculture and Industry in China's Economic Development: Economic Growth and Structural Change," *Shijie jingji daobao*, 11 January 1988, p. 7, translated in *JPRS-CAR-88-011*, 8 March 1988, pp. 26–29. The World Bank has estimated that between 1980 and 1986, nonagricultural rural employment grew 14 percent per year; during this period, the nonagricultural labor force increased by 124 percent, or over 30 million people. The World Bank figure, however, includes only laborers in nonagricultural material-producing sectors (i.e., industry, construction, transportation, and commerce) and excludes the service sector. William Byrd and Qingsong Lin, "China's Rural Industry: An Introduction," p. 18.

7. This is most closely associated with Western economists such as Jeffrey Sachs. See, for example, his *Poland's Jump to the Market Economy*.

8. Privatization of large state-owned firms was a topic of intense debate up to the time of China's decision to begin the process in 1997. See, for example, "Maoist Document Criticizes Reforms," *South China Morning Post*, 18 July 1997, p. 10; and "Jiang's State Sector Reform Strategy Revealed," *South China Morning Post*, 29 July 1997, p. 9.

rapid industrial growth. The book also seeks to understand the political consequences of such growth.

STATE AND DEVELOPMENT

To suggest that government intervention leads to successful economic development is nothing new. The many studies of state-led development in Japan and the East Asian newly industrializing countries (NICs) have highlighted the importance of government policies and institutions.[9] What is new is to cast *local* government in the lead role of the development process. Even more surprising is that these governments are communist. Such systems have generally been assumed to be incapable of reform.[10]

At the beginning of China's reform era, believers in a rapid market transition assumed that local cadres would simply fade from the scene or become "regulators" in an economy of household entrepreneurs, as the distribution of power shifted to producers.[11] Those who focused on how reform would rob communist officials of their power, which was rooted in the Leninist system of central planning and control,[12] argued that local cadres would resent and resist the reforms.[13]

Those who hold to the accepted wisdom about communist systems would probably think China's economy is booming because local officials are merely taking advantage of opportunities to line their own pockets. This is consistent with numerous stories of cadre corruption.[14] While one cannot discount such explanations, the spectacular and sustained

9. Among the earliest and best known is Chalmers Johnson, *MITI and the Japanese Miracle.* Johnson's more recent views on the Asian capitalist model and the role of the state in the economy are summarized in his "Capitalism: East Asian Style." Other works include Daniel Okimoto, *Between MITI and the Market;* Robert Wade, *Governing the Market;* and Kent Calder, *Strategic Capitalism.*

10. János Kornai, *Road to a Free Economy;* Jan Winiecki, "Soviet-Type Economies"; and Merton Peck and Thomas Richardson, eds., *What Is to Be Done?*

11. Victor Nee, "Theory of Market Transition."

12. Barrett McCormick, *Political Reform in Post-Mao China.*

13. See, for example, Helen Siu, *Agents and Victims in South China;* Richard Latham, "Implications of Rural Reform"; and David Zweig, "Opposition to Change."

14. Among the numerous reports of cadre corruption and profiteering, see "Party Members, Cadres Resign to Enter Private Business," *Chiu-shih nien-tai,* 1 January 1993, translated in *FBIS-CHI-93-017,* 9 March 1993, p. 1; "Vice Minister Called 'Culprit' in Bribery Case," *Ming pao,* 19 June 1993, translated in *FBIS-CHI-93-117,* 21 June 1993, p. 24; "Officials Arrest Cadres for Illegal Fund Raising," *Wen wei po,* 17 June 1993, translated in *FBIS-CHI-93-115,* 17 June 1993, p. 11; and "Anhui Village Cadres Arrested for

growth of China's economy suggests that corruption alone is an insufficient explanation.

Believers in the market might argue that a better place to look for an explanation of China's rural industrial success (and the NICs' success in general) is the rapid growth in inputs into the system, such as the huge amount of surplus labor available in China.[15] Some have suggested that China's rural industry would be just where it is today, even without state intervention, simply as a result of market forces.[16] Inputs and market demand must be taken into account, but neither explanation addresses the timing of the take-off or the dominance of publicly owned township and village enterprises over private ones.

Others who have explicitly rejected what they see as the "statist" view of China have gone to the other extreme, attributing the success of China's rural reforms wholly to "society." Some of these observers have attributed the changes to the "unorganized power of the peasants";[17] others refer to a "societal takeover."[18] While such conclusions are fashionable in the wake of the demise of communism, they fail to answer the crucial question of where peasants obtained capital and resources to fuel China's economic takeoff when personal savings were meager and the market in its infant stage of development.

Given the failures and problems associated with state intervention not only in Leninist systems but more recently in the East Asian NICs, it is not surprising that some would resist the notion of a successful state-led development effort in post-Mao China. But not all state intervention is the same. Market economies also have some form of state intervention.[19]

The experiences of Eastern Europe and Russia suggest that the lack of institutional support forced many new private firms to sink before they learned to swim. As Evans has pointed out, "The appropriate question is not 'how much' but 'what kind' [of state intervention]."[20]

A different explanation might posit that China properly laid the foundation for reform by first ridding the bureaucracy of possible opposition

Abuses," *Zhongguo qingnian bao*, 22 April 1993, translated in *FBIS-CHI-93–081*, 29 April 1993, p. 9.

15. Paul Krugman, "Myth of Asia's Miracle."

16. Edward Steinfeld, *Forging Reform*.

17. Kate Xiao Zhou, *How the Farmers Changed China*.

18. Minxin Pei, *From Reform to Revolution*. Pei's "takeover coalition" includes local officials as well as peasants.

19. For two insightful essays on this issue, see Paul Streeten, "Markets and States," and Kiren Aziz Chaudhry, "Myth of the Market."

20. Peter Evans, *Embedded Autonomy*, p. 10.

and installing a new breed of farsighted, well-educated officials eager to serve the interests of reform. The reason China's local officials have responded more positively to reform is that they are not the same communist officials of the past. Such a hypothesis, while useful, can take us only so far. China's reformers did try to eliminate the deadwood in its bureaucracy to improve and revitalize its cadre force, but their success was limited and appears to have been most evident at the higher levels of government.[21] Many of the local officials who are now leading rapid economic development are the same people who presided over a minimally functioning economy during the Maoist period.

Alternatively, one might also argue that because China is a communist system, its local officials have what Murrell and Olson call an "encompassing interest" that is much stronger than that held by officials in democratic regimes to make their economy grow rapidly. In such situations, the person with dictatorial power has "a property right in his society. . . . Just as the owner of a firm has an incentive to make the firm as valuable and productive as possible."[22] Murrell and Olson have dictatorial leaders such as Stalin in mind, but they state that "any leader with complete control over a society has an encompassing" interest in the productivity of that society. To the degree that such arguments are valid, they would apply primarily to the *lowest* level of the political system (i.e., the villages) where one-person rule is common. Some village leaders do seem sincerely to believe in the superiority of collective ownership.[23] But villages alone are not responsible for the rapid growth of industry. The theory does not explain the behavior of the supporting cast—the bureaucracy at different levels of local government above the village—in the growth process.

One other explanation is that China is still a mobilization system. Rather than taking local initiative, officials are being forced by administrative fiat to pursue growth to meet central-level targets. The success of the one-child policy certainly suggests that mobilization has not disappeared from the political scene.[24] Such an explanation, while plausible, could never sufficiently explain the degree of enthusiasm with which

21. See the work on bureaucratic reform by Hong Yung Lee, *Revolutionary Cadres to Party Technocrats;* and Tyrene White, "Political Reform and Rural Government."

22. Peter Murrell and Mancur Olson, "Devolution of Centrally Planned Economies," p. 253.

23. Zweig found this to be the case early in the reform period. See his "Opposition to Change." In my interviews I found cadres with similar beliefs, even at much later stages of the reform process.

24. Tyrene White, "Postrevolutionary Mobilization in China."

local governments have spearheaded growth. We know that local cadres during the Maoist period only minimally complied with central directives. An explanation needs to be given for why communist officials at the local levels departed dramatically from their previous patterns of behavior.[25]

A PROBLEM OF AGENCY

There is no need to make assumptions about the nature of communist officials—either that they are corrupt or that they are motivated by lofty ideals that lead them to want to enrich their communities. Compliance with central directives in a communist system cannot be assumed. Whether officials comply is an agency problem like that in any bureaucratic hierarchy.[26]

For China the issue was not whether its bureaucracy was capable of generating economic growth but whether it had the incentive to do so. During the Maoist period, the constraints of the state plan and fiscal system provided localities with little inducement to generate additional revenues. Localities were required to turn over all or most of their revenues to the upper levels, which in return provided budget allocations for expenditures. The use of whatever surplus that remained within the locality was subject to higher-level approval. Rather than initiate growth, localities had incentives to try to extract as much bureaucratic slack as possible from the upper levels in the form of larger budget allocations.

China's bureaucrats could be mobilized to action, but Maoist ideology distorted incentives. Words and actions became manifestations of political attitude—what is termed *biaoxian*. Expression of such attitudes became intertwined with economic performance and was measured by ability to meet and exceed economic quotas.[27] Pressure to exaggerate economic performance contributed to the massive famine during the Great Leap Forward as rural cadres exaggerated production and sought to outdo each other in the sale of grain to the state, even when their own village populations had little or no grain for their own use.[28]

---

25. There is the problem of inflation of statistics, but even if that is taken into consideration, the growth is still significant.

26. See Terry Moe, "New Economics of Organization," on the usefulness of agency theory for understanding bureaucratic control.

27. Examples of this in rural and urban areas can be found respectively in Oi, *State and Peasant in Contemporary China* and Walder, *Communist Neo-Traditionalism*.

28. Bernstein, "Stalinism, Famine, and Chinese Peasants." On the famine itself, see Banister, *China's Changing Population*.

It was not the Maoist state's inability to foster economic development but the ideology and the goals of state intervention that undermined its effectiveness. Chalmers Johnson calls communist systems "plan ideological" and the capitalism of developmental states such as Japan "plan rational." [29] He notes that using similar policy instruments, the latter fosters market competition whereas the former, guided by a socialist ideology, replaces the market and fosters an egalitarian distribution of resources and income. [30] China had an "industrial policy," but its all-inclusive rather than selective scope hindered rather than promoted economic efficiency. Unlike a "plan rational" economy like Japan's, wherein state intervention is limited by a commitment to private property and the market, the Maoist state closed free markets in 1957 and created a state monopoly for the procurement and sale of most goods and services. Factories were told which products to make and in what quantities, given the materials for production, at what price to sell their finished products, and to whom the products were to be sold.

Like East Asian NICs, China had the power to "get the prices wrong," but the purpose of price setting was to ensure inflation control and an equal distribution of goods and resources within a socialist ideological context, not to provide manufacturers a comparative advantage in a competitive world market. Production hinged not on costs or on sales but on the state agencies' plan. The plan determined demand and limited consumer choice.

This book examines what happened when China's local officials were presented with a new set of incentives in the reform period. It begins with the simple premise that local officials in a communist system, like officials in any political system, are rational actors who respond to incentives and existing constraints within the limits of their cognitive ability to evaluate alternatives and process information. [31] Their response to reform can be determined only by looking at the concrete circumstances that affect their behavior as *agents:* incentives, constraints, skills, and resources available to those who are responsible for implementing reform and the effectiveness of monitoring by the central state as the principal. It cannot be predicted on the basis of past performance or ideological orientation.

29. Chalmers Johnson, *MITI and the Japanese Miracle.*
30. Applebaum and Henderson, in "Situating the State in the East Asian Development Process," try to refine Chalmers Johnson's distinction between plan rational and plan ideological by further dividing systems into "market ideological" and "market rational." China remains in the "plan ideological" quadrant.
31. I am here assuming bounded rationality. Herbert Simon, *Administrative Behavior.*

Bureaucratic behavior is a consequence of whether "net incentive effects upon key officials are positive or negative, and to what degree." [32]

This study thus departs from previous work that focused either on the center or on the peasants.[33] It shifts the focus of inquiry from the center to the localities, and from the peasants to those officials charged with the day-to-day implementation of the reforms. To be sure, the reforms would not have succeeded to the extent that they have if China's peasants had not enthusiastically responded to calls to "dare to stand out" and to "get rich first." But one cannot extrapolate from the response of the peasants to decollectivization and growth of the agricultural sector to explain the rise of rural industry. To understand the latter, one must examine the role of local governments.

A local-level approach to the study of reform and development recognizes the role of the central government and its political elite in the formulation of policy—it is the center that establishes the institutions of rule.[34] The successful economic reform process in China began with the formulation of policies at the national levels of government by a fairly small political elite led by Deng Xiaoping.[35] Without the green light from above, or at least from key elements within the central leadership, it is unlikely reform would have occurred.[36] But although enlightened reform initiatives from the center are a prerequisite for institutional change, well-intentioned policies do not ensure successful implementation, as the failures in the Soviet Union and elsewhere suggest.[37] While it is useful to understand how different elites and factions within the central leadership

32. Anthony Downs, *Inside Bureaucracy*, p. 201.
33. An exception is the wide-ranging study of local government and its economy during the reforms by Marc Blecher and Vivienne Shue, *Tethered Deer*.
34. As Robert Bates, *Miracle of the Market*, p. 149, notes for other developing contexts, "whether the interests animating political conflict in agrarian societies results in ideologically motivated clashes or in private struggles among competing particular interests depends at least in part upon the structure of political institutions and the incentives they generate for politicians. The analysis of political change in rural societies thus must explicitly incorporate the study of national political settings."
35. On elite-level politics involved in the formulation of China's reforms, see Joseph Fewsmith, *Dilemmas of Reform in China;* also Susan Shirk, *Political Logic of Economic Reform.*
36. For a contrasting view, see Daniel Kelliher, *Peasant Power,* who argues that once the peasants instituted the household responsibility system, the leaders had no choice but to follow. Zhou, *How the Farmers Changed China,* takes a similar, if more extreme, position.
37. For comparative discussion and examples, see Merilee Grindle, ed., *Politics and Policy Implementation;* and Merilee Grindle and John W. Thomas, *Public Choices and Policy Change.*

jockeyed for power and to be aware of the support that each gave to policies regarding rural industry,[38] that information fails to provide a satisfactory explanation of how these ideas were transformed into rural industrial growth and why that growth took the form that it did in different parts of the countryside. One needs to zoom in on the local levels, to those whose responses in the end determined whether China's policies toward rural industrialization were implemented.

The statist literature rescued the "state" from "society," but it is necessary to heed Lowi's reservations about viewing the "state" as "a unitary, solitary reality that can be brought into theory as some kind of a measurable force."[39] This is doubly important when the state in question is usually categorized as a "strong" state.[40] The assumptions underlying such a label do little to illuminate the process of political and economic transition that is occurring in the former communist countries or in a reforming communist system such as that of China.[41] Local-level officials in China are members of the official bureaucracy and professionals in a "well-bounded" system;[42] they act as part of the administrative apparatus, as part of the "state," but local governments are distinct entities apart from the central state and society, with their own agendas, and increasingly with their own resources.

This study is an institutional analysis of economic development at the local level that views local officials as political and economic actors distinct from the central state.[43] It delves into the process of economic development to examine the changing political and economic contexts in which local officials operate. It asks how institutional incentives affect the adoption of certain development strategies and how local governments calculate and maximize their interests. It explores the mechanisms by which localities have satisfied diverse interests and dealt with their su-

---

38. See, for example, Dali Yang, *Calamity and Reform in China*, chap. 8.

39. See Theodore Lowi, p. 891 in Eric Nordlinger, Theodore Lowi, and Sergio Fabbrini, "Return to the State." See also my *State and Peasant*, chap. 1.

40. Joel S. Migdal, *Strong Societies and Weak States*.

41. For a useful critique of the artificial line drawn in the literature between state and society, see Timothy Mitchell, "Limits of the State."

42. They are not those whom Eric Nordlinger, *Autonomy of the Democratic State*, identifies as coming in and out of the state.

43. In this study, I adopt North's broader definition of institutions as "a set of the rules, compliance procedures, and moral and ethical behavioral norms designed to constrain the behavior of individuals in the interest of maximizing the wealth or utility of principals." This definition focuses attention not only on existing structures but also on policies, such as reform initiatives, adopted at the center and passed on to the local governments for implementation. Douglass North, *Structure and Change*, pp. 201–2.

periors at higher levels of government and with subordinates below. It considers the effect of the resource endowments that local officials have had at their disposal, the constraints they have faced in making their choices, and the changes that have occurred over time.

PROPERTY RIGHTS AND ECONOMIC GROWTH

North and Weingast, among others, point to the importance of secure property rights for economic development.[44] Scholarly discussion has been limited, to a large extent, to market economies, with a focus on law that protects the assets and income flows of companies or individuals — those who own and operate the firms within a market economy — from arbitrary expropriation by government. The importance of this principle underlies the felt need in formerly socialist countries such as Poland and Russia to privatize. There is, however, no inherent reason why only individuals or privately held companies, as distinct from governments, can be entrepreneurs. Similarly, there is no inherent reason why property rights are effective incentives only if they are assigned to non-government entities.

Privatization need not be the sole path to economic growth in reforming communist systems — and, in any event, it has nowhere yielded results approaching those obtained in China. Publicly owned firms may be capable of playing the same role as privately held firms. This study examines the impact of the assignment to local governments of new property rights over surplus revenues beginning in the 1980s. It assumes that growth can occur when property rights are given to such organized entities under a regime that provides sufficient incentives to pursue growth.[45] Furthermore, given that these rights were granted to local governments by the central state pursuant to a policy change and were not guaranteed by law, this study raises the question of how secure these rights have to be. Are predictability and stability of property rights — what is sometimes called *credible commitment*—sufficient? This is most puzzling in light of the dramatic growth of the private sector in the 1990s. All evidence suggests that China still lacks what most in the West would see as "clear and secure" property rights for private business.

44. Douglass C. North and Barry Weingast, "Constitutions and Commitment."
45. For a theoretical statement on this aspect of property rights as an incentive, see Yoram Barzel, *Economic Analysis of Property Rights*.

This study is intended to provide some insight into how to reconcile the lack of such protection and the growth of both collective and private business.

LOCAL STATE CORPORATISM

Property rights and incentives are essential but not sufficient to explain China's rural growth story. There remains the question of how such growth was achieved in a state that was still communist. Accepting the view that communist officials want to maintain their power, one would expect them to spur economic development only to the extent that it does not jeopardize their political positions. This study examines how collectively owned industrial enterprises better served both the political and the economic interests of local cadres during the initial stages of reform. It also examines the more puzzling shift in strategy in the 1990s when local governments turned from their earlier strategy and began promoting the private sector, even selling some of the collectively owned enterprises for private operation. This study details how in China the administrative power of local officials helped to facilitate rather than hinder the rapid economic development, first of the collective and then of the private sector.

My answers to these questions center on the merger of government and economy in the reform period, resulting in an institutional development that I label *local state corporatism*. The term *corporatism* requires some elaboration, because the way I use it differs from the way it has been used in previous studies and because my own use of the term has evolved over time. First, I am not concerned with the role of the central state in the vertical integration of interests within society as a whole. This departs from general uses of the term by such writers as Schmitter,[46] as well as from the recent use of the term by those studying China.[47]

46. Philippe Schmitter defines *corporatism* as "a system of interest representation in which the constituent units are organized into a limited number of singular, compulsory, noncompetitive, hierarchically ordered and functionally differentiated categories, recognized or licensed (if not created) by the state and granted a deliberate representational monopoly within their respective categories in exchange for observing certain controls on their selection of leaders and articulation of demands and supports." "Still the Century of Corporatism?" pp. 93–94. Joseph Fewsmith, *Party, State, and Local Elites*, following Schmitter's definition, uses a similar understanding of corporatism to describe China during the Republican period.

47. Others have recently begun using the term *corporatism* in Schmitter's sense to understand the relationships between different interest groups and the central state. See Anita Chan, "Revolution or Corporatism?"; Mayfair Yang, "Between State and Society"; Peter

The corporatism that I describe is constituted and coordinated by local government—specifically counties, townships, and villages—not central authorities.

The central state set the reform process in motion and provided localities with the incentives and the leeway to develop economically, but local government has been the activist state that has determined the outcome of reform in China. My use of the term *corporatism* follows those who stress that corporatism need not refer to the unit that does the organizing and aggregating, but denotes a form of state-society relations where narrow interests within society are organized and integrated so as to achieve higher-order goals—namely, stability and economic growth for the state and society as a whole.[48] *Local state corporatism* is my attempt to describe a context that exhibits the essence of the category "corporatism" as it has been traditionally used, but contains sufficient differences to warrant a separate category. The modifiers *local* and *state* are meant to specify these differences.[49]

Second, in this book my use of the term *corporatism* is intended to convey both a "corporate" and a "corporatist" meaning. In my earlier formulation, local state corporatism was used primarily to highlight the workings of local government and the economy that it oversees as a corporation.[50] That stemmed from the dominance of the collectively owned enterprises in the 1980s. It was primarily the corporate nature of growth that first led me to adopt the term. I used it to highlight the ability of local government to intervene directly by virtue of its ownership of these firms. Local governments ran their firms as diversified corporations, redistributing profits and risks, and thereby allowing the rapid growth of rural industry with limited resources. Local governments took on many

---

Nan-shong Lee, "Chinese Industrial State"; and Jonathan Unger and Anita Chan, "China, Corporatism." While these studies provide some useful insights, it is questionable whether the central state at this point is corporatist. Local governments are much more able, because of the smaller size of the community, to exercise control and offer effective inducements to create a corporatist relationship. The center may formulate guidelines, but it is the localities that hold the power to decide which groups are actually treated as legitimate and what treatment they will receive.

48. Ruth Berins Collier and David Collier, "Inducements Versus Constraints."

49. This is what David Collier and James E. Mahon would call a second-category specification of the broader term *corporatism*. "Conceptual 'Stretching' Revisited." Giovanni Sartori would probably call this "traveling," but it is not "concept stretching." "Concept Misformation in Comparative Politics."

50. My earlier formulation is contained in "Fiscal Reform and Economic Foundations."

characteristics of business corporations, with officials serving a role equivalent to that of a board of directors.[51]

In the 1990s a new aspect of local state corporatism emerged as local governments moved from simpler and more cadre-centered forms of governance to a mixed model appropriate to a vastly larger industrial economy consisting of both private and collectively owned firms. The degree to which the local corporate state has been able to restrain the private sector from becoming an independent economic class points to the emergence of a corporatist rather than a free market system, at least at the local levels. This feature of the local corporate state has led me to broaden my initial focus to accentuate and incorporate the corporatist meaning of the term *corporatism*. I see the Chinese case as a subcategory of *state* corporatism.

Corporatist groups in Schmitter's definition of state corporatism "were created by and kept as auxiliary and dependent organs of the state which founded its legitimacy and effective functioning on other bases."[52] Collier and Collier highlight the point that in state corporatism, interest associations are "dependent and penetrated."[53] What needs clarification in the Chinese case is the interest associations that are being penetrated and made dependent. Most instances of corporatism have been found in historical situations where the interest groups are fully formed and a central state steps in to control the existing organizations.[54] The corporatist nature of the local state-society relationship in China is obscured because the local state, as part of a functioning Leninist state, has the ability to prevent the formation of independent groups.

The most politically significant group, and the group that historically has contained the seeds of a civil society and has been a precursor to a more democratic system of rule, is the private entrepreneurs.[55] Theories

51. I present a preliminary version of this argument in "Chinese Village, Inc." Others have made similar analogies between local governments and business entities. See, for example, articles in William Byrd and Qingsong Lin, eds., *China's Rural Industry: Structure, Development, and Reform.*
52. Schmitter, "Still the Century of Corporatism?" pp. 102–3.
53. Collier and Collier, "Inducements versus Constraints," p. 978.
54. See, for example, Alfred Stepan, *State and Society*, especially part 1. Stepan uses *corporatism* to refer to "a particular set of policies and institutional arrangements for structuring interest representation. . . . In return for such prerogatives and monopolies the state claims the right to monitor representational groups by a variety of mechanisms so as to discourage the expression of 'narrow' class-based, conflictual demands. Many . . . have used such corporatist policies for structuring interest representation" (p. 46).
55. For a classic statement of the link between an independent economic elite and democracy, see Barrington Moore, Jr., *Social Origins of Dictatorship*.

of market transition predicted that these "producers" would wrest power from local officials.[56] But as of now, this has yet to occur in China's countryside. The present study will investigate the constraints that local government applies to the private sector, but it will also show that inducements are offered to private firms under local state corporatism.[57] The corporatist nature of this relationship offers an explanation of how communist cadres in China can promote the emergence of an economic elite that in other settings would be independent and therefore threatening. It provides clues to interpret the loosening of control in a Leninist system.

INSTITUTIONAL REFORM, INCENTIVES, AND CHANGE

John Zysman argues that "by following the money flows in the market economy and in the institutions that structure that flow we can learn a great deal about the uses to which the society's resources are put, the people who make the allocative decisions, and the process through which control is obtained and exerted."[58] I utilize this approach to study the impact of changes in China's fiscal flows on local governments and on those who serve within them.[59]

Fiscal flows were altered by two institutional changes in the early 1980s. One was decollectivization, the second was fiscal reform. The enthusiasm with which local officials embraced economic development stemmed directly from these two policies. Decollectivization and the return to household production robbed villages and townships of rights to the income from agricultural production. The fiscal reforms hardened budget constraints on local governments while, at the same time, granting local governments rights to and use of surplus revenues generated from development. The conjuncture of fiscal reforms and decollectivization in the early 1980s presented officials at the county, township, and village levels with both the necessity and opportunities for economic growth.

56. This development is explicit in Nee's theory of market transition. "Theory of Market Transition."
57. On corporatism as a combination of constraints and inducements, see Collier and Collier, "Inducements Versus Constraints."
58. John Zysman, *Governments, Markets, and Growth,* pp. 7–8.
59. There are a number of macro-level studies of financial control in transition systems, including Ronald McKinnon, *Order of Economic Liberalism* and *Gradual versus Rapid Liberalization;* and Richard Bird and Christine Wallich, "Local Finance and Economic Reform."

But whether economic growth takes place depends on more than incentives. The particular configuration of resource endowments, political constraints, skills of local leadership, and severity of budget constraints determined the variations in responses to institutional incentives in different localities in China. Consequently, no single pattern adequately describes development during the reform period.

Finally, the successful use of one set of incentives may undermine the effectiveness of another. The incentives offered to the localities to pursue rapid growth have had unintended political consequences in the behavior of local officials as agents of the central state. The last part of the book analyzes the corollaries of rapid rural industrialization, as well as the effects of the buildup of local resources, on the central state's ability to control the development process that it has unleashed so successfully.

PRÉCIS OF THE STUDY

Chapter 2 describes how decollectivization and fiscal reform changed the rules for the disposition of locally generated revenue. It presents the institutional framework that has allowed localities to benefit from the residual revenue generated by economic growth. Interests and incentives created by these new rules are shown to have provided the impetus for the rapid development of rural collective industry. The discussion is limited to the county, township, and village levels—those most directly involved in rural industrialization.

Chapter 3 considers the intervening variables that determined the response of different localities to the institutional reforms and the incentives embedded within them. This chapter sketches the geographical and temporal variations in the development of rural industry. In an attempt to unveil the logic of local development, it considers factors that affected the selection of particular types of strategies. It considers how changes in the political and economic context influenced the evolution of management and ownership forms in rural industry from a predominance of collectively owned enterprises to today's more varied mix of collective, private, and shareholding systems.

Chapter 4 examines the sinews of the local "corporate" state. It details the mechanisms that have allowed local governments to foster rapid rates of growth. It lays out the constraints and inducements local governments use to mobilize and co-opt different types of rural industry—including the private sector—to serve their own interests. It stresses that key strategies and tools used to achieve economic growth are derived from central planning, but it also makes clear that local governments have adapted Maoist institutions for market production.

Chapters 5 and 6 consider the political consequences of local economic growth for central-state control. Chapter 5 analyzes the nature of local regulation. Using agency theory, it considers the degree to which locally based agents serve central and local interests. Chapter 6 considers the effectiveness of the monitoring systems when central policy conflicts with local corporate interests. It takes as a case study the effectiveness of central control over local rural enterprise growth during the retrenchment period of 1988–1989. At the crux of the analysis are the increasing amounts of locally owned funds that are outside the bounds of existing central regulations. Both chapters reveal the weaknesses of central-state control by examining how local governments have been able to circumvent central controls and pursue their own interests. In the concluding chapter, I consider some of the broad implications of local state corporatism for China's political future.

CHAPTER 2

Reassigning Property Rights over Revenue

Incentives for Rural Industrialization

Bureaucratic compliance is a principal-agent problem in China, just as it is in other types of political systems.[1] The challenge for the central state, as the principal, has been to design a compensation system (a contract) that motivates local officials, its agents, to act in the principal's interest.[2] The literature on agency theory says that "under a range of conditions, the principal's optimal incentive structure for the agent is one in which the latter receives some share of the residual in payment for his efforts, thus giving him a direct stake in the outcome."[3] The failure of the Maoist

---

1. The literature on principal-agent theory is extensive in both economics and political science. Moe, "New Economics of Organization," provides a useful review of the earlier economics literature and its relevance for political science. For an overview of the assumptions behind agency theory, see Debra Friedman and Michael Hechter, "Contribution of Rational Choice Theory." Among the earliest works to use agency theory to understand China are Scott Rozelle, "Economic Behavior of Village Leaders" and "Decision-Making in China's Rural Economy." James Tong, "Central-Provincial Fiscal Relations," uses the framework as a backdrop for a statistical study of the effects of different revenue-sharing programs on local fiscal activity by provinces and municipalities. Shirk, *Political Logic of Economic Reform,* employs a variant of the principal-agent model to understand administrative control within the Chinese political system, taking the party as the principal and the government as the agent. Yasheng Huang, *Inflation and Investment Controls,* in one of the more rigorous uses of agency theory, examines the effectiveness of the central personnel and appointment system in controlling investment spending by provincial-level agents of the central state. A preliminary version of my arguments in this section can be found in Oi, "Fiscal Reform, Central Directives."

2. Adapted from Joseph Stiglitz's definition of "principal and agent (ii)" in *The New Palgrave,* p. 966.

3. Moe, "New Economics of Organization," p. 763.

system to sustain high levels of growth illustrates the political and economic consequences when these rights are denied those who generate the residual. Peasants and production team leaders colluded to hide grain from the state and manipulated grain reserves policies to gain a larger share of the harvest.[4] The outcome was an agricultural system that met basic state-set procurement quotas, but little more. Local governments similarly fulfilled state-set revenue quotas, but they lobbied for larger budget allocations rather than generating increased revenues. Scott's observation that "what is important is not what is taken out, but what is left"[5] holds true as much for revenue as it does for grain.

This chapter seeks to explain how the decollectivization of agriculture and the 1980s fiscal reforms reassigned property rights over the residual, and why they provided strong incentives for officials at the county, township, and village levels to undertake rural industrialization eagerly.

DIVIDING PROPERTY RIGHTS

Property rights are in actuality a bundle of rights.[6] The right to sell property—what in the literature is termed the right of alienation—is only one type of property right. In addition, there are rights to manage the property and rights to the income from the property. Within the rights to the income from the property is the right to the residual, that is, the surplus income that remains after expenses have been paid. In Leninist systems such as Maoist China, "ownership" entailed none of these rights.[7]

Land and enterprises were categorized as either *state owned* (*quanmin suoyou*) or *collectively owned* (*jiti suoyou*). The former indicated "ownership by the whole people," while the latter restricted "ownership" to a smaller group known as a collective. In practice, the people, either as a whole or in smaller collectives, had none of the three property rights. The de facto owners were the local governments in the areas where the land or enterprises were located. Down to the level of the county, governments had under their jurisdiction (and therefore "owned") both state and collective enterprises. Below the county, communes and brigades had collectively owned enterprises within their respective jurisdictions. Production teams, subordinate to brigades, were the legal owners of the

---

4. See Oi, *State and Peasant*, chap. 6.
5. James Scott, *Moral Economy of the Peasant.*
6. Demsetz, "Structure of Ownership."
7. One of the best discussions of these rights in socialist systems is János Kornai, *Socialist System*, particularly chap. 5.

agricultural land and the harvest produced on that land, as well as of any team-level enterprises.

But the administrative units that "owned" the property also lacked the full range of rights over it. First, local governments had no right to sell property under their jurisdiction or "ownership." Second, they had only restricted rights to manage their property; central planning dictated the limits of those rights. Third, the rights to the residual rested not with the owner but with the central state. Neither the production team nor the peasant who produced the harvest had rights to decide its disposition, nor did they have rights to the residual.[8] Similarly, local governments lacked the right to keep revenues generated within their locality and the right to decide how this revenue would be used. Provincial and county governments, like state-owned factories, submitted their profits upward and received a budget allocation from the upper levels to cover set operating expenses.

The decollectivization of agricultural production and the 1980s fiscal reforms fundamentally altered the allocation of property rights in China's countryside. The sections that follow will first examine how decollectivization transferred rights to the income from the sale of agricultural production from the village to individual household producers. Later sections will detail how the fiscal reforms gave *new* rights over revenue to local governments down to the township level. While the impact on local coffers was negative in the case of decollectivization and positive in the case of fiscal reform, the reassignment of property rights ultimately provided the incentive for village, township, and county officials to pursue rapid rural industrialization.

DECOLLECTIVIZATION AND THE LOSS OF INCOME

Prior to the early 1980s, when decollectivization was completed in most parts of China, villages were known as brigades, the second of a three-tier administrative hierarchy in the commune system. Brigade income was derived from brigade-level enterprises, from limited funds sent from the commune, and from income submitted by the production teams from the sale of the collective agricultural harvest. The harvest was owned by the production team, the level below the brigade. Revenue belonged to the production team, which paid one portion of its income to

8. I elaborate on this point in *State and Peasant*.

the individual peasants who worked the collective land and sent another portion of its income to the brigade and commune.

Decollectivization and the institution of the household responsibility system changed the unit of accounting from the collective to the individual household. Ownership of the harvest was transferred from the collective to the individual producer. With the agricultural reforms, ownership, for the first time, meant rights not only to the income but also to the residual and its disposition. Peasants were free to do as they pleased with their harvest after they had met the basic obligations to the state. This change, together with the dramatic rise in agricultural procurement prices, improved incentives for grain production and increased peasant incomes in the early 1980s.

But the reassignment of property rights had an adverse effect on village (brigade) government because it eliminated agriculture as the source of village income. Villages that failed to develop alternative sources of revenue were left with little or no funds in their collective coffers. Property rights over the income from agricultural production were reallocated from the collective to the individual household. When the household became the basic production and accounting unit, the relationship between collective and household was reversed: the collective village government became dependent on its members for a share of the harvest. Peasants still paid an agricultural tax and sold a set amount of grain to the state, but their payments were made at township stations and were remitted to the upper levels, not to the village government.

Unlike the townships and the counties, villages were not considered an official level of government, nor were they considered a fiscal accounting unit. They did not participate in any kind of revenue sharing with the upper levels, nor did they receive a budget allocation from those levels. Their officials were considered local, not state, cadres and were therefore paid from village funds. The villages paid taxes, but they had no rights to any tax revenues. Decollectivization thus created a critical fiscal situation for them.

Villages with a primarily agricultural economy had few sources of revenue. They could collect rent from collectively owned property, but this excluded most crop land up until the 1990s.[9] Only orchards, fishponds, forest land, and village-owned enterprises were subject to contracting fees that yielded revenue.

9. In the early 1990s some villages began to auction off fields to those willing to pay the highest rent. See James Kung, "Property Rights in Chinese Agriculture."

The primary source of revenue for many village coffers was ad hoc surcharges, known as *tiliu* (retained funds), levied by the village on its members.[10] The *tiliu* was levied on a per capita basis and was usually taken as a percentage of income.[11] The *tiliu* extractions officially were not supposed to exceed 5 percent of a peasant household's income, but in practice they often did. For example, in one area where levies should have totaled about 12–13 yuan per person, they actually amounted to 30 yuan.[12]

Peasants, particularly those in poor areas, were understandably resentful of these local extractions. The degree of their discontent became evident in the 1990s when peasants in some localities staged protests against "increases in the peasants' burden."[13] The taxes that local officials in poor areas in Guizhou levied for the construction of roads and for irrigation were necessary, but from the perspective of the already poor peasants any increase in taxes and fees was much more of a burden than it was in richer areas where the cushion was much greater.[14]

The fiscal crisis faced by villages was heightened by the center's decision to shift the burden of infrastructural investment to the localities. Figure 1 shows that central-level agricultural investment dropped from over 9 percent of total central investment in 1980 to only 3 percent in 1988, in spite of the center's verbal support and emphasis on grain production.[15] The center expected localities to support agriculture with profits from rural industry, under the "using industry to subsidize agriculture" (*yigong bunong*) policy.[16] But only some had the resources to do so.

Industrially developed villages have plowed substantial investments into agriculture, even if the rates are lower than they were during the Maoist period. For example, in highly industrialized Wuxi, 1.1 billion

10. The *tiliu* consists of about ten items, including funds for education, roads, "five guaranteed households" (those who have no one else to provide for them), health, and so on. The amounts are set by the county for each item. These funds are considered extrabudgetary. China Interviews (hereafter cited as CI) 8791.

11. There seems to be substantial variation in how the *tiliu* was calculated.

12. Special funds (*zhuanxiang jizi*), which are not included in the *tiliu* limit, are also often collected. Although technically these are not *tiliu*, peasants still refer to them that way. The villages do not have to report this revenue to the upper levels; however, the finance bureau has tried to be stricter about regulating these funds by requiring biannual accounting. CI 8791.

13. Examples are noted in Sheryl WuDunn, "China Is Sowing Discontent with 'Taxes' on the Peasants," *New York Times,* 19 May 1993, pp. A1, A6; and Anthony Blass, Carl Goldstein, and Lincoln Kaye, "Get off Our Backs." For analysis of peasant protests, see Kevin O'Brien and Lianjiang Li, "Villagers and Popular Resistance."

14. Examples of the hardships caused are vividly described in Sheryl WuDunn, "As China Leaps Ahead, the Poor Slip Behind," *New York Times,* 23 May 1993, p. E3.

15. *Zhongguo nongye nianjian, 1989,* p. 9.

16. "Yindao nongcun," pp. 20–25.

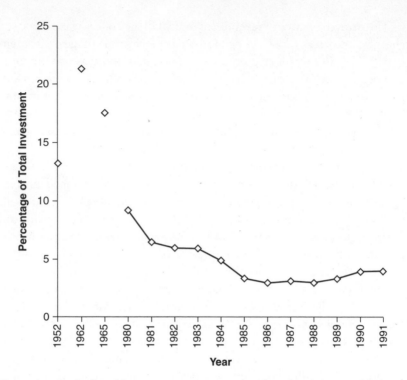

Figure 1.   Agricultural investment as percentage of total investment, 1952–1991 (Source: *Zhongguo xiangzhen qiye nianjian, 1992,* p. 158)

yuan of profits were taken from rural industry to support farming between 1979 and 1986. This amount was four times that of central state investment.[17]

For the nation as a whole, however, the percentage of profits designated at the local levels to support agriculture has decreased.[18] In spite of a growing collective economy, collective investment of capital in agriculture as a percentage of total collective investment in fixed assets declined from close to 40 percent in 1982 to less than 10 percent in 1988.[19] Contrary to the mandates of state policy, the decline was particularly sharp in the use of rural enterprise funds. There was more than a 70 percent decline in the amount used for agriculture between 1979 and 1988.

17. "Rural Industry Provides Base for Economic Growth," *China Daily,* 5 August 1987, p. 1, in *JPRS-CAR-87–045,* 9 September 1987, p. 42.
18. *Zhongguo tongji nianjian, 1987,* p. 205; and *Zhongguo tongji nianjian, 1988,* p. 287.
19. "Yindao nongcun."

Disaggregating these figures, one finds that from 1979 to 1983, when the communes still existed, subsidies for agriculture averaged a little more than 3.3 billion yuan per year. But from 1984 to 1988, after the communes were disbanded and township enterprises began to develop rapidly, such subsidies averaged only 1.5 billion yuan per year.[20]

For the poor agricultural regions, where the collective has little income, the shift to local funding has been devastating. These areas either wait for what little central-level investments exist or thrust the costs of maintaining the agricultural infrastructure onto the shoulders of the local population, through corvée labor (*yiwu gong*) and various surcharges levied at the township and village levels.[21] This basic lack of revenue lies at the root of the growing "peasant burdens" that have received substantial press coverage as the cause of discontent. These are seldom issues in the rich areas, where the collectives often pay such costs for the peasants from industrial profits.[22]

VILLAGE INDUSTRY AND RIGHTS TO REVENUE

Decollectivization negatively affected fiscal flows for village government, but this institutional change is at the crux of why village cadres who wanted to survive and get ahead sought to develop village industry. It is easy to understand why the rights of the village to income from its enterprises made this an attractive strategy to pursue. What needs to be explained is how these collectively owned enterprises could be lucrative to village coffers when they were contracted out for individual management, as they all were, in the process of decollectivization. The answer lies in the details and actual operation of the contracting system.

ENTERPRISE CONTRACTING

The term *contracting* (*chengbao*) is used for both the contracting of collectively owned land to individual farm families and the contracting of collectively owned enterprises, but the rights entailed in the two types of contracting are different. In the contracting of enterprises, the contrac-

20. "Yindao nongcun."
21. Albert Park, et al., show the negative impact of the fiscal reforms and the diversion of resources from agriculture in poor areas of Shaanxi province. "Distributional Consequences."
22. Most peasants are responsible for corvée labor, but they can use money to buy themselves out of the obligation. The collective often pays the *tiliu* in industrialized villages.

tor pays taxes to the state and the contract fee (rent) and perhaps a management fee or surcharge to the village, as the owner of the enterprise. On paper, it appears similar to the contracting of land—peasants pay a tax and sell quotas of grain to the state for the right to use the land. This similarity has no doubt led some to conclude that when collectively owned enterprises are contracted, a semiprivate form of ownership results. In practice, the rights and limitations governing the contractors of enterprises and village government are much less clear than they appear on paper.

Separating Management Rights and Rights to the Residual

Contracting implies both management and residual rights, the latter being the rights to decide the disposition of profits. When it contracts land from the collective, a peasant household has both. Only the right to sell or transfer the land remains with the village. When a peasant contracts an enterprise, however, only day-to-day management rights are transferred to the contractor. Crucial rights to the residual—the profits—and the disposition of revenues remain with the village authorities.[23] Retaining these rights enables local authorities to limit management autonomy and use of enterprise profits.[24] Key decisions about personnel, investment, and product line must be approved by the village. The contractor is merely an employee of the collective—that is, the village.

Johnson identifies "administrative guidance" as an important part of Japan's growth strategy during the 1960s and 1970s, when its economy grew rapidly and successfully. The Japanese government induced independently owned firms to conform to certain strategies of growth through the preferential allocation of inputs. In China, continued ownership of enterprises by the village gave village government not only influence but the ability to intervene directly in the internal affairs of those enterprises, even after they were contracted out to individual management.

Village officials controlled enterprise revenues either directly or indirectly. Profits that were not extracted were strictly regulated. Rules stipulated how the retained profits were to be used. Strict formulas limited

---

23. The right of alienation (i.e., the right to sell) also remains with the village.
24. Christine Wong makes a similar point. See "Interpreting Rural Industrial Growth."

the amounts to be used for worker benefits (*fuli*) and bonuses, designating the majority of the profits for reinvestment. Some regulations specified that 50 percent of after-tax profits had to be plowed back into the factory to expand production, and only 20 percent could be used for bonuses and benefits.[25] Interviews with factory managers reveal that in some areas 70 percent of a factory's retained profits had to be used for reinvestment.[26] Local regulations further mandated that the remaining 30 percent of the profits that went to the collective had to subsidize agriculture and provide for village welfare (see chapter 3).[27]

Those who contracted to run the enterprises were dependent on the village officials. There was competitive bidding, but local officials decided who would be given a contract. Trust, reputation, and loyalty were as important as promises of high returns. Factory managers who made good suggestions and ran factories effectively received large bonuses, and some became quite powerful (and wealthy). These managers had a stake in the economic performance of their enterprises, but the lack of rights to the surplus revenues prevented them from becoming an independent elite with their own resource base. Local officials remained in a position to drive the engine of change and development.

Remuneration and Rent

The contractor's remuneration was determined by which of the three major types of rental arrangements was in force: (1) a fixed rent; (2) a floating rate calculated as a percentage of profits; or (3) the factory manager responsibility system.[28]

---

25. Nationwide, the average percentage of reinvested profits in 1985 was 46.3. In 1986 this increased to 49.8. *Zhongguo tongji nianjian, 1987,* p. 205. Whether factories in fact followed the local guidelines is another issue. For an account of the illegal use of profits, see "Survey of 107 Small- and Medium-Sized Enterprises Shows That Improper Use of Retained Profits Affects Enterprises' Staying Power," *Jiangxi ribao,* 20 November 1987, translated in *JPRS-CAR-88–005,* 18 February 1988, pp. 21–22.

26. CI 72388.

27. This is sometimes paid to the village and sometimes to the township. In Nanjiao, outside Tianjin, village industry paid only to the township, which then distributed funds to all of its villages. Local officials argued that this ensured a fairer distribution. The township in this area also took care of those villagers who had no one else to provide for them. CI 71886.

28. The precise method varied among villages and over time. For accounts of the process in the early years of reform see Thomas Bernstein, "Local Political Authorities," which

A fixed rent was the type most commonly used during the early stages of the reforms, when local officials had little idea of the profitability of their enterprises. Villages simply set a profit target and allowed the contractor to keep the over-quota profits. But as the reforms took hold and villages came to understand how successful some of their enterprises could be under private management, local officials developed more sophisticated ways to reap income.

Some governments turned to the floating rent or percentage system, where all profits up to a set amount were divided between the legal owner—the village—and the contractor according to a set ratio.[29] For example, prior to 1985, a village outside Shenyang contracted its enterprises on a fixed-rent basis, regardless of profits. In 1985, however, when profits rose, the village adopted a floating rent. It set the ratio at either 7:3 or 8:2, with the collective getting the larger share. When the profits were expected to be particularly high, the latter ratio was used.[30]

Others adopted the factory manager responsibility system (*changzhang ziren zhi*), wherein the enterprise was contracted technically to both management and workers—the factory as a collective entity. Because it was difficult to deal with all members of the collective, the factory manager, along with his top staff, acted as the principal contractors and legal representatives of the collective. These individuals had primary responsibility for meeting the village-set quotas. This was essentially a work responsibility system that enabled the village to control the distribution of profits and make the major decisions.

Under the factory responsibility system there was no preset remuneration. The factory manager and his staff were awarded a bonus by the village government if the factory met the preset targets. The bonuses given to factory managers were limited, but the amounts varied substantially. In the latter part of the 1980s, some Shandong villages limited a factory manager's salary to an amount no more than 20 percent above that received by the highest-paid worker.[31] During the same period in other Shandong villages, the factory manager/contractor was allowed to make three to four times the salary of the average worker.[32] In the late 1980s,

---

gives details of one county in Shandong and one county in Anhui; and on contracts in villages in the Pearl River Delta see Graham Johnson, "Fate of the Communal Economy."

29. For village enterprises, the enterprise management committee set the ratio and determined the percentage of over-quota profits; at the township level, this was done by the economic commission.

30. CI 72986.   31. CI 6488.

32. CI 72388.

factory managers in Daqiuzhuang, outside Tianjin, earned as much as 10,000–20,000 yuan per year.[33]

Regardless of the precise terms of the contract, rents were subject to renegotiation. Contracts could be declared null and void at any time; unlike contracts in the Western legal context, they seem to have been nonbinding. Contractors were sometimes left with no legal recourse, even though in theory they were protected by law. This was especially the case for those enterprises that became unexpectedly profitable.[34] But even when the contracts were honored, local authorities had ad hoc access to enterprise revenues because the rights to the residual income remained with the village.

It was this continued access of village governments to nontax revenues that made collectively owned firms more attractive than private ones. Because villages were not entitled to keep any state taxes, private firms were of little fiscal use. Village authorities could (and no doubt some did) resort to predatory rent-seeking behavior, but that likely had detrimental effects on growth.

FISCAL REFORM AND RIGHTS TO THE RESIDUAL

Townships, like villages, had strong incentives to develop their collectively owned enterprises. Counties were eager to promote development at both levels. But the incentives at the township and county levels centered on fiscal reform, not decollectivization. Reform granted county and township governments—unlike village governments—new rights over revenues. The 1980s fiscal reforms created a revenue residual and granted the rights to that residual to local governments down to the level of the township.

CREATING THE RESIDUAL

A residual, simply put, is an economic surplus. The potential benefits from this surplus make it an effective tool for hierarchical control in organizations. Yet those who study public bureaucracies note that

33. This was actually less than the 80,000 yuan to which some were entitled. The village leadership decided that it would be better to use more of the profits for development and subsidies, especially because they felt that the managers were making so much more than they could possibly need. CI 11888.

34. For examples, see Jean C. Oi, "Commercializing China's Rural Cadres." Also see David Zweig, et al., "Law, Contracts, and Economic Modernization."

there is no residual in the ordinary sense of the term. The typical bureau receives a budget from governmental superiors and spends all of it supplying services to a nonpaying clientele. Regardless of the agency's performance or how it changes over time, the results are not reflected in an economic surplus accruing to bureau heads, and this major incentive for the efficient monitoring of employee behavior fails to operate. Incentive plans that give employees a share of the 'profit' in partial payment for their effort . . . are also ruled out.[35]

The closest thing to a residual that exists in most public bureaucracies is "slack."[36]

The above description was written by a student of American politics, but it describes accurately the situation in China prior to the 1980s fiscal reforms. The slack, to the extent that it existed, was the amount of revenue that the local governments could save from their budget allocations. To get ahead, local governments lobbied the upper levels for larger budgets.

The 1980s fiscal reforms dramatically changed the incentives for local governments. First, the central state no longer guaranteed upper-level budget allocations to meet local expenditures. China converted a vertical (*tiao*) apportionment system that had allocated revenues from the upper to the lower levels into a system in which localities had to rely primarily on horizontal flows (*kuai*)—that is, on income that they generated themselves. The impact of the 1980s reforms is captured by the colloquial phrase "eating in separate kitchens," the antithesis of the situation during the Maoist period when everyone "ate from one kitchen."

Second, behaving more like a business organization than a public bureaucracy, China began to motivate its agents by granting local governments clear rights to any economic surplus that they were able to generate. Contrary to what some observers have argued, this surplus was not simply more "organizational slack"; it was a residual.[37] The 1980s fiscal reforms eliminated the organizational slack for local governments, but it granted them rights to a residual. Even though these rights were granted to governments, not individuals, the re-allocation of property rights gave localities positive inducements to promote rapid economic growth, which became not only a necessary strategy for bureaucratic survival but a *viable strategy for getting ahead.*

35. Moe, "New Economics of Organization," p. 763.
36. Ibid., p. 763. See Richard Cyert and James March, *Behavioral Theory of the Firm,* for the original discussion of the role of slack; also William Niskanen, "Bureaucrats and Politicians."
37. See Shirk, *Political Logic of Economic Reform,* p. 160.

DEFINING THE RESIDUAL

Let me now turn to the details of the 1980s revenue-sharing system to explain how the residual was generated at the township level and above and to describe the property rights that different levels of local government had over these revenues.[38] The terms of revenue sharing are technical (some readers may prefer to skip these sections), but the details of the system are important in that they reveal why localities found certain development strategies more attractive than others. Disparate types of revenues were treated differently. Some, by definition, had to be shared with the center; others fell directly into the category of the residual.

Revenue-Sharing Contracts

Revenue sharing is a process in which local governments down to the level of the township have the responsibility for collecting all nationally set taxes and then turning over a portion of this revenue to the next higher level. Those who have increased their tax revenues are allowed to keep the major portion of the increase. The more a locality collects, the more it can keep. The provisions of revenue sharing are formalized in fiscal contracts between the central state and each of its provinces, between each province and its prefectures, between each prefecture and its counties, and between each county and its townships.[39] The terms of the contracts vary. Some areas employ an overall ratio, such as 70:30; the level of government from which the taxes are collected keeps 70 percent and 30 percent is sent to the next higher level. In other cases, a level of government pays a fixed lump-sum quota to the next higher level, but,

38. Differences that have appeared as a result of the 1994 reforms will be treated separately later in the chapter.

39. When revenue sharing was first instituted in 1980, only governments down to the county level were eligible to participate. Up until the mid-1980s, townships collected taxes, but they had no right to keep any of them. The effort to establish township-level finance departments began in 1983. A National Financial Work Conference advised all prefectures to select two counties to set up experimental township finance departments. All taxes were turned over to the county, and the county then continued the old system of allocating a budget for the township's expenses. Only in April 1985, when the State Council approved a directive issued by the Ministry of Finance, "On Township [xiang/zhen] Fiscal Management Experimental Methods," was the fiscal system extended to the townships. Official reports state that by the end of 1986, 91.4 percent of all townships (xiang and zhen) in the country had established finance departments that paved the way for revenue sharing. Caizhengbu caishui tizhi gaigesi, Caishui gaige shinian, pp. 14–15, 205–6. My fieldwork revealed that in 1996 some townships were still not subject to revenue sharing.

once that quota is met, the level of government that has collected the revenue retains all, or the bulk, of the over-quota tax revenues. Regardless of the system of revenue sharing in effect, increased tax collection guarantees a locality an increase in retained tax revenues.

Revenue sharing is premised on localities producing sufficient revenues to meet their own expenses and producing a surplus that they will share with the upper levels. Localities that fail to generate a surplus need not share tax revenues with the upper levels. Unlike fiscal systems being tried in former socialist economies such as Russia, the Chinese system headed off potential opposition to the reforms from poorer areas by building in a revenue "safety net."[40]

Within each level of administration, there are those who make payments, those who do not, and those who receive subsidies. The status of each locality is determined by a complex calculation involving (1) fixed expenditures; (2) fixed receipts; (3) fixed payments upward, and (4) fixed subsidies. Fixed expenditures are the amount that the higher authorities determine to be the "minimum essential budget" items for the local government. What constitutes the minimum essential budget is the subject of intense negotiations between the levels, but at a minimum, fixed expenditures include the payment of base salaries to state cadres on the local payroll[41] and the funding of primary services, such as education, health, roads, and housing. How much is provided for each expense reflects past expenditures, with some provisions for increases based on population. Fixed expenditures also include "development needs," an amorphous category that, as explained by a finance bureau head, encompasses costs for agriculture, irrigation, and forestry, and the vague category of "developing the rural commodity economy," which includes expenses for rural enterprises engaged in mining, seed production, and animal husbandry, among other activities. Once the fixed expenditures are set, this amount is compared with the "fixed receipts," which are equal to the tax collection quota set for the locality.

A locality makes a "fixed payment upward" to the next higher administrative level only if its fixed receipts are greater than its fixed expenditures. If expenditures and receipts are equal, the locality neither pays revenue to the upper level nor receives a subsidy. If the fixed receipts are

40. On Russia, see Bahl and Wallace, "Revenue Sharing in Russia"; Jon Craig and George Kopits, "Intergovernmental Fiscal Relations"; and Jorge Martinez-Vazquez, "Expenditure Assignment."

41. Some cadres who work at the local-government level are not considered state cadres; thus they are not paid from the official budget but from extrabudgetary funds.

less than the fixed expenditures, the difference is the "fixed subsidy" for the area.[42] This becomes the subsistence ceiling or social safety net for the locality.

At every level, from province to township, some units failed to generate sufficient revenues to cover expenditures.[43] Nationwide, in 1991, out of thirty-five listed provinces, autonomous regions, and municipalities, fourteen received fiscal transfers from the center.[44] Table 1 describes the revenue-sharing systems in twenty-seven provinces and municipalities in 1992 and indicates which received fiscal subsidies. The picture is similarly diverse at the local level. For example, throughout the 1980s and into the 1990s in one Shandong prefecture with six counties and one municipality, only one county and the one municipality paid revenues to the prefecture; within that one county, only seven out of the seventeen townships paid revenues to the county.[45]

An obvious question is whether subsidies result in the continuation of the "iron rice bowl" mentality. Do localities that receive subsidies have an incentive to develop? There is evidence that while local budget constraints are softened by the existence of subsidies, the pressure to increase revenue remains strong. One North China county's production and income statistics show that over a ten-year period when fiscal contracting was in effect, all subsidized townships pursued economic growth and increased income. Moreover, while the output value of tax-paying townships was higher than that of the subsidized townships, the growth rate of subsidized townships was significantly higher than that of tax-paying townships.[46] A similar pattern of more rapid revenue increase in poor areas is noted in twenty-five counties nationwide, including those in poorer provinces.[47]

---

42. Caizhengbu, *Caishui gaige shinian*, p. 13, explains that if the locality's set income is less than expenditures, a prescribed ratio is used to determine how much of a locality's other revenues will be retained; when the local set revenue and the central-local shared revenue together are not sufficient to cover expenses, the center will give a fixed subsidy to the locality. Once this is established, it will not change for five years.

43. Drawing on a report by China's minister of finance, Christine Wong has noted that in 1989 localities remitted a total of 44.7 billion yuan to the central budget while receiving central subsidies of 56.3 billion yuan. "Central-Local Relations," p. 698.

44. Agarwala, *China*, p. 68.   45. CI 8791.

46. These findings emerged from a regression analysis on tax and output time series data for 1984–1993 for seventeen townships in one county. The results were highly significant (at 0.1 level). I would like to thank Tony Chung, Hong Kong University of Science and Technology, for his help with the statistical work that derived these findings.

47. Cited in Park et al., "Distributional Consequences," p. 761. Park et al. found a similar trend for Shaanxi. The growth of revenue per capita in poorer counties outpaced that of the nonpoor counties. They found that the counties that received the most subsidies grew the fastest in terms of revenue per capita (p. 758).

TABLE 1. AMOUNTS OF REVENUE RETAINED
ACCORDING TO CENTRAL–LOCAL REVENUE-
SHARING CONTRACTS (SELECTED PROVINCES
AND MUNICIPALITIES, 1992)

| City/Province | Basic Sharing (%) | Basic Sharing with Growth | | Fixed Quota to State (100 mil. yuan) | Fixed Quota with Growth | | Fixed Quota Subsidy (100 mil. yuan) |
		Basic Retention Rate (%)	Contracted Annual Rate of Increase (%)		Initial Amount to State (100 mil. yuan)	Contracted Annual Rate of Increase (%)	
Shanxi	87.6						
Anhui	77.5						
Henan		80.0	5.0				
Hebei		70.0	4.5				
Beijing		50.0	4.0				
Harbin		45.0	5.0				
Jiangsu		41.0	5.0				
Ningbo		27.9	5.3				
Shanghai				105.0			
Heilongjiang				3.0			
Shandong				2.0			
Guangdong (inc. Guangzhou)					14.1	9.0	
Hunan					8.0	7.0	
Inner Mongolia							18.4

(continued)

TABLE 1. *(continued)*

Xinjiang	15.3
Tibet	9.0
Guizhou	7.4
Yunnan	6.7
Qinghai	6.6
Guangxi	6.1
Ningxia	5.3
Hainan	1.4
Gansu	1.3
Shaanxi (inc. Xi'an)	1.2
Jilin	1.1
Fujian	0.5
Jiangxi	0.5

SOURCE: Adapted from Christine P. W. Wong, Christopher Heady, and Wing T. Woo, *Fiscal Management and Economic Reform in the People's Republic of China*, p. 89.

Such findings are not surprising. The subsidies are barely sufficient to pay basic expenses. In the really poor areas, these subsidies are in fact often insufficient to meet even essential expenditures.[48] In most areas no slack exists for the improvement of services or bureaucratic growth.[49] The fixed subsidies generally pay only for a set number of bureaucratic positions; no funds are provided for cost overruns.[50] Furthermore, townships in the North China county cited above had the added security and incentive of knowing that they could keep additional revenues over the "fixed receipt" quota and continue to receive the agreed upon "fixed subsidy." Ten out of the county's seventeen townships that had the status of fixed-subsidy townships were allowed to keep that designation over a number of contract periods, even as their tax collection—the "fixed receipts"—exceeded the contract amount.[51]

Taxes

Under the 1980s revenue-sharing schemes, the nationally set taxes that the localities had to collect fell into two major categories: income tax and industrial-commercial taxes. Appendix B provides a full list of taxes and how they were shared under the 1980 (table 10) and 1985 (table 11) systems.

Income Tax

In the Maoist period, state-owned industries had little incentive to be profitable. Factories were required to turn over all profits to the state. In return, their wage bills and other budgeted expenses were met by the state. These profits rather than taxes provided the bulk of government revenue from state-owned enterprises.[52] A "tax for profit" (*ligaishui*) reform was instituted in the 1980s simultaneously to provide the state with revenue and to give state-owned enterprises an incentive to be more efficient and profitable.

48. Park et al., "Distributional Consequences."
49. Exceptions are minority areas classified as "poor," such as those that Xiaolin Guo studied in "Variation in Local Property Rights"; local officials in northwest Yunnan found the subsidies to be sufficiently lucrative to warrant hiding the number of township-owned enterprises from the upper levels.
50. On the growth of local governments, see White, "Political Reform and Rural Government" and "Below Bureaucracy."
51. CI 8791.
52. A World Bank report states that until 1983, approximately 60 percent of government revenue was generated from the remittance of profits from state-owned enterprises. *China*, p. 2.

The enterprise income tax (*giye suode shui*) was the mechanism devised for this purpose. In actuality it was a profit tax. The rate was based on an eight-grade progressive scale that ranged from a low of 10 percent for profits under 1,000 yuan to a high of 55 percent on profits over 200,000 yuan. In 1985 this income tax was extended to township and village enterprises, replacing the industrial-commercial income tax (*gongshang suode shui*).[53]

Local governments were required to collect income tax from all enterprises located in their administrative jurisdictions. Rights to this tax revenue depended on the level of government to which the enterprise belonged. Enterprises were divided between central and local governments. Central-level enterprises included, among others, all banks and post offices. All income tax from these enterprises had to be given to the center. All income tax from local enterprises remained in the locality.

Industrial-Commercial Taxes

The second category of taxes collected by the localities is loosely termed "circulation taxes" (*liuzhuan shui*) or "industrial-commercial taxes" (*gongshang shui*). The category primarily includes product (*chanpin*), value-added (*zengzhi*), and turnover/business (*yingye*) taxes.[54] Each of these taxes is based on production, income, or sales, irrespective of profits. Together, they make up the bulk of total tax revenues. These taxes are levied on private, state, and collectively owned enterprises, including township and village firms.[55] The revenue from these taxes is shared between the center and the localities.

Prior to the 1980s, the primary source of industrial tax revenue was county-level state or collectively owned enterprises. Since the post-Mao reforms, county-level industry continues to be the bedrock of county-level income and taxes, even in those counties with relatively high success in developing rural industry, but its tax contribution has decreased as a proportion of total revenues as rural enterprises have grown.[56] Aggregate statistics show that the lion's share of the increases in circulation/

53. Wang Xiaoxu, ed., *Nashui shiyong shouce*, p. 49.
54. For details on the evolution of these taxes see Caizhengbu caishui tizhi gaigesi, *Caishui gaige shinian*.
55. Under the 1985 system, the income tax from county-level state-owned enterprises was shared, but not that from townships, villages, or privately owned enterprises. With the change to the total-revenue–sharing system after 1988, this distinction became meaningless.
56. See Wong, "Central-Local Relations"; and Barry Naughton, "Implications of the State Monopoly."

industrial-commercial taxes came from township and village enterprises. Between 1978 and 1987, these taxes from township and village
enterprises increased from a little over 2 billion yuan to 17 billion yuan;
in 1988 alone, there was a 40.7 percent increase in tax revenue from
these enterprises.[57] In 1990 these taxes totaled 34.4 billion yuan, and by
1995 they were up to 205.8 billion yuan—almost a fivefold increase.[58]

MAXIMIZING THE RESIDUAL

Given the pressures imposed on local governments to be fiscally self-
sufficient and the incentives to increase revenues under the new fiscal
system, one might have predicted that these governments would engage
in predatory taxation.[59] Yet my fieldwork strongly suggests that some
Chinese local governments have been relatively generous in the assessment and collection of state taxes. One such example is counties that allow their poorer townships to keep increased revenues when it is time to
sign new fiscal contracts. Another example is local governments that
grant generous tax breaks to their local enterprises.

While the growth of tax contributions from collective rural enterprises
is impressive, local governments failed to obtain the maximum amount
of taxes from their firms. Some of this failure may have been due to tax
evasion, but it was not a case of outside tax collectors having the wool
pulled over their eyes. Collection and assessment were done by local tax
officials who had intimate knowledge of local enterprises.[60] The evidence
suggests that minimum rather than maximum taxation was the result of
conscious local policy to underassess taxes on favored enterprises.

National regulations allow township and village enterprises favorable
tax treatment. Factories that meet certain criteria, such as serving agriculture or hiring the handicapped have special exemptions.[61] Village
factories for the disabled, for example, have tax-free status.[62] New enterprises were exempt from income tax for their first year of business.
Old factories that started a new product line also qualified to receive a
one-year tax holiday on those profits. But some localities went beyond

57. Detailed statistics on the early years of rural enterprise development are in *Zhongguo xiangzhen qiye nianjian, 1978–1987.*
58. Nongyebu xiangzhen qiyesi juhua caiwuchu, *1995 nian quanguo xiangzhen,*
pp. 2–8.
59. See, for example, Margaret Levi, *Of Rule and Revenue.*
60. This will be examined in chapter 6.
61. Those located in old revolutionary base areas also fall into this category.
62. See *Zhongguo xiangzhen qiye nianjian, 1978–1987,* p. 270, for a list of the official
exemptions.

official regulations to extend this favorable treatment to two and three years.

In some areas, across-the-board cuts were granted as standard practice; some provinces were particularly generous. In Zhejiang province, if the tax rate for an enterprise came to more than 30 percent according to the nationally set scale, the amount taxed at the higher rate was cut in half. In Guangdong province, if the tax rate was above 20 percent, the tax levied above that level was also cut in half.[63] In addition, county officials allowed ad hoc tax breaks for local enterprises. For example, in 1987 a county outside Tianjin collected 59.3 million yuan in taxes but allowed almost half as much, 26.65 million yuan, in tax breaks.[64] Nationwide in 1987, out of 20.7 billion yuan in profits earned by township and village enterprises, 17.4 percent, or 3.6 billion yuan, was exempt from taxes.[65]

Local officials are constrained in their largesse by nationally set tax rates. But, as a World Bank study notes, "Provincial governments cannot vary the nominal rates of tax, nor may they redefine the legal tax base. However, they have almost complete autonomy in assessing and collecting taxes, and along with the lower level county government can and do give tax relief without having to seek approval from the center. One can fairly say that subnational governments can substantially alter the level and pattern of effective tax rates by enterprises."[66]

My interviews at the county level show that local officials can and do manipulate the tax base to lower indirectly the taxes that enterprises must pay. This strategy works particularly well with the income tax. Local officials can redefine certain items as factory costs, which are then deducted prior to assessing the income tax—remember that this is a tax on profit, not on total income. In some cases, enterprises have been allowed to negotiate an agreement whereby loan repayments are deducted from the tax base before the income tax is calculated.[67] There is less leeway to manipulate the industrial-commercial taxes, but sometimes reductions and exemptions are given for these taxes also.

63. He Xian, "Woguo."   64. CI 8888.

65. *Zhongguo xiangzhen qiye nianjian, 1978–1987*, p. 270. On tax reductions and exemptions nationwide, see Yuan Dong, "Problems in the Financial Relationship Between the Central Government and Local Governments and Ways to Resolve Them," *Zhongguo jingji wenti*, 20 January 1992, no. 1, translated in *JPRS-CAR-92–035*, 2 June 1992, pp. 35–40.

66. World Bank, *China*, p. 84.

67. In 1990 this arrangement was abolished for collectively owned enterprises but was still allowed for state-owned enterprises.

How much local officials allow enterprises and subordinate levels to get away with depends on how much revenue is available. Local governments can ill afford to be too lax about tax collection. A fine line must be walked that balances tax breaks with tax needs. The degree to which local officials pursue tax collection will vary according to local conditions. The county outside Tianjin that gave almost half of the collectible tax amount in breaks contained one of the highest income-generating villages in China. In contrast, poor counties have little ability to provide their enterprises leeway given the tremendous difficulties that these areas have in raising enough revenue to meet minimum expenses. This may explain why poor provinces exert greater tax efforts than rich ones.[68] Local governments must in the end meet their tax quotas specified under the revenue-sharing contracts. But in a context where the economy is growing and there is a surplus, local governments may tax at minimum rather than maximum levels.

Within-Budget and Extrabudgetary Revenues

In trying to understand why local governments give tax breaks, one must realize that these governments have access to a number of different types of revenues. This is where the technical terms of revenue sharing become relevant. Revenue is divided into two major categories: within-budget and extrabudgetary. The taxes that have been described so far—the income and industrial-commercial taxes—fall into the category of within-budget funds (*yusuannei zijin*). But in addition to these state tax revenues that are subject to revenue sharing with the upper levels, there are also revenues that are not—the extrabudgetary revenues (*yusuanwai zijin*). These include a category of taxes known as "local taxes" (see below) and all money that falls into the category of *nontax revenues*—including fees, surcharges, retained profits and other revenue that local governments are entitled to collect from their enterprises and other sectors of their economy on top of state taxes. Localities have the right to retain these revenues in their entirety. Table 2 shows the major sources for these two types of revenue.

The distinction between within-budget and extrabudgetary funds existed during the Maoist period, but extrabudgetary funds were mini-

---

68. Park et al., "Distributional Consequences," offer this as an explanation for their findings of increased revenue growth in the poorer counties in Shaanxi.

TABLE 2. MAJOR WITHIN-BUDGET TAXES
AND EXTRABUDGETARY REVENUES, PRE-1994

Within-Budget Taxes	Extrabudgetary Revenues
Income Tax	Local Taxes
Industrial-Commercial Taxes/ Circulation Taxes	Agriculture–animal husbandry tax
Product tax	Special agricultural and forestry products tax
Value-added tax	Property tax
Turnover/Business tax	Land-use tax
	Animal sales tax
	Animal slaughter tax
	Collective and individual enterprise sales tax
	Collective and private enterprise income tax
	Stamp tax
	Urban maintenance and construction tax
	Other
	Nontax Levies and Revenues
	Contracted profits
	quota
	over-quota
	Management fee
	Ad hoc charges
	Loans and voluntary contributions
	Enterprise retained profits

mal,[69] at best, and they were subject to upper-level controls. The attractiveness of these funds to localities is reflected in their extraordinary growth in the 1980s. The reported average annual increase of extrabudgetary funds for the 1978–1987 period was 21.67 percent.[70]

The growth and significance of these extrabudgetary revenues become readily apparent when they are compared with the within-budget revenues. In 1978, extrabudgetary revenue was 34.7 billion yuan, or 31 percent of within-budget revenues (112.1 billion yuan). By 1987, extra-

69. See Wong, "Fiscal Reform and Local Industrialization," p. 205.
70. This rate exceeds that of the growth of the total national product (*chanzhi*) for the same period by 10.6 percent, of the national income (*guomin shouru*) by 8.9 percent, and of the national within-budget revenue by 8.1 percent. Caizhengbu, *Caishui gaige shinian*, p. 322. Tam On Kit, "Fiscal Policy Issues in China," estimates that nationwide between 1978 and 1988 there was a sixfold increase in the amount of extrabudgetary revenue. One Chinese source indicates that in 1990 extrabudgetary funds equaled 275 billion yuan, a figure that represents a 79.7 percent increase from 1985. It also reports that the average annual increase exceeded the average annual increase for the same period of within-budget income. Xiang Huaicheng, ed., *Jiushi niandai caizheng*, p. 296.

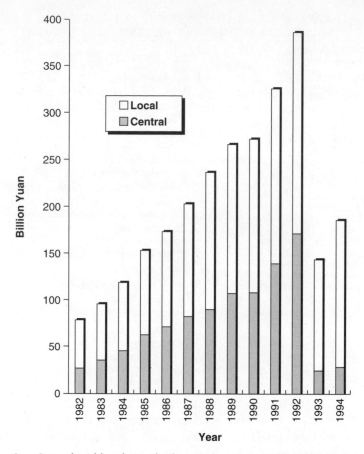

Figure 2.   Central and local extrabudgetary revenues, 1982–1994 (Source:
Zhongguo tongji nianjian, 1996, p. 236)

budgetary revenues were 89.66 percent of within-budget revenues.[71]
However, it is not just the growth of these revenues that is notable but
the fact that over time the localities were getting a larger portion (see
figure 2). The growth of local extrabudgetary revenues was the result of
strategic planning on the part of localities to develop those sectors and
activities that yielded not only the most revenue but also the most extrabudgetary revenue.

The economic logic behind the general pattern of local growth is

71. Caizhengbu, *Caishui gaige shinian*, p. 323.

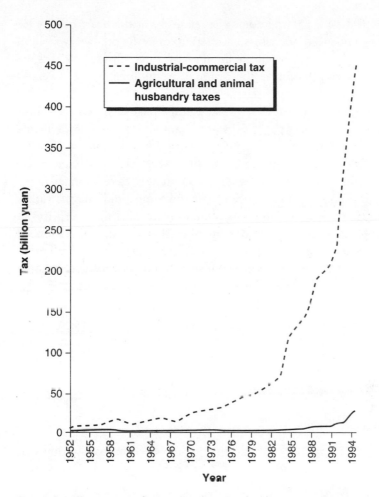

Figure 3.   Tax revenue from agriculture and industry, 1952–1994
(Sources: *Zhongguo tongji nianjian, 1991*, p. 213; *Zhongguo tongji
nianjian, 1996*, p. 228)

revealed in the following sections, which enumerate the sources of extrabudgetary funds at the county, township, and village levels. Sources of
both tax revenue and extrabudgetary revenues cluster around industry
and commerce. As figure 3 shows, agricultural taxes remained relatively
flat while the industrial-commercial tax on industry grew steadily and
rapidly. Not surprisingly, the composition of the rural economy moved
noticeably from agriculture to industry and commerce in the 1980s.

Rights to these local and nontax revenues lie at the heart of why lo-cal governments need not assess national taxes in the predatory fashion that would be expected given the fiscal constraints imposed by revenue sharing. Localities maximize the residual by minimizing the revenues subject to revenue sharing—that is, national taxes.

This is especially true at the township and village levels where collec-tively owned enterprises pay a substantial amount of nontax payments to local coffers.[72] County government has the most to lose from mini-mum rather than maximum taxation on township and village enter-prises. But counties in the 1980s seemed content to take a longer-range view that promoted growth within their townships and villages rather than capturing maximum amounts of taxes from existing enterprises in the short term. One must also remember that county officials were judged not just by the amount of taxes collected but by the overall pros-perity and growth of the county. Moreover, the county had its own sources of extrabudgetary funds.

The County Residual

The residual accruing to county coffers consists of funds officially au-thorized as "extrabudgetary" and taxes defined as "local."

Extrabudgetary Funds

The total of a county's extrabudgetary funds is a composite of individ-ual accounts. This includes

1.   revenue belonging to local finance departments

2.   income of institutional and administrative units not counted in within-budget funds

3.   various specialized funds held by state-owned enterprises and their leading organs

4.   income from enterprises belonging to the localities and income of central departments that is not included in within-budget funds.[73]

---

72. All after-tax revenues fall into the residual category.
73. These categories are defined in the tax handbook, Wang Xiaoxu, ed., *Nashui shiyong shouce*, p. 27.

As figure 4 shows, the bulk of extrabudgetary funds consists of the retained enterprise funds.[74] Nationwide, retained enterprise funds increased almost nineteenfold from 1978 to 1987.[75] The most important of these are the profit, depreciation, welfare, and bonus funds. The increase in these funds was due to the profit retention (*liuli*) and tax for profit (*ligaishui*) reforms, and the various responsibility systems designed to reinvigorate the fiscal reserves of enterprises. A 1985 regulation allowed some industrial sectors (*hangye*) and enterprises to raise their depreciation rate. Because depreciation could be written into costs, this change also served to decrease income taxes by reducing profits.

The next largest holdings are the miscellaneous extrabudgetary revenues of individual departments and administrative units that are overseen by the county finance bureau. The management fee that the rural enterprise management bureau receives from township-owned enterprises is an example of such extrabudgetary revenue. Another bureau-held extrabudgetary fund is the "individual entrepreneur's industrial-commercial management fee" (*geti gongshang yehu guanli fei*) that individual and private entrepreneurs pay when they are licensed.[76] This fee is collected jointly by the county Administration for Industry and Commerce and the Individual Entrepreneurs Association.[77] The latter also collects an association fee (*huifei*) that belongs entirely to the association and has grown quite substantial.[78] In one county in 1990, it amounted to almost 1 million yuan.[79] Another source of extrabudgetary funds is the profits from commercial companies set up by county agencies. For example, when the rural enterprise management bureau sets up a material supply company, the company's after-tax revenues fall into the extrabudgetary category.

74. A 1990 World Bank report states that extrabudgetary revenues of the government generally accounted for only about 3 percent of total extrabudgetary funds; agencies retained about 17 percent, while enterprises retained about 80 percent. *China*, pp. 85–86.

75. Caizhengbu, *Caishui gaige shinian*, p. 322.

76. The rate varied according to sector: the rate for commerce (*shangye*) was .05 percent of total sales (*xiaoshou e*), and for transport (*yunshu*) 1.5 percent of total business (*jingying e*). One North China county where private enterprise developed only gradually collected in 1989 over 700,000 yuan from these fees; by 1990 the amount reached almost 1 million yuan. CI 81291.

77. Each receives 50 percent after a percentage of the total is sent to the prefectural level. CI 81291.

78. This fee was instituted in 1984, abolished in 1985–1986, and then reinstituted. In 1991 it was 6 yuan per year and was designated for the welfare and relief of association members. CI 81291.

79. CI 81291.

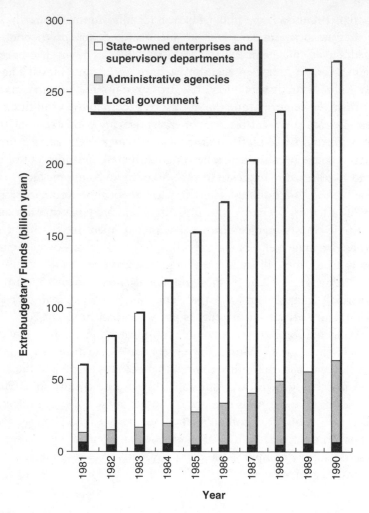

Figure 4.   Extrabudgetary funds by source, 1981–1990 (Source: Adapted from Christine P. W. Wong, Christopher Heady, and Wing T. Woo, *Fiscal Management and Economic Reform in the People's Republic of China,* pp. 236–37)

Local Taxes

Local taxes are those designated by the central state as belonging exclusively to the localities. Table 2 lists the main items that county-level finance and tax bureau officials in the late 1980s enumerated as local taxes. The potency of the residual as an incentive for shaping local growth is highlighted by the rise in the revenues that are defined as "local taxes."

The tremendous upsurge in extrabudgetary funds stems primarily from the increase in originally allowed local taxes, not the addition of new items into the category of extrabudgetary items.

When tax designations were drawn, most of the items classified as local taxes were fairly inconsequential sources of revenue—which may explain why the center granted the rights over these to the localities in the first place. Tax revenue from private enterprises is a good example. It has grown enormously. In one county, taxes on the private sector, starting from almost zero in the early 1980s, had grown to 17.6 percent of total county taxes by 1984; and by 1990 they were almost one-quarter of that total.[80] Given the importance of these taxes, it is not surprising that in 1990 this county issued quotas for the development of private enterprises to each of its townships.

The Township Residual

The residual at the township level was minimal, if there was any at all, prior to the reforms. Known as communes before decollectivization, townships generally had few revenue sources other than fees levied on its brigades and teams and the agricultural tax. Some commune-level enterprises existed, but townships received only limited income from such industries. Some commune factories did not even pay profits to the commune; the income remained within the factories, perhaps because it was minimal.[81] Most factory income went to pay for expenses, including food rations for workers.[82]

Yet by the latter part of the 1980s, total extrabudgetary revenues in some townships exceeded within-budget revenues. The sources of the township residual included a portion of the fees assessed by villages on their residents, the *tiliu*, and various fees (*tongchou*) that were levied by the township on villages. However, the primary source of township extrabudgetary funds was collectively owned township enterprise.

---

80. Statistics provided by the county tax bureau, 1991. This does not include the agricultural tax.

81. In one township, factories began to pay profits to the commune beginning in 1976, when they paid 40 percent. They also paid an income tax of 20 percent of total profits. By 1988, when the eight-grade scale employed for urban enterprises was put into effect, if the profits were more than 100,000 yuan, the factory paid a set rate of 53 percent; if profits were over 200,000 yuan, the rate was 55 percent. CI 22688.

82. For further details of the collective agricultural work system, see Oi, *State and Peasant*.

The amounts of nontax extrabudgetary fees and ad hoc surcharges extracted from the collectively owned enterprises differed by locality; but overall the amounts were excessive enough to prompt press warnings that "township enterprises should not be treated as 'small cash registers' from which money can be taken at will."[83]

Standard Assessments

Township-owned enterprises pay nontax levies to both the township government and to the specialized bureaucratic agency within the government responsible for township enterprise development, the township economic commission (*xiang jingji weiyuan hui*) (see chapter 4).

The township government receives a set percentage of the gross income of all township-owned enterprises before any rent or taxes, including income tax, are extracted. National regulations stipulate a rate of 10 percent, but in some cases the amount is as much as 20 percent.[84] All townships require this payment.[85] In addition, most township governments also receive a portion of the after-tax profits of their enterprises.

The township economic commission receives the bulk of nontax payments made by township-owned enterprises. First, the commission levies a management fee on total sales.[86] Second, it collects a contract fee (rent) from each of its township-owned enterprises. The rents paid by the contractors (factory managers) are determined and stipulated in contracts

83. "Township Enterprises Should Also Implement Reform," *Jingji cankao,* 18 November 1988, p. 1, translated in *JPRS-CAR-88-005,* 18 February 1988, pp. 20–21. Christine Wong, "Interpreting Rural Industrial Growth," p. 23, also refers to this problem.

84. This was the case in a Shandong township. CI 72188.

85. Some areas also levy an additional amount, *bunong bufu jijin* (aid agriculture, aid sidelines fund) before taxes. Sidelines include such activities as pig raising. In the vicinity of Shanghai, this charge is 10 percent. In the same region, there is yet a third levy, on enterprise workers, that also goes into the "aid agriculture, aid sidelines fund." He Xian, "Woguo."

86. The fee varies. In parts of Sichuan, for example, it is 1 percent of total income. There the money is collected by the tax office from both village and township enterprises. The township receives the money, but then gives a portion to the economic commission. CI 81786. However, in one county near Ji'nan, Shandong, 1 percent of total sales is levied by the township economic commission as the management fee, but only on township-owned enterprises. Different portions are then allotted to the township and county governments. CI 53188. In this same county in 1993, the rate was reduced to between .5 and .7 percent, with the township allowed to keep 40 percent of the total while 30 percent went to the county, 20 percent to the prefecture, and 10 percent to the province. CI 62296. In another Shandong county, this one near Qingdao, the township government levies a fee of 20 percent of enterprise profits and then pays the township economic commission a percentage as the management fee. CI 72388. In Jinghai county outside Tianjin, perhaps because it includes the highly industrialized Daqiuzhuang, the economic commission takes only .6 percent of sales as a management fee.

in ways similar to those described for the village enterprises. Total after-tax profits, quota profits, and over-quota profits are treated differently, and a percentage is taken of each. National regulations stipulate that township governments are limited to 20 percent of after-tax profits, but again, in practice, the amounts may be larger.[87]

Ad Hoc Surcharges

On top of the standard management fee and the contracted profit (rent), township governments, like village authorities, institute a variety of other ad hoc levies to meet shortfalls in local revenue. It is because of these levies that enterprises have been dubbed the "cash registers" of local authorities. The heads of various economic commissions admit that they take profits from rich enterprises when they need extra funds. In one case, between 1986 and 1988 a township economic commission took over 3 million yuan when it needed extra funds.[88] Although some of my interviewees denied engaging in these practices, they all had heard of such instances and knew of areas where the practices had been employed.

The local variations and ad hoc nature of these levies make it difficult to determine how much is extracted by township governments and their economic commissions. A national study shows substantial variation among regions in the amounts paid to township governments.[89] How much is extracted also depends on the availability of other sources of capital. Chapter 6 will show that when bank credit was tight, as it was in 1988–1989, such within-township levies were prevalent.

CREDIBLE COMMITMENT

Creating a residual and holding it out as an incentive to local governments may not be enough to motivate state agents to pursue economic development. Strictly speaking, there was a residual during the Maoist

87. There are regional variations even within the same county.
88. CI 71988.
89. This study divides the payers of after-tax profits to township governments into three groups: (1) those areas that give the largest portion of their enterprise profits to the township; (2) those areas that give only a small portion to the township; and (3) those areas that give almost nothing to the township, except for the management fee. The amounts were correlated to the extent to which the government was involved in investment and development of production. Unfortunately, the study does not tell us which method of extracting revenue was the most common. However, one should note that a "small" amount, including examples from Hebei, Jiangsu, Zhejiang, is actually about 30 percent of after-tax profits. A "large" portion, 56.99 percent, is turned over in the Beijing area, while in Shanghai the average is 71.6 percent. He Xian, "Woguo."

period. For most of the Maoist period expenditures and revenues were linked, and some form of revenue sharing was in effect.[90]

For a residual to be effective in generating local economic growth there must also be *credible commitment* on the part of the principal, the central state, to its agents at the local levels that it will not renege on its contract. The agents must have reasonable assurances they will (1) be granted the right to a minimum residual; (2) have autonomy over its use; and (3) be able to collect that residual for a predictable and sufficiently long period so that they will be able to reap the rewards of their increased effort. (See table 12 for a summary of the changes in these conditions over time.)

The Mao period fiscal policies failed to provide such commitment to the localities on all counts. As table 12, shows, localities had little assurance that they would benefit from increased revenues. Pre-1980 fiscal contracts were valid for only one year.[91] No clear limits applied to the central share; that left uncertain the residual for the localities. Use of what little surplus revenue remained at the local levels required upper-level approval.

The above sections have shown how the residual was created, defined, and allowed to expand with increases in revenue without preset limits in the reform period. The post-1980 decision by the central state to divide revenue into (1) income specifically assigned to the center, (2) income assigned to the localities, and (3) income to be shared[92] effectively capped the center's share and thus identified the point at which the localities could claim their residual. The remaining sections will examine how the state dealt with the last two requirements to show credible commitment.

USE RIGHTS AND CADRE BONUSES

The attractiveness of a residual, no matter how large, is diminished if those who generate this surplus lack the rights to decide its use. During the Maoist period, not only were the extrabudgetary funds meager in

90. Michel Oksenberg and James Tong, "Evolution of Central-Provincial Fiscal Relations."

91. An exception was the experimental Jiangsu fixed-rate responsibility system between 1977 and 1980. This system, which also included effective incentives, did not become the standard in most provinces until 1982–1983.

92. Technically, the income was actually divided into four categories. The amount shared consisted of "income to be divided" and "adjustment income" to be divided between the center and its localities. Caizhengbu, *Caishui gaige shinian*, p. 195.

amount but localities had no right to use the funds left at the local levels without prior upper-level approval. In contrast, the 1980s fiscal reforms granted local governments autonomy over the use of their residual. Localities no longer had to submit a detailed budget for the use of the residual or wait for approval before the money could be spent.[93]

This reform allowed the residual to act as an incentive for development on two levels. On a professional level, increased revenues enabled cadres to ease the severe budget constraints created by revenue sharing and to command the resources necessary to increase administrative effectiveness.[94] On a personal level, increased revenues in local government coffers directly translated into lucrative (and legal) economic rewards for local officials. Local governments used the residual for bonuses. Linking cadre bonuses to the size of the residual gave local officials a direct stake in economic growth.

Cadre bonuses were dependent on the completion of specific tasks and targets.[95] Each higher level of government set quotas for its subordinates.[96] Fulfillment of targets was the core of the cadre evaluation system. In the 1980s, county cadre evaluation offices (*ganbu kaohe bangongshi*) set the levels of the bonuses.[97] Each year the achievements of the townships and their enterprises were measured against the target figures (*jihua shu*); officials of these units were rewarded accordingly with bonuses for fulfilled or overfulfilled targets. If a branch of the Agricultural Bank, for example, went over its quota for growth of savings deposits, it was recognized at the prefectural level and its officials rewarded with a bonus.[98] The size of the bonuses varied. In the late 1980s, bonuses of officials in a township industrial-commercial management office were

93. Later, as the size of the extrabudgetary funds grew, attempts were again made to regulate spending, but the budgets were simply submitted to the local finance office. The major criterion used for approval was that spending not fall into prohibited categories. See discussion later in chapter 6.

94. For a description of the fiscal crisis that ensued in poor areas where there were insufficient revenues after the fiscal reforms, see Park et al., "Distributional Consequences."

95. The cadre bonus system is examined in depth by Susan Whiting, "Micro-Foundation of Institutional Change."

96. CI 8891.

97. In one county, units were divided into three categories or classes, with the "first class" as the highest designation. Enterprises within the same class received the same bonuses. The finance bureau allocated a lump sum for bonuses to the unit, which then determined the division among its members. The cadre evaluation office also decided award bonuses (*jiangli gongzi*) that were given at year-end to those units that had achieved the rank and title of "advanced unit" (*xianjin danwei*).

98. One county in 1990 had a quota to increase deposits by 16 million yuan. In 1991, another 17.6 million yuan was to be added. CI 8991.

5 percent of the private entrepreneurs' management fee (*geti guanli fei*).[99]
People hired to help collect fees on market days received a cut of the receipts—in one case, it was 13 percent of the fees collected.[100] The head
of a township finance office could receive two bonuses, one based on
whether the revenue collection quota had been met and the other on
whether expenses had been held within the limits prescribed by the plan.
A tax official who received a base salary of 1,038 yuan in 1987 received
a total salary of 2,400 yuan when his various bonuses were included.[101]

Although villages were not subject to the revenue-sharing system, the
salaries of their officials were similarly affected by their economic performance. In fact, both their salaries and bonuses were directly tied to the
collective's total income. One village party secretary of a successful North
China village in 1995 received a basic wage of 900 yuan per month, or
10,800 yuan per year. That in itself was fairly good for the countryside,
but it was only a portion of his income. His bonuses were more than
50 percent of his base wage, or more than a third of his total income,
which totaled 16,000 yuan for the year.[102]

The successful economic growth that led to a monetary reward also
had a political payoff. After Mao, political advancement became linked
to entrepreneurial skills. Local cadres had to manage their economies
well, find opportunities for their firms, and raise revenues to build up local infrastructure. Even village party secretaries could achieve promi-
nence by building village industry and wealth. Yu Zuomin, the party secretary of Daqiuzhuang, is perhaps the most notorious.

STABLE CONTRACTS

The central state's declaration that fiscal contracts would be valid for
five years rather than for one year further increased the credibility of the

99. This figure varied between sectors: in commerce, it was .05 percent of sales; in the
food and beverage industry, it was 1.5 percent; and in the service sector it was 2 percent.
CI 23688.

100. The percentage was decided by the county. CI 23688.

101. Local offices went out of their way to help enterprises grow, with the hope that
such assistance would eventually yield more revenues. For instance, when a brick factory
was low on funds, the tax office provided a one-year, interest-free loan of 5,000 yuan to
buy coal with which to continue operations. CI 24688.

102. The bonuses seem to constitute a smaller proportion of total income for lower-
ranking cadres at the village level. For example, the head accountant in the same village
received a basic wage of 700 yuan per month; with bonuses, his total income was 9,000
yuan for the year. The lowest-paid cadres in the village received 4,000–5,000 yuan per
year. While these amounts are substantially lower than that paid to the party secretary,
they are still relatively generous. CI 23696.

state's commitment. This five-year term stands in sharp contrast to policies in Russia in the early 1990s, where revenue-sharing contracts reportedly expired every three months and the ratios sometimes changing retroactively. Such uncertainty left local governments paralyzed by their inability to know how much revenue they would retain and therefore how much they would have to spend.[103]

China's commitment to the rights of the localities to a residual did not, however, preclude fiscal policy changes after 1980. The history of the post-1980 fiscal reforms has been marked by a number of different systems and policy changes (see table 12).[104] Yet the outcome was different from that in Russia. The locality's rights to the residual were not "secure" in the legal sense—either in Russia or in China—and the reassignment of property rights in China similarly hinged on policy change. The difference is that in China there were reasonable assurances of credible commitment. The insecurity in China was mitigated by the longer tenure of the fiscal contracts. Moreover, the policy shifts that did occur never violated the rights of the locality to a fixed local share.

Post-1980 policy shifts in China adjusted only the amount that the localities could retain; continuity in the overall division of revenues remained. The permutations clustered around two methods for apportioning revenues. The first designated revenues as central, local, or shared.[105]

---

103. Roy Bahl and Sally Wallace, "Revenue Sharing in Russia."

104. Attempts at fiscal reform have been numerous. As Oksenberg and Tong note, "In the twelve years from 1968 to 1979 six [fiscal] regimes, each lasting one to three years, were adopted and aborted in rapid succession: 1968 (total centralization), 1969–70 (sharing total revenue), 1971–73 (lump-sum transfer), 1974–75 (decoupling expenditure from revenue), 1976–78 (sharing total revenue) and 1979 (sharing above-plan revenue)." "Evolution of Central-Provincial Fiscal Relations," p. 31. One of the most comprehensive studies of the early periods, up until 1960, is Audrey Donnithorne, *China's Economic System.* The literature on the later fiscal reforms is extensive. The Oksenberg and Tong work is one of the most useful reviews of the evolution of the fiscal reforms up to 1984. World Bank, *China,* provides a detailed discussion of the system after 1985. See also James Tong, "Fiscal Reform, Elite Turnover"; Christine Wong, "Fiscal Reform and Local Industrialization" and "Central-Local Relations"; also Audrey Donnithorne, *Centre-Provincial Economic Relations.* For a study of the tax situation in Shanghai, see Lynn White III, *Shanghai Shanghaied?* Other studies include Shaoguang Wang, "Rise of the Regions"; and Penelope Prime, "Taxation Reform." Shirk, *Political Logic of Economic Reform,* discusses the bargaining between central and provincial leaders over tax reforms. Details of various types of taxes and changes in the tax system are found in Christine Wong, Christopher Heady, and Wing T. Woo, *Fiscal Management and Economic Reform.* On the 1994 tax reforms, see Jae Ho Chung, "Beijing Confronting the Provinces," and Xiaolin Guo, ed. and trans., "Readjusting Central-Local Relations."

105. The 1980 and 1985 fiscal systems are examples of the first type, which fixed the amount of revenue subject to sharing between the localities and the center, designating central and local taxes. The 1980 system designated local and central revenue according to the level of government to which the enterprise belonged. The 1985 reforms made more

The second method was a much simpler total-revenue–sharing scheme that specified either a percentage (fixed rate) or a lump sum to be turned over to the central state, leaving the remainder to the locality.[106]

For example, when the Jiangsu experimental model that shared total revenues was instituted nationally in 1983, the share rates remained stable and the localities continued to benefit, even though they were required to share more sources of revenue with the center. When the lump-sum system was put into effect for all provinces in the late 1980s, localities were given even more incentives to increase revenue, because they were allowed to keep all, or the bulk, of the revenue beyond the set quota, which was fixed for a number of years.

FROM LIMITED INDIRECT EXTRACTIONS TO DIRECT TAXATION

While it can be said that the center was faithful to its commitment to grant the localities a residual, it also attempted to right the imbalance between the growing local residual and the center's diminishing share of total revenues. However, because of the danger of dampening the enthusiasm for growth that the residual generated in the 1980s, the state took a fairly passive position with regard to extrabudgetary funds. It legislated for itself a few measures to extract a share of the local residual, but it relied mostly on administrative regulation of these funds, which largely remained at the local levels. Only in 1994 did the state take more direct measures.

---

explicit which revenues would be shared, designating categories of taxes as either local or central. This system was only selectively implemented in some experimental areas. Oksenberg and Tong attribute this to a lack of progress in replacing enterprise profits with taxes. "Evolution of Central-Provincial Fiscal Relations," p. 2. As will be discussed later, the 1994 reforms were a return to this type of system.

106. Oksenberg and Tong's study, "Evolution of Central-Provincial Fiscal Relations," shows that the lump-sum system in effect in the early 1970s did contain potential incentives. However, this system was abandoned in favor of a more restrictive total-revenue–sharing policy. The lump-sum system eventually reappeared in a limited form in Guangdong and Fujian provinces, but not until the early 1980s. Under this arrangement, rather than certain funds being designated as local and therefore as part of the residual, a proportion was given to the center. The residual then took the form of the share that was given to the localities. This lump-sum system provides the clearest residual as far as tax revenues are concerned. Guangdong's rapid economic growth is often attributed to the lump-sum system. For a wide-ranging study of Guangdong's economic success, see Ezra Vogel, *One Step Ahead*. The fixed-rate system, in contrast, provides the center and the localities fixed proportions of the total revenues. With the lump-sum system, the center must settle for a preset amount of revenue, regardless of future increases in revenue, while the localities are left to enjoy any future increases. In both systems, the nontax revenues are beyond the reach of the center.

SURCHARGES ON THE RESIDUAL

In the first few years after the beginning of the reforms, the central state tried to amass a portion of the extrabudgetary funds and other "socially idle" (*xiansan*) capital through indirect measures, such as the selling of treasury bonds.[107] In 1983, it instituted various surcharges, including a "state energy transport key projects fund" (*guojia nengyuan jiaotong zhongdian jianshe jijin*) and a "self-finance basic construction fund" (*zichou jiben jianshe jijin*).[108] These funds were ostensibly to protect national resources, transportation, and other key projects, but both were in fact levies on the extrabudgetary funds of a locality. The latter fund was a direct assessment on construction projects financed by extrabudgetary funds. The bonus tax (*jiangjin shui*) and the wage adjustment tax (*gongzi tiaojie shui*) were similar mechanisms to take a portion of the increased revenues retained in enterprises.

There were set rates for these taxes and surcharges, but they were inconsistently enforced. For example, the state energy transport key projects fund tax was supposed to be 15 percent of the extrabudgetary revenue. However, according to one county-level finance official, instead of having to adhere to a set rate, the county was assigned a quota. If the quota was fulfilled, the percentage rule was not upheld. The only advantage to the quota system was that it allowed counties and townships some discretion as to who was subject to the tax. Richer units could be required to pay more while selected other units were allowed to retain more funds for development.

In addition to the standard levies on the extrabudgetary revenues, the central state also resorted to trying to extract a bigger share of these revenues by taking "loans" from the localities. In one county, the center in 1990 took 900,000 yuan as a "central loan" (*zhongyang jiekuan*), an increase of 400,000 yuan over the 1988 levy.[109] Local officials were quite pessimistic about such "loans" ever being repaid.[110] In recent years, at least in some areas, the central state has no longer even made a pretense that such sums would be repaid. Instead of a "loan," the payment of these funds to the center is now called a "contribution."

107. Caizhengbu, *Caishui gaige shinian*, p. 328.
108. These taxes also served other purposes: for instance, to control capital investments financed from extrabudgetary funds.
109. CI 19696.
110. In principle, these loans went for construction of central-level projects. A quota was set for the province as a whole. The prefecture then divided this quota among the counties in proportion to the numbers of their respective construction projects. CI 8791.

1994 FISCAL REFORMS

The institution of the 1994 tax reforms signaled a shift in strategy for controlling extrabudgetary funds. These reforms switched to a more direct means of reducing the amount of such funds: taking more in taxes from the localities. This most recent round of reforms reclassified categories of income and subjected more revenue to revenue sharing, declaring some categories the property of the central state (see table 13). Included was a reclassification of a key portion of extrabudgetary revenues—enterprise retained profits.

Even so, the 1994 fiscal reforms were not a major departure from other post-1980 policies. Many features of fiscal contracting continued to exist, and at the local levels, the old contracts with the townships remained essentially the same. Those who had received subsidies under the old system continued to do so.[111] In many ways, the 1994 reforms were a return to the 1985 method of dividing up revenues between center and locality. This time the lines were based not simply on who owned an enterprise but also on a division of property rights over certain taxes. Under the 1994 changes, the center was given exclusive rights over the taxes of central enterprises, such as the post office and the banks, and over a newly established consumption tax (*xiaofei shui*) with a hefty rate that tapped into once-lucrative products for local governments, such as beer, hard liquor, and cigarettes. In addition, the new regulations assigned 75 percent of the value-added tax (*zengzhi shui*) to the center, leaving only 25 percent to the localities. To ensure adequate collection, quotas were set for the value-added and consumption taxes.

The 1994 assignment of taxes resulted in a substantial increase in the amount that the localities had to pay to the center. In one county, finance and tax officials revealed that in 1994 they paid roughly 9.56 million yuan more to the center in taxes. Out of a total within-budget revenue of over 44 million yuan, they paid approximately 11.5 million yuan in taxes. This was in addition to 440,000 yuan that the county loaned to the center each year. In 1995, having collected over 54 million yuan in within-budget revenues alone, the county paid almost 20.5 million yuan to the center.[112]

But these figures alone provide only a partial picture of the division

---

111. On the national level, the subsidy system is undergoing change. It involves a complex pattern of revenue transfers and returns from the central state after taxes are paid. See Xiaolin Guo, ed. and trans., "Readjusting Central-Local Relations."

112. Unless otherwise noted, this section is based on CI 19696.

of revenues. When it instituted this system, the center guaranteed each locality a minimum base revenue. It used the 1993 tax revenue as the base, which is one reason why there was a big push in all localities to maximize revenues in that year. If the amount now demanded by the center leaves the locality with less than this guaranteed amount, the center is required to return the difference back to the locality. The county cited above was guaranteed a revenue base of 49 million yuan each year. On top of this, it was also granted 30 percent of all revenue above the base amount. This is beyond whatever additional subsidies the center may provide a locality. The old practice also persists of allowing the locality to retain a set budget allowance for minimum expenditures. In 1994 the county was allowed 10.2 million yuan, and in 1995 it was allowed 18.7 million yuan. This allocation is used, as under the previous system, to calculate whether a locality is entitled to any subsidies.

Most important for the purposes of this discussion is that in spite of increased payments to the center, the 1994 system, like its predecessors, leaves the localities a clearly defined residual over which they have exclusive rights. As table 13 in Appendix B shows, the sales tax, local enterprise income tax, individual income tax (*geren suode shui*), property tax (*fangchan shui*), urban maintenance and construction tax (*chengshi weihu jianshe shui*), slaughter tax, agriculture–animal husbandry tax, and special agricultural products tax, along with nontax revenues still belong to the localities.[113] In the example cited, the county paid substantially more to the center under the new system, but it still had 29 million yuan just in the nontax extrabudgetary funds in 1994 and 50 million yuan just in the nontax extrabudgetary funds in 1995.

Some localities are left with a still sizable residual, but the 1994 reforms have had a significant impact on local finances and have resulted in a reconsideration of development strategy. The obligation of localities to pay substantially more revenues to the center has caused massive problems for some of them, as they now face difficulties in paying for basic expenditures, including basic wages. But some localities are taking countermeasures to ensure that local revenues increase. In line with arguments made earlier in the chapter that the definition of the surplus directly affects which sectors become targets for growth, astute local officials have quickly adjusted their strategies to maximize those revenues that are still assigned to the localities. One county, after strongly pursuing a strategy

---

113. Xiaolin Guo, ed. and trans., "Readjusting Central-Local Relations," provides a useful discussion of the 1994 reforms.

of developing rural industry in the 1980s, has since 1994 started to develop commercial agriculture. One reason for this shift is that most of the taxes that are levied on agricultural goods fall entirely into the category of local taxes. In this county, the special agricultural products tax increased over 40 percent in one year.[114]

FISCAL INCENTIVES FOR LOCAL DEVELOPMENT

The experience of Russia and the Eastern European countries has led some to argue that in transitional Leninist systems, enterprises must first be depoliticized—the party and officials must be removed from the factories—before economic growth can occur.[115] While these measures may have been necessary in Russia and the Eastern European countries, the case of China suggests that publicly owned firms can grow without privatization. The key variable is not the form of ownership but the incentive structure for the officials who manage these firms. This chapter has shown that in China, the political interests of local officials, instead of being at odds with local economic interests, became institutionally tied to them.

Moe points out that in organizations "slack is only available to the extent that the bureau as a whole operates inefficiently by producing at greater than minimum costs, with [the] budget exceeding the true costs of production. The greater this inefficiency, the greater is the slack."[116] When China eliminated the organizational slack that its localities had come to rely on, it changed the operating context of officials. Decollectivization and fiscal reform tightened the budget constraints of local governments and created a need to increase revenues. At the same time, they offered localities, and officials within each locality, positive inducements to benefit from lucrative sources of income—the economic surplus generated from local development. The central state thus successfully created a situation where the way to survive and get ahead was to develop the local economy, both to swell local government coffers and to receive bonus payments. There was little reason for local officials to obstruct the reforms. The incentives presented a legitimate alternative to corruption. The lure of the residuals allowed opportunities that led to growth at the township and village levels.

114. CI 23696.
115. Boycko, Shleifer, and Vishny, *Privatizing Russia.*
116. Moe, "New Economics of Organization," p. 763.

To make the incentive package attractive, the central state has had to minimize rather than maximize its claim to revenues generated from the growth process. In contrast to schemes in Eastern Europe and Russia, China during the first decade and a half of reform allowed the local residual to grow to maximum proportions, even at the cost of denying the central state maximum tax revenues. Localities were allowed to benefit disproportionately from local economic growth. Amsden argues that the NICs were successful because they did not get the prices right.[117] A case can be made that the Chinese reforms succeeded in generating local economic growth because the central state did not get the taxes right.

Such an incentive package has carried with it considerable costs. For the central state, the most obvious is the disproportionate size of the local residual—the ballooning extrabudgetary funds. This deprived the center of revenues, put strains on the central treasury, and eventually led to a new set of fiscal policies. A later chapter will show that this strategy also has had far-reaching political implications for the balance of power between the center and the localities. Before turning to that issue, I will first examine how local governments tried to increase revenues and how political costs and resource constraints affected the economic calculations of local officials in determining the patterns and timing of rural economic growth. Officials were presented with strong incentives to pursue economic growth, but the local political and economic context determined the degree to which these incentives were actualized.

117. On the NICs "getting the prices wrong," see Alice Amsden, "Theory of Government Intervention."

Strategies of Development

Variation and Evolution
in Rural Industry

All parts of China's countryside were subject to the incentives embedded in decollectivization and the fiscal reforms, but only a portion of the countryside has successfully developed rural industry. Some areas have been left out of the overall trend of industrial growth and the prosperity that has come with it. In those areas that have succeeded in industrializing, various forms of ownership have been adopted. Some counties, townships, and villages have relied primarily on collectively owned enterprises, whereas others have favored private ownership.

Collectively owned enterprises dominated in most townships and villages in the 1980s, though in a few locales such as Wenzhou[1] and spots in Fujian,[2] private enterprise prevailed.[3] In the early to mid-1990s, the trend began to reverse. The collective model of development started to wane, and private firms grew in number, size, and output value. Moreover, collectively owned firms began to be privatized. What explains this variation and pattern of growth?

1. On the private sector in Wenzhou, see Susan Whiting, "Regional Evolution of Ownership Forms," and her dissertation, "Micro-Foundation of Institutional Change"; Yia-Ling Liu, "Reform from Below"; and Kristen Parris, "Local Initiative and National Reform."
2. On the private sector in Fujian, see Chih-jou Jay Chen, "Local Institutions," and David Wank, "Social Networks and Property Rights."
3. Pockets of private enterprise also existed from a fairly early date in other parts of the country, such as Sichuan and areas of Hunan.

INTERVENING INCENTIVES

The revenue imperative was a necessary but not a sufficient condition for rural industrial growth. Intervening incentives and constraints determined the degree to which local governments could pursue the revenue imperative and the types of strategies they could adopt. Local officials are rational actors who seek to maximize their interests, but theirs is a bounded rationality.[4] They are limited in the information, skills, and resources that they bring to bear on their choices. In China, such officials are further bound in their actions by political constraints. Unlike pure administrators or entrepreneurs, local officials in China are economic actors with administrative and political responsibilities. The logic of China's economic development reflects the intersection of economic and political interests as these officials try to balance multiple, and sometimes conflicting, agendas.

Politics still intervenes to shape economic development in China, even though the campaigns and radical shifts in policy characteristic of the Maoist period have been greatly moderated since 1978. Resources may circumscribe the extent of local growth, but political constraints deter localities from adopting certain courses of development, even when they have the necessary economic resources to do so.

Rather than grow grain themselves, many villages and peasants would have preferred to buy it and concentrate their limited resources on industry. But politics made that an unacceptable strategy of development. Neither localities nor individual peasant producers have had much choice.[5] In spite of the more relaxed atmosphere of the post-Mao period, quotas from the center continued to force localities to maintain minimal levels of grain production.[6] Regardless of the success with which locali-

---

4. Simon, *Administrative Behavior.*
5. Anticipating that localities would increasingly turn away from grain, the center instituted rules requiring provinces to be responsible for their own grain supplies, and it kept in place mandatory grain sales quotas to the state. Some peasant households can pay their agricultural tax in cash, but all must fulfill their sales quotas in grain. If a peasant has not planted any grain, he must go to the market to buy grain to sell to the state. To further ensure that peasants actually sell to the state, some areas close all free grain markets until the state has collected its grain.
6. From the mid-1960s until the end of the Cultural Revolution period in 1976, the economic activity of rural local communities and the individual peasants within them was strictly controlled—little choice existed as to development strategy. The central state dictated that everyone was to "take grain as the key link" to achieve the victory of socialism. Grain production was mandatory, regardless of whether a locality could have more profitably pursued sideline production or cash cropping. Those caught trying to engage in sideline activities or in small-scale industry were labeled "capitalist roaders." Selling grain to

ties pursued rural industry, the center mandated that grain production be maintained. Even one of the most industrialized villages in China, Daqiuzhuang, outside Tianjin, was not exempt. With more than 120 village enterprises in the mid-1980s, this village, capable of providing industrial employment to all its members—as well as to those of surrounding villages—and yielding more than sufficient income to buy on the market all the grain that its members needed, instead had to grow all its own grain.[7]

Politics has likewise dictated the ownership forms of rural enterprises and whether private or collective ownership would grow faster. In theory, the revenue imperative could have been met through either form of ownership. But in practice the collective sector was given preferential treatment while the private sector was at best ignored and at worst ostracized. It was not a question of which type of ownership might yield more efficient use of resources or which was better suited to market production. As Robert Bates has noted in other developing contexts, efficient methods for development do not work if they threaten the political interests of the power elite.[8]

China's development strategies represent compromise solutions that "satisfice"[9] competing interests, with consideration given to resources, opportunities, and costs. For much of the 1980s, political and economic constraints led to the prevalence of a development strategy centered on *collectively owned* rural industry—namely, township- and village-owned enterprises[10] Whether or not this was the most economically efficient course of development, it was the most politically and economically feasible strategy given the resources and constraints of the time. Only gradually, as economic *and* political conditions changed, was there significant movement toward the private sector.

Chapter 2 shows why fiscal incentives prompted China's local officials to seek economic growth as a means of increasing local revenue. This

---

the state was more than an economic action; it was also a measure of political reliability. For details on the way that the need to grow and sell grain shaped rural politics, see Oi, *State and Peasant.*

7. CI 11988.

8. Robert Bates, "Macropolitical Economy."

9. This term refers to the adaptive mode of behavior of boundedly rational individuals. See James March and Herbert Simon, *Organizations.*

10. Byrd and Lin, *China's Rural Industry: Structure, Development, and Reform,* provides one of the most comprehensive studies of rural enterprises based on survey data. See also Wong, "Interpreting Rural Industrial Growth"; Jean Oi, "Fate of the Collective"; David Zweig, "Rural Industry"; and John Wong, Rong Ma, and Mu Yang, eds., *China's Rural Entrepreneurs.*

chapter moves the analysis one step further by examining those incentives in the local contexts that determined which strategies would optimize relevant interests. It seeks to understand how political constraints affected China's rural industrialization and to explain variations in the patterns of rural industrialization across geographical regions and over time. As the following sections will show, China's model of local development has been a dynamic one that has allowed for the changing weight of political and economic interests over the course of reform, as well as for a reassessment of the costs of that reform by local officials whose resource endowments have changed during this period. The variation and evolution of ownership forms in rural industry have followed these changes.

THE CHARACTER OF RURAL INDUSTRIAL GROWTH IN THE 1980s

No one pattern accurately characterizes the process of economic change in China's countryside. Areas with rural industry have generally enjoyed higher incomes and higher standards of living.[11] Some individual peasants left in agriculture get by, some in cash cropping do well, but others remain below the poverty line as defined by the Chinese authorities themselves: seventy million people live in abject poverty.[12] In twelve provinces in western and central China, where rural output was still primarily agricultural as of 1993, the rural net average income was below the national rural average of 922 yuan.[13]

UNEVEN DISTRIBUTION OF RURAL INDUSTRY

The prevalence and higher output value of rural industry have been concentrated in the eastern coastal provinces. The differences among regions in the percentage of total rural output represented by industry are stark. Whereas in the eastern areas nonagricultural production was more than 80 percent of total rural output in 1994, in the central regions it was 15.5 percent and in the western regions 19.5 percent. The differ-

11. See Rozelle, "Rural Industrialization," and Azizur Rahman Khan et al., "Household Income and Its Distribution."

12. Figure cited in He Kang, "Woguo," and Wang Qiang, "2000 nian zhongxibu."

13. The twelve provinces were Gansu, Guizhou, Shaanxi, Ningxia, Yunnan, Henan, Sichuan, Shanxi, Xinjiang, Hubei, Hunan, and Jiangxi. Wang Qiang, "2000 nian zhongxibu."

ences are less sharp but nonetheless clear in employment terms. In the eastern regions, the nonagricultural labor force was 35 percent of the total rural labor force in 1994, while in the central regions it was only 23.5 percent and in the western regions 17.9 percent.[14]

VARIATION IN OWNERSHIP FORMS

In areas that have succeeded in industrializing, various forms of ownership can be found. In fact, the common term *xiangzhen qiye,* which literally means "township enterprises," is understood by all to include ventures owned by local governments at the township or village level as well as those owned by individuals, either singly or in partnerships.[15]

In the 1980s, much of China's post-Mao rapid rural industrialization occurred in *local government-owned enterprises at the township and village levels.* This fact is sometimes forgotten. Perhaps because of the dismal performance of the state in managing economic development during the Maoist period or because of the image of communist cadres as likely opponents of reform, some commentators have glossed over or ignored the government role, leaving the impression that all these industrial enterprises were private.[16]

As figure 5 shows, after 1983 the number of private enterprises far outstripped that of township- and village-owned firms. However, if one considers the average number of people employed per firm under the different types of ownership (figure 6) and the output of each type of enterprise (figure 7), it is clear that collective township- and village-owned firms were dominant. They were the largest and most economically significant enterprises in the Chinese countryside for most of the 1980s, in spite of their smaller numbers.

Other commentators, adhering to the conventional economic view that only privatization could lead to such dramatic growth, have tried to explain away China's unexpected growth by asserting that collectively owned firms are quasi- or secretly "private."[17] While some township and

14. He Kang, "Woguo," p. 14.
15. These different types of enterprises are referred to as the "four wheels of rural enterprise."
16. Zhou, *How the Farmers Changed China,* for example, denies the role of the state and asserts that these enterprises owed their existence entirely to the "revolutionary power of unorganized farmers." For an excellent critique of this view, see David Zweig, "Rural People."
17. See, for example, Victor Nee and Sijin Su, "Institutional Change."

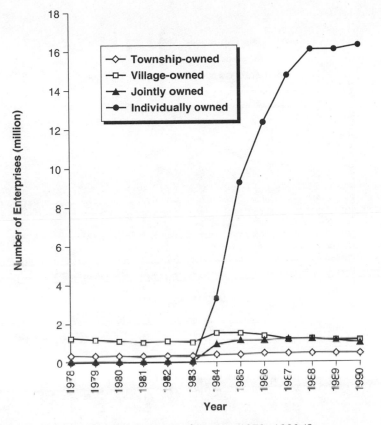

Figure 5.   Rural enterprises by ownership type, 1978–1990 (Source: *Zhongguo xiangzhen qiye nianjian, 1991*, p. 137)

village enterprises, such as those in Wenzhou and parts of Fujian,[18] were "fake collectives" that used the collective label only for protection and economic benefit, lumping together all rural firms as "nonstate firms" [19] or (as in one instance) using them to indicate a "capitalist revolution" [20] misrepresents the character of these enterprises and misidentifies the pivotal actors in the process of China's rural industrialization. Moreover, it is necessary to acknowledge that even in Wenzhou and Fujian, the suc-

18. Liu, "Reform from Below," on Wenzhou; and Chen, "Local Institutions," on Fujian.
19. This is sometimes done in a casual and shorthand manner. See, for example, John McMillan and Barry Naughton, "How to Reform a Planned Economy." In other cases, such as Pei, *From Reform to Revolution,* this categorization underlies a basic argument that these firms are essentially all the same, that is, not owned by the central state.
20. Pei, *From Reform to Revolution,* especially chap. 3.

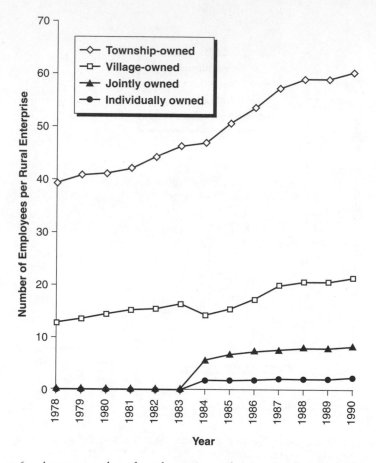

Figure 6.   Average number of employees in rural enterprises by ownership type, 1978–1990 (Source: *Zhongguo xiangzhen qiye nianjian, 1991,* pp. 137–38)

cess of the private sector was fostered by a close relationship with local authorities. Those authorities shielded their private businesses under the "red umbrella"—that is, by allowing private firms to be called "collective." While the precise role of local authorities has varied and some have played a more active role than others, government support has been crucial to both the collective and the private sectors.

Firms under the two types of ownership—collective and private— differ in the access they have had to resources and in their relationship to those who are in a position to provide privileged access to production inputs. In the 1990s, when some of the collectively owned firms began to institute new management systems, some fuzziness between public

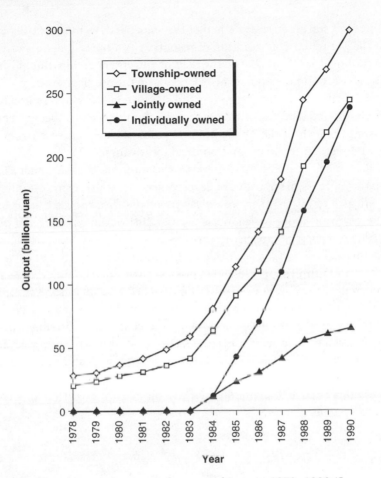

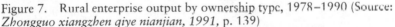

Figure 7.   Rural enterprise output by ownership type, 1978–1990 (Source: *Zhongguo xiangzhen qiye nianjian, 1991,* p. 139)

and private enterprises began to appear, but certainly when rural industrialization was taking off—that is, for most of the 1980s—they were analytically distinct entities.

THE LOGIC OF COLLECTIVELY OWNED ENTERPRISE DEVELOPMENT

The question is why collectively owned enterprises developed first. The answer follows both an economic and a political logic. The economic argument is consistent with Alexander Gerschenkron's observation that when the risks and costs are too great for private individuals, the state steps in to start industry.[21] Whether the state needs to intervene depends on the particular configuration of resources and the willingness of various political actors to take on the risks of entrepreneurship. But in China access to economic resources also depends on the political context, which either facilitates or hinders successful development by different actors. The following sections will show that the dominance of collective enterprises for much of the 1980s in most parts of the country mirrors the private sector's economic and political disadvantages.

The political argument centers on the interests of local officials. To say that successful strategies of development do not threaten established political interests is to make only part of the case for such strategies. Bates, writing about Africa, observes that "[g]overnment intervention in markets creates the capacity to form patron-client networks, or political machines. Through the controlled market, public officials can organize groups of faithful supporters who possess the valued commodity—now rendered scarce by government policy—because of official favor."[22] Such a description aptly characterizes the situation that local officials faced during the Maoist period, when the centralized distribution system provided them with a personalization of authority.[23] Its relevance remains for the post-Mao context, where township and village enterprises allowed local officials to keep their control over the economy and to use this control to maintain their patron-client networks and personalized systems of authority.

RESOURCE CONFIGURATION IN THE 1980S

During the early to mid-1980s, when the reforms began, peasants, eager for alternative sources of income, looked toward rural industry. Some became small entrepreneurs, and large numbers served as the labor force for rural enterprises. But in the early years of the industrialization process, the private sector had neither the right political nor the right economic conditions for takeoff. In contrast, the collectively owned enterprises had advantages in their access to resources and in the favored treatment they received from local authorities.

21. Alexander Gerschenkron, *Economic Backwardness in Historical Perspective.*
22. Bates, "Macropolitical Economy," p. 52.
23. On the clientelist nature of Chinese politics, see Jean C. Oi, "Communism and Clientelism," as well as *State and Peasant;* and Walder, *Communist Neo-Traditionalism.*

Limited Private Resources

Regardless of how much peasants may have wanted to start rural enterprises, the configuration of resources after the decollectivization of agriculture made it unlikely that many could have the inputs needed to start a firm of any scale. After three decades of Maoist collective production, some peasants were only minimally skilled in farming, especially in the cultivation of cash crops. They certainly had neither the skills nor the resources to develop enterprises capable of employing more than a few family members. Not only market information, connections, and technical skills were necessary, but substantial sums of capital too. Given the low cash income of team members during the collective period,[24] few peasants could have had much capital in the early 1980s. Figure 8 shows that peasant savings built up only gradually in the years immediately following decollectivization.

Individuals could and did pool their resources and borrow from relatives what small savings could be spared to start family enterprises. One might think that peasants could also have borrowed from banks, but they received extremely limited bank credit during the early years. According to official government statistics, in 1985, private (and jointly owned) enterprises received a total of 2.8 billion yuan in bank loans. In contrast, during the same period, township enterprises received 20.1 billion yuan in loans and village enterprises 5.9 billion yuan, with a much smaller number of enterprises competing for these loans.[25] The limited capital of the private sector is reflected in the large number but generally small scale of private businesses during much of the 1980s. Most were in the service trades, handicrafts, or small manufacturing—enterprises that required minimal capital.

Wenzhou and places in Fujian are obvious exceptions. A close look at these cases, however, shows that special circumstances intervened to affect the configuration of resources and opportunities. In the area of Fujian studied by Chih-jou Jay Chen, strong clan ties and overseas remittances yielded the private sector extraordinary access to the resources and political protection necessary for successful rural industrial devel-

---

24. I document this in *State and Peasant*. In some teams, peasants never received the money that was owed to them.
25. The total number of private and joint enterprises at the time was 10.65 million, whereas there were only 420,000 township-owned and 1.13 million village-owned enterprises. Nongyebu xiangzhen qiyesi jihua caiwuchu, *1995 nian quanguo xiangzhen.*

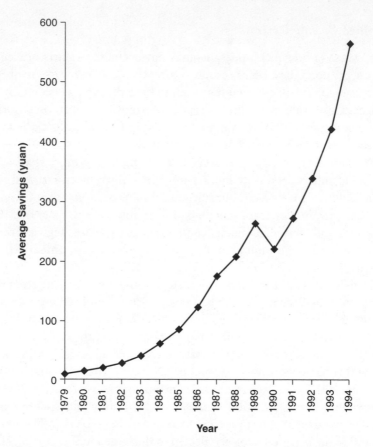

Figure 8. Average peasant savings, 1979–1994 (Sources: *Zhongguo nongcun jinrong tongji, 1979–1989*, p. 1285; *Zhongguo nongcun jinrong tongji nianjian, 1995*, p. 241)

opment.[26] An unusually active kinship network kept money flowing into the area throughout the post-1949 period, even during the height of radical campaigns. Once the political environment became hospitable to economic development, substantial funds flowed in from Taiwan, Hong Kong, and Southeast Asia, and these were used as capital for private business. In addition to outside funds, considerable sums were pooled and managed by strong lineage organizations encompassing large numbers of clan members within Fujian. These funds were plowed into enterprises owned by clan organizations.

26. Chen, "Local Institutions."

In contrast, the collective village and township governments in this area were relatively weak, with few resources to compete with the private sector. Moreover, the thick social and personal kin or clan ties encompassed officials. These social ties mediated a relationship between local officials and the new entrepreneurs that might otherwise have been characterized by fear and hostility. It made both economic and political sense for local officials to let private individuals simply take the risks and assume the costs of entrepreneurship rather than to compete with or repress this sector.

Various explanations have been offered for the early rise of the private sector in Wenzhou,[27] but mounting evidence suggests that there, too, the private sector was much better endowed than local governments. In Wenzhou there is the added factor of a very mobile population that started migrating from an early date in search of labor opportunities and remitted funds home. From 1982 to 1984, migrant workers remitted 465.4 million yuan back to Wenzhou.[28] By 1986 nearly one-tenth of its rural labor force worked outside Wenzhou, earning approximately 900 million yuan. No available statistics allow us to know how much of this money actually was plowed into private enterprise, but the earnings of the migrants alone suggest that peasants in Wenzhou were in a class of their own during most of the late 1970s and early 1980s. In addition, as in Fujian, large amounts of overseas remittances were sent to Wenzhou. In the two-year period 1983–1984, overseas Chinese remittances amounted to 12.68 million yuan. This figure represented 30 percent of the total remittances sent to the entire province of Zhejiang.[29] While these isolated facts are not conclusive, they suggest that in Wenzhou, as in Fujian, individuals had substantial funds to undertake entrepreneurial activities. Also as in Fujian, local governments were poor, with a long history of relative financial neglect by the center during the Maoist period,[30] so that collectively owned assets were comparatively meager.[31]

27. Earlier studies have stressed its relative isolation from and neglect by the center, which they argue led to a rebelliousness of local authorities resulting in their support of private enterprise. See, for example, Liu, "Reform from Below."

28. Zhang Renshou and Li Hong, *Wenzhou moshi*, cited in Jacky Tsang Wai Chun, "Private Sector in Wenzhou."

29. Zhang Renshou and Li Hong, *Wenzhou moshi*, p. 32. Fei Xiaotong, "Nongcun, xiaochengzhen chuyu fazhan," argues that the returned migrants were a key to the Wenzhou model.

30. One source lists 559 million yuan as the total amount of investment by the state from 1949 to 1978 in Wenzhou. Cha Zhenxiang, "Lun woguo nongcun gufen hezuozhi."

31. Local governments in Wenzhou during this period had considerably less in fixed assets than other areas where the collective model was strong. Whiting finds that in Songjiang

Thus, in Wenzhou and parts of Fujian, the private sector had the re-sources and was willing to assume the risks of entrepreneurship, thereby obviating the need for local governments to intervene and take on the task directly.

Expanding Corporate Resources

In contrast to private firms, township- and village-owned enterprises were part of a larger corporate entity, the township or the village. The unit responsible for capital outlay and risks was the corporate com-munity—the village or township—not an individual firm. Village and township authorities used their administrative power to pool capital and risks, thereby permitting individual firms within them to grow faster than would otherwise have been possible given the limited resources available during the early years of reform. Township and village officials redistributed income and debt among sectors and enterprises within their corporate community. No single individual needed to assume the risks of entrepreneurship. Local officials took the initiative to start firms, made the investment decisions, and, when necessary, found ways to bail enterprises out of financial problems, but the collective—that is, the township or village as a collective entity—bore the risks.

Below is a partial list of the resources that collectively owned enter-prises could draw on within their own corporate community. Chapter 4 will examine the resources supplied by the county and higher levels of government.

Collective Funds

The amount of funds a village redistributed depended on how much was already in collective coffers and whether there was an existing group of profitable firms within the collective. If the village possessed sufficient funds, officials had the authority to use them to develop village industry. If such funds were not available, village authorities could mobilize re-sources from profitable enterprises either to fund a new enterprise or to expand an existing one. This is where rights to the residual became relevant.

---

county, Shanghai, the assets of township and village enterprises amounted to 280 million yuan in 1985; in Yueqing county, Wenzhou, the figure was only 25 million yuan. Whiting, "Regional Evolution of Ownership Forms."

As I argue in chapter 2, the rights to profits ultimately remained with the owner of the enterprise, either the village or the township. However, because of the contracting system and the need to maintain the incentive of the contractor, village and township officials often phrased their requests for funds in terms of "borrowing" from an enterprise to further the collective good. Depending on how these loans were handled, whether they were repaid, and whether they earned interest, they might be better seen as examples of the ad hoc surcharges described in chapter 2. In some cases, the term used was not "loan," but "rent paid in advance." In one township, the local government took 400,000 yuan and 200,000 yuan in two separate years from its wealthier enterprises.[32] Interviews with factory managers and village officials reveal that this was not an easy task. Enterprises being asked for funds tried to resist handing over their profits. Yet this approach to raising capital was often successful. Aside from the power that the village or township had over factory managers through its ability to assign contracts, those being asked for a loan also knew that someday they might be on the other side of such a request.

When factory managers did approach the banks for loans, especially large loans, they were accompanied by the township or village head; in some cases, the latter might already have obtained the bank's approval for the financing. Interviewees from a number of localities stated that when a collective enterprise failed and defaulted on its loans, the debt was paid off by the remaining solvent collective enterprises. In one township in 1987, four enterprises closed, leaving a debt of 120,000 yuan. The township economic commission had funds to repay 60,000 yuan to the bank, but the remainder of the debt was divided among its other enterprises.[33] These firms paid, however grudgingly, because their own future depended on the goodwill of the local authorities who controlled credit and investment opportunities.

Enterprise Self-Raised Funds

Once an enterprise was set up, funds could be raised within the enterprise to be used exclusively for its own purposes. This effort took various forms. The most familiar method was to require new workers to give the factory a lump sum (*daizi ruchang*) before they were hired.[34] The

32. CI 72388.   33. CI 17788.
34. The amounts workers were required to pay varied. For example, in one factory workers were required to pay 300–500 yuan. CI 6690.

workers received interest on this money, and the principal was returned after they had fulfilled their minimum work contract, be it one year or a few months.

In the late 1980s, an innovative job bonding system was instituted in some areas to raise funds.[35] An employee would put down a cash deposit (*diya*), which the enterprise then used as circulation funds. Each worker—and most important the factory manager—of a township enterprise put down a deposit to ensure that the requirements of a contract would be met.[36] If the factory manager or the workers failed to meet their quota, they lost their deposit;[37] if they met the quota, they received their basic wage plus the interest on the deposit; and if they exceeded the contract quota, they received interest, their basic wage, and a bonus. The amount of the deposit was based on a person's position. In one county, this system accumulated over 3 million yuan from the county's 366 township enterprises. Interest on the deposits was paid by the enterprises at a rate at least equal to that offered by the banks. The catch was that a deposit had to remain in the fund as long as the worker remained on the job.[38] In some of the townships, the collateral was turned over to the township economic commission, which pooled the money and distributed it within the township. The head of one rural enterprise management bureau reported that this was the procedure in about one-quarter of the townships in his county. In such cases, an enterprise had to apply to the commission to use the funds.[39]

Loans from Collective Members

When village governments failed to raise sufficient capital from their enterprises, or if they had no enterprises, they could borrow from their members. This practice was criticized as placing extra burdens on peasants, especially in poor areas, but it was an important way to raise funds for enterprise development. The methods that were used varied widely across regions and over time.

35. Examples of this were found in Shandong and Guangdong.
36. The amounts varied. For example, some factory managers gave as much as 1,500–2,000 yuan, whereas others gave only 500–800 yuan or less.
37. I have no evidence that any deposits were actually forfeited when a worker or factory manager failed to meet a quota. Officials hoped that the system would give workers a direct incentive to complete their contracts, but the tight credit situation may have been the more important consideration.
38. Interest rates varied among factories. CI 6490.
39. CI 6690.

Some townships and villages sold bonds to enterprise workers and crafted savings schemes offering high interest rates.[40] These opportunities were usually offered only to workers within an enterprise, but sometimes they were extended to other village members. Fairly large sums could be raised in these ways, as I discuss in Chapter 6. Some of the savings strategies seem to have evolved into shareholding systems in the 1990s. But in addition to dividends, a number of these systems continued to pay interest. These schemes became aggressive attempts to generate capital for the enterprise.[41]

POLITICAL CONSTRAINTS AND CADRE INTERESTS

While the configuration-of-resources argument yields insights into whether the private sector was economically viable when relying on its own resources, it does not explain why the private sector was not selected for preferential treatment by local authorities, which had the power and the resources to help it grow. The state could have favored the private sector by giving it tax breaks and loans to bolster the resources available for investment, as localities finally did in the 1990s. But this path of development was initially bypassed because of political bias against the private sector.

Political Constraints on the Private Sector

Officially, prohibitions against private enterprise were removed early in the reform period, but suspicions lingered and constraints remained.[42] In many counties, where for most of the period prior to 1979 not a single license was granted for private enterprise, the private sector was a foreign concept and not readily accepted.[43] Until 1987 the hiring of more than seven employees was banned.[44]

In some areas, the private sector remained vulnerable to political attacks throughout the 1980s. During the retrenchment period of 1988–1989, the center issued general directives to reduce the number of rural

40. This began in 1988. In 1991 the average interest rate on these savings plans in one Shandong village was around 12 percent.

41. This was apparent in a number of collectively owned enterprises where I interviewed, as well as in some state-owned firms in large urban areas.

42. See Dorothy Solinger, *Chinese Business Under Socialism*.

43. CI 23688.

44. See Willy Kraus, *Private Business in China*.

enterprises. In the North China heartland, including Shandong, more often than not the private enterprises were closed first (see chapter 6). Further south, as late as 1988, in one area in Jiangsu (known for the success of the collective model of development), a local gazetteer states that any township or village worker who quit his or her job to open a private firm would be denied a license and face severe consequences, as would the worker's immediate family.[45]

The hostility and suspicion that lingered for much of the 1980s between local officials and private businesses are further apparent in the abusive language local officials used to describe private businesspeople. Rural officials in a county with a history of a strong collective mentality and development strategy referred to private entrepreneurs as "underground snakes" (*ditou she*). Township tax offices in the 1980s complained that private businesses kept incomplete or inaccurate records, or none at all; and once taxes were levied, it was difficult to collect them from private businesses. They reportedly had to be chased down three, four, or five times, and then only grudgingly did they make payments.[46]

Collective Ownership and Cadre Power

While some may have believed in collective ownership of rural industry for ideological reasons, this form of property rights best served the political and economic self-interest of most local officials. Observers of communist officials are correct in saying that cadres do not give up their power easily, but, fortunately for China, the desire of cadres to maintain power did not preclude their supporting economic reform and development. Rather than be undermined by economic reform, local officials had the option of leading growth in the countryside by directing local government-owned enterprises.

The development of collectively owned enterprises yielded little threat of an economic elite that would be independent of the existing power structure. Established bureaucratic mechanisms, including the use of plans and targets, could easily be employed to monitor the activities of collectively owned firms and their managers. The contracting system allowed townships and villages to decentralize management and to use economic incentives to spur performance while keeping a tight rein on the enterprises and their profits. Local officials at the county, township,

45. Zweig, "Rural People."   46. CI 24688.

and village levels could maintain the fusion of economic and political power while furthering economic growth.

In the County

For county governments, collectively owned enterprises were preferable to private ones for a number of reasons. Administratively, township and village enterprises were easier to monitor than private firms. Not only were there fewer of them, but the people who ran the firms were bureaucratic subordinates, not independent entrepreneurs. Public ownership of these firms allowed the county to use routine bureaucratic methods to oversee their management and operation. Such oversight was particularly effective with township-owned enterprises. County authorities continued to regulate the activity of enterprises through plans and targets, even though China was steadily moving away from central planning.[47] Targets for profit, output, and revenue were formulated and transmitted by the county to subordinates at the township level. The county finance bureau, for example, issued revenue quotas to its townships, with built-in growth rates based largely on the number and performance of the township and village industries. These were the targets on which the bonuses for local cadres, discussed in chapter 2, were based.

Rather than have to chase down large numbers of private entrepreneurs, who might or might not keep accurate books, the county could use the extensive reporting system inherited from the Maoist period to monitor how well its plans and targets were being implemented. All township enterprises sent reports to the township economic commission, which then submitted reports to the county, along with the reports from other parts of the township government. Only at the village level was the required preparation of reports attenuated, but villages were still subject to township supervision.

Collectively owned township and village enterprises were also preferable to county-level enterprises in terms of costs. They offered a lucrative opportunity to increase a county's tax base with a minimum of county-

47. Local plans may or may not have been mandated by central quotas. Provinces sent plans to the prefectures, which sent them to the counties, which then sent them to the townships. For example, the county apportioned annual procurement quotas for agricultural goods, such as grain and cotton, and allocated the agricultural tax that it received from the upper levels to the townships. Each of the specialized banks was given growth quotas for deposits by the prefectural banks. In addition, localities, from the province on down, could also set local annual industrial production and fiscal targets.

level investment. The county was free of the financial responsibility for benefits, wages, and other costs associated with state-owned enterprises. Moreover, profits from these township and village enterprises were higher because of lower social overhead costs and the absence of regulation regarding wages and benefits.[48] Even when profits of township and village factories were low, the county still stood to benefit through the collection of the circulation or industrial-commercial taxes, which were levied on total income, production, or sales, not on profits. Unlike workers in state-owned factories, during downturns in the economy workers in township- and village-owned enterprises could simply be sent back to the fields. To a great extent, development costs for the county were low, while the returns were relatively high. The same would also be largely true for the private sector, but private enterprise did not become a viable option until the 1990s.

In Townships and Villages

The cadres who benefited most from collective ownership of enterprises were those at the township and, particularly, the village levels. Collective enterprises constituted a crucial part of their personal power base. After decollectivization, local cadre power was no longer guaranteed, but neither did it come to an end. Some cadres may have felt powerless and ignored by peasants, particularly in poor areas, after decollectivization.[49] But the degree to which this was true depended on how important the resources controlled by the cadres were for the peasants who still lived in the villages.[50] The power of cadres was strongest in those villages with successful collectively owned industry, which provided officials with new resources—replacing those lost with decollectivization—to carry out their administrative and economic responsibilities.

48. There were some exceptions in highly developed areas like Wuxi, which provided some of its workers with such benefits as pensions. See Wong, Ma, and Yang, eds., *China's Rural Entrepreneurs*, especially chaps. 9 and 10. This is also beginning to occur in areas outside of Wuxi. By the mid-1990s, a Shandong village provided retirement pay to its enterprise workers of 70–170 yuan per month, depending on their tenure. CI 62394.
49. For the early years of reform, see Latham, "Implications of Rural Reform," and Siu, *Agents and Victims*.
50. In my own earlier work, I assumed that cadres in villages without industry would be less powerful. See "Fate of the Collective." Yan Yunxiang finds cadres in an agricultural village in Heilongjiang province to be relatively ineffective and powerless. *Flow of Gifts*. However, some preliminary research in other agricultural areas suggests that this is not always the case. Heilongjiang is land-rich, but where land is in short supply and cadres have kept control of its allocation, even where there is no industry, local cadres retain considerable power.

The Need for Jobs

Decollectivization created a large surplus labor problem.[51] While not required by law to provide jobs, officials were under local social and political pressure to find alternative sources of income for their "constituency." Work in township and village enterprises was the major source of jobs in China's countryside in the reform period. The number of workers employed in rural enterprises rose from 32.4 million in 1983 to 87.8 million in 1987.[52] In 1988, the nonagricultural rural labor force constituted almost 18 percent of the total national labor force and almost one-quarter of the rural labor force.[53] The former ideological emphasis on strict egalitarianism was rejected, but it was common for village officials to allow at least one member from each household to work in the village's industrial enterprises.[54] Findings by economists that township and village enterprises tend to overemploy workers support this generalization.[55] However, whether a family received a position was up to local officials.[56]

Jobs in township and village enterprises were coveted by peasants because they were more lucrative than farming.[57] From 1984 to 1988, net income per workday increased 45.9 percent for nonagricultural industries, compared to 15.1 percent for grain production.[58] In addition to

51. Jeffrey Taylor, "Rural Employment Trends."
52. *Zhongguo tongji nianjian, 1988,* p. 293. There is disagreement among economists about the precise numbers. According to Wong, "Interpreting Rural Industrial Growth," the figures from the State Statistical Bureau tend to undercount the number of persons actually working in rural industry. At any rate, the trend is clearly toward more workers employed in rural industry.
53. *Zhongguo nongye nianjian, 1989,* p. 19.
54. There remained a sense that income disparities should not be extreme. A village official outside Shenyang had to return some of his bonus pay because it was so much in excess of the average village member's income. CI 1986. For an interesting account of the social-leveling process from an anthropologist's perspective, see Ann Anagnost, "Prosperity and Counter-Prosperity."
55. Mark Pitt and Louis Putterman, "Employment and Wages."
56. Some did not when extreme clan rivalry was rife within a village. Such examples have been found by Gregory Ruf, "Collective Enterprise and Property Rights."
57. Economists have shown that the greatest inequalities in peasant income are due to wage labor. See Khan et al., "Household Income and Its Distribution." Rozelle, "Rural Industrialization," similarly finds that wages from rural industry account for rural income inequalities, but he goes further to provide a breakdown of the sources of income inequality by region. For a Chinese account, see, for example, "Broad and Profound Impact of the Development of China's Township Enterprises," *Jingji daobao,* 20 October 1987, pp. 34–35, translated in *JPRS-CAR-87–061,* 31 December 1987, pp. 23–25.
58. "1984–1988 nian liangshi shengchande weiguan tanshi." From 1979 to 1986, 20 percent of the peasants' increased income was from rural industry. "Rural Industry Provides Base for Economic Growth," *China Daily,* 5 August 1987, p. 1, in *JPRS-CAR-87–045,* 9 September 1987, pp. 41–42.

paying higher wages, many jobs in rural enterprises had the advantage that, unlike cash cropping jobs, they did not require any special skills.[59]

Profits from collectively owned enterprises underwrote subsidies and community projects that won cadres respect and gratitude from their constituents and political recognition from their superiors. Village officials successful in industrialization found themselves in powerful political positions and they were honored with the title "entrepreneur" (*qiye-jia*). Some village party secretaries were promoted to township posts. For example, after leading his village to industrialization and wealth, one village party secretary was made a party vice secretary of the township.[60]

But the ability to generate increased revenues did not merely give township and village officials recognition and power. Nontax revenues from enterprises paid cadre salaries and bonuses and a host of other expenses that fell to the localities after decollectivization, particularly in villages where officials needed revenue to fund basic services as central investment in agriculture declined.

The Need to Support Agriculture

The politically dictated decision to maintain grain production created problems and costs for villages intent on industrialization. If nothing else, it required factories to alter their work schedules to accommodate the agricultural cycle. Sometimes township as well as village factories had to close during the harvest season, when workers returned home to tend family plots. But the cost to villages involved more than merely adjusting work hours. Those trying to mount successful rural industrial efforts had to allocate resources to enable village members to be both industrial workers and farmers. Local subsidies and support for agriculture determined how costly or profitable agriculture was for individual peasant households, which were now responsible for paying the agricultural tax and meeting the grain sales quotas.

Providing subsidies to support agriculture was a minor burden for rich, industrialized villages. Where the majority of peasant households no longer farmed, authorities provided special incentives to persuade a small

59. Opportunities to pursue nonagricultural jobs varied as a result of disparities in the growth of rural enterprises throughout the country. Overall, the number of areas with a sizable output from rural enterprises increased. By 1988, 46.6 percent of all counties in China had rural enterprises with an output value exceeding 100 million yuan, and some counties had rural enterprises with an output value of more than ten times that amount. *Zhongguo nongye nianjian, 1989*, p. 20.

60. CI 62394.

segment of the population to remain in agriculture. For example, the village might offer to pay the agricultural tax or management fee (*tiliu*) for peasants who continued to farm. In some rich, highly industrialized villages, the collective subsidized the costs of agricultural equipment purchased by specialized farm households. In the 1980s, outside Shenyang, when a specialized household wanted to buy a reaper for 4,000 yuan, the village provided a subsidy of 3,000 yuan.[61] In rich villages like Daqiuzhuang, special subsidized teams of agricultural workers grew all the grain that was consumed in the village and met annual quotas of grain sales to the state. In rich villages, where most peasant households still farmed, if only on a part-time basis, authorities provided services to handle the more onerous agricultural tasks, such as plowing, so that older or weaker members of the family could grow grain while the stronger family members worked in the local factories. Households often paid for these services, but the collective needed sufficient funds to make the initial investment in equipment.

Redistributive Corporatism

Byrd and his collaborators at the World Bank characterize the dilemma of local officials as that of wanting to be good businessmen as well as good government administrators responsible for village welfare.[62] Holding property rights over the collective enterprises allowed village leaders to extract and redistribute profits legitimately and directly for the development of the community infrastructure. The rich, industrialized villages used profits from collective enterprises to provide an impressive array of services and benefits to villagers, whether these individuals worked in rural industry or remained in agriculture.[63]

In highly industrialized villages, the reforms have led not to the end of redistributive socialism but to a new form of redistributive corporatism. The collective is strongest precisely in those areas where the economy is diversified, where agriculture is performed by specialized households, where the contract responsibility system is flourishing, and most important, where industry is booming. In such environments, the power of the local government has grown along with the provision of collective welfare. It is common for highly industrialized villages to build schools,

61. CI 72886.
62. Byrd and Lin, "China's Rural Industry: An Introduction."
63. Graham Johnson, working in the Pearl River Delta, was one of the first to find that villages after decollectivization still provided substantial funds for collective welfare benefits. See "Fate of the Communal Economy."

housing, movie theaters, and community centers for their members. In the mid-1980s, some provided the community with free water, electricity, and liquid fuel as well as subsidies for education ranging from 600 to 3,000 yuan for each student who passed the college entrance examination.[64] In one village, each student who enrolled in a vocational school received 200 yuan; in another village, each student received 2,500 yuan.[65] In 1986 a village near Shenyang provided 60 yuan annually per student and per toddler in nursery school, 1,000 yuan for any student admitted to university, and 20 yuan per month in pensions for men over sixty and women over fifty-five. In one of China's most industrialized villages, over 2 million yuan was spent per year in the late 1980s on various subsidies, excluding services; this village was earning over 30 million yuan in profits.[66]

MANAGEMENT AND OWNERSHIP FORMS
IN THE 1990s

Collective ownership and the contracting system worked remarkably well in generating rural industrial growth in the 1980s. Yet by the early to mid-1990s, problems began to emerge. The success of township and village enterprises in the 1980s had been facilitated by the gaps in production left by the large state-owned enterprises. The pent-up demand provided a niche for these small, low-technology enterprises. Using relatively backward and inexpensive technology, resourceful local officials could make a success of these enterprises in a growing market. By the 1990s, however, the international as well as the local economic environment for rural industry had changed (see table 3). Beginning with the economic retrenchment of 1988, tight credit made loans expensive and difficult to obtain. At the same time, rising competition from the expansion of rural enterprises nationwide increased competitive pressures on rural firms.[67] As table 3 shows, by the early 1990s, production costs— and labor costs—were increasing at higher rates. To be successful in the lucrative export market necessitated higher production and technological standards, both of which required higher input costs and thus reduced profits. The low cost of the technology, a factor that initially allowed these enterprises to grow rapidly in the 1980s, in the 1990s has taken its

64. CI 6488; CI 72886; CI 81786.   65. CI 81786; CI 6488.
66. CI 72886; CI 11888.
67. See Naughton, "Implications of the State Monopoly."

toll as the market has grown and standards have risen.[68] Those who cannot afford to upgrade technologically face increasing difficulties.

The question confronting local authorities is how best to meet these new challenges—whether to continue to promote a narrow policy of favoring collectively owned enterprises or to broaden the development strategy to encompass a strong private sector that can operate in a new economic and political context. Most localities have some mixture of collective, private, and jointly owned enterprises. It is a matter of which sector to support. For every locality, each strategy has its costs and benefits. Each strategy is shaped by the constraints, resource endowments, and benefits of a particular period of time. Changes in conditions alter the feasibility or desirability of a chosen strategy. The key to China's continued growth has been the ability to adapt to broader market and political conditions, including adopting new ownership forms better suited to current conditions.

NEW STRUCTURES OF MANAGEMENT

In the 1990s, higher levels of government beginning with the county have encouraged collectively owned township and village enterprises to adopt new forms of management to make them more competitive and more efficient. Instead of relying mainly on contracting, authorities are pushing a variety of new arrangements. Some more closely approximate private ownership, with the manager possessing more autonomy and clearer rights to the residual. Others remain nearer the collective model but have been upgraded to the level of large-scale corporations to take advantage of scale of production and concentration of resources. These forms include leasing (*zulin*), shareholding (*gufenzhi*), and the formation of corporations (*gongzi*) and conglomerates (*jituan*).

Leasing

Compared with contracting, leasing grants more complete management rights over collectively owned firms, as well as rights to dispose of the

---

68. Changing market conditions, backward technology, and lack of technological expertise were cited by a leading county bank official, as well as by officials in a rural enterprise management bureau, as reasons for the current difficulties of collectively owned enterprises. CI 21696; CI 24696.

TABLE 3. CHANGES IN RURAL ENTERPRISES, 1985–1995

Indicator	Ownership	1985	1990	1995	1985–1990		1990–1995	
					Total Rate of Increase (%)	Annual Rate of Increase (%)	Total Rate of Increase (%)	Annual Rate of Increase (%)
Number of Enterprises (10,000)								
	Township	42	39	42	−7.14	−1.47	7.69	1.49
	Village	115	107	120	−6.96	−1.43	12.15	2.32
	Joint & Private	1,065	1,727	2,041	62.16	10.15	18.18	3.40
	Total	1,222	1,873	2,203	53.27	8.92	17.62	3.30
Fixed Assets (billion yuan)								
	Township	43	128.6	530.8	199.07	24.50	312.75	32.78
	Village	20.1	77	381.5	283.08	30.82	395.45	37.72
	Joint & Private	19.2	62.6	371.8	226.04	26.66	493.93	42.81
	Total	82.3	268.2	1,284.1	225.88	26.65	378.78	36.78
Bank Loans (billion yuan)								
	Township	20.1	80.6	268.9	301.00	32.02	233.62	27.25
	Village	5.9	29.2	110.4	394.92	37.69	278.08	30.47
	Joint & Private	2.8	11.7	64.7	317.86	33.11	452.99	40.78
	Total	28.8	121.5	444	321.88	33.36	265.43	29.59
Total Cost of Production (billion yuan)								
	Township	74.2	220.3	1,510.8	196.90	24.31	585.79	46.97
	Village	44.4	173.8	1,490	291.44	31.38	757.31	53.68
	Joint & Private	72.5	240.9	2,276	232.28	27.15	844.79	56.70
	Total	191.1	635	5,276.8	232.29	27.15	730.99	52.73

(continued)

TABLE 3. (continued)

Number of Employees (10,000)							
Township	2,111	2,333	3,029	10.52	2.02	29.83	5.36
Village	2,041	2,259	3,031	10.68	2.05	34.17	6.06
Joint & Private	2,826	4,670	6,801	65.25	10.57	45.63	7.81
Total	6,978	9,262	12,861	32.73	5.83	38.86	6.79
Total Wages (billion yuan)							
Township	14.1	28.8	111.4	104.26	15.35	286.81	31.07
Village	9.8	26.4	107.8	169.39	21.92	308.33	32.50
Joint & Private	2	45.9	218.9	2,195.00	87.14	376.91	36.67
Total	25.9	101.1	438.1	290.35	31.31	333.33	34.08
Net Profit (billion yuan)							
Township	6.9	8	58	15.94	3.00	625.00	48.62
Village	6.7	13.7	91.7	104.48	15.38	569.34	46.26
Joint & Private	10.1	33	175.5	226.73	26.72	431.82	39.69
Total	23.7	54.7	325.2	130.80	18.21	494.52	42.83
Total Tax (billion yuan)							
Township	6.3	14	67.1	122.22	17.32	379.29	36.81
Village	3.6	10.7	63.1	197.22	24.34	489.72	42.60
Joint & Private	3.9	9.7	75.7	148.72	19.99	680.41	50.82
Total	13.8	34.4	205.9	149.28	20.04	498.55	43.03
Total Losses (billion yuan)							
Township	0.5	3.8	12.6	660.00	50.02	231.58	27.09
Village	0.3	1.2	4.2	300.00	31.95	250.00	28.47
Joint & Private	n.a.	n.a.	31	n.a.	n.a.	n.a.	n.a.
Total	0.8	5	47.8	525.00	44.27	856.00	57.07

SOURCE: Nongyebu xiangzhen qiyesi jihua caiwuchu, 1995 nian quanguo xiangzhen qiye jiben qingkuang ji jingji yunxing fenxi, pp. 1–43; 2.1–2.15.

residual after rent is paid to the township or village owners. This option has existed since the early days of the reform period, but at first it was infrequently used. In the 1980s, it was reserved usually for very small, relatively unprofitable firms in which the management responsibilities had become burdensome to the village. While aggregate statistics are not available, isolated case studies suggest that in recent years leasing has become more prevalent at both the township and the village levels. A highly industrialized village in Shandong had until the mid-1990s leased only one of its seventeen enterprises, a flour mill that had lost considerable sums of money by 1987 and fallen into deficit. Originally, like the village's other enterprises, it had been contracted out for individual management.[69] In 1994 the village leased out four enterprises in one year.[70]

Shareholding

Shareholding cooperatives have become one of the most popular new forms of ownership in recent years, although there is some evidence that the form is still somewhat unstable. In 1995, 182,400 enterprises were employing this system—11.26 percent of all township and village enterprises.[71] However, statistics for 1996 show a decrease, with only 143,477 enterprises using this form.[72]

It is hard to characterize the impact of this change. Various studies have shown that in practice shareholding has taken on different meanings, which may account for the relatively sharp decrease noted above.[73] Some of the companies were originally collectively owned; others are essentially private firms formed with investments from a number of stockholders—something like the original joint ownership firms. As more detailed studies of these new ownership forms show, their precise meaning remains vague, and their adoption is not necessarily intended to improve

69. CI 4688. The situation was similar to that in another highly successful village: only one of the village's ten enterprises, a transport operation, was leased. CI 62494.

70. CI 23696.

71. Nongyebu xiangzhen qiyesi jihua caiwuchu, *1995 nian quanguo xiangzhen,* p. 25.

72. This total comprises 47,923 township enterprises and 95,554 village enterprises. Nongyebu xiangzhen qiyeju jihua caiwuchu, *Quanguo xiangzhen qiye,* p. 47.

73. For a detailed discussion of the history of the formation of shareholding, see Vermeer, "Shareholding Cooperative System"; for a discussion of how two different types of enterprises, formerly collective and formerly private, have converged in the adoption of shareholding, see Whiting, "Regional Evolution of Ownership Forms."

efficiency. Shareholding, like hiding under the "red umbrella" of the collective label, may be yet another device for political convenience and economic benefit. In some cases, the purpose is to approximate private ownership more closely and to clarify property rights. In places like Wenzhou, private firms are using this method to gain greater political acceptance and to improve on their earlier strategy of adopting the collective label, which provided them with a degree of protection but accorded few legal property rights to the actual investors in the firm. However, in the case of former collectively owned factories, shareholding seems to be more a device to raise funds through the sale of shares to workers and managers while the collective retains primary control of the enterprise.

Corporatization

In recent years, highly industrialized wealthy villages have begun to formalize the corporate character of their operations. These villages have changed their names to industrial corporations (*gongzi*); some that are sufficiently large have become industrial conglomerates (*jituan*).[74] Again, it is unclear whether this is a movement toward more private forms of ownership, as ownership remains public, within the village. The impetus seems driven by the desire of local officials to improve the performance of enterprises by increasing the scale of operations and command of resources. Village authorities also seek to upgrade the image of their enterprises from that of "village firms" to that of "corporations." They believe this will put them on a more equal footing with the larger and more prestigious urban, state-owned firms with which they are trying to compete.

THE PRIVATE SECTOR RECONSIDERED

The most dramatic change in the 1990s has been the support that local governments have accorded private enterprise. The existence of a strong private sector is no longer limited to traditional citadels like parts of Fujian or Wenzhou; it is growing in North China and in places like Wuxi, the heartland of the collective model of rural industrial development. Sta-

---

74. This is quite rare for villages. In one county, only seven villages qualified for such a classification. CI 24696.

tistics from one county in Shandong, which had exhibited a strong ad-
herence to the collective development model, illustrate the phenomenal
growth of the private sector in the last few years. The first private entrepreneur was licensed in 1978 in this county about two hours by car from
the provincial capital of Ji'nan. In 1980 there were just over five hundred
private firms, but by 1990 the number had risen to close to fourteen thousand and by 1996 to approximately twenty thousand. The growth of
registered capital is even more dramatic. In 1981, the first year for which
there are statistics, registered capital totaled 610,000 yuan. By 1990 it
had risen to 44.34 million yuan, an increase of over 7,000 percent.[75]
In 1978 the total product value from individual enterprises was only
900,000 yuan; by 1988 it had risen to 247.13 million yuan.[76] Table 3
shows the nationwide increase in the number and scale of private enterprises, although their rate of growth has slowed, suggesting that the overall tougher economic environment has hit the private sector as well.

More significant than the increase in numbers—there have always
been more individual than collectively owned enterprises—is the growth
of large-scale private industrial enterprises.[77] Nationwide, by 1991 the
number of private enterprises (*siying qiye*) exceeded 100,000, employing
1.75 million people and with 10.6 billion yuan in registered capital.[78]
Most of these larger businesses (some 80 percent) were engaged in construction and manufacturing, mining, and transportation. Sixty-two percent of the newly established private enterprises were industrial, and only
25 percent were commercial. By June 1992, there were 110,000 private
firms, the majority of which were in rural areas.[79] As table 3 shows, the
fixed-capital investment of private firms increased at an average annual

75. Calculated from statistics provided by the county industrial-commercial management bureau.
76. Shandong tongjiju, *Huihuang chengjiu*, p. 328.
77. In China, the "private sector" encompasses both individual (*geti*) and private (*siying*) enterprises. These two differ with respect to the size of their labor force. The former
refers to small individual entrepreneurs. The latter refers to businesses of eight employees
or more. *Siying* were legalized in November 1987, when it was announced that the state
would not impose upper limits on the number of workers in private enterprises in the
countryside. Cited in Kraus, *Private Business in China*, p. 95. Other specialized studies on
the private sector include Ole Odgaard, *Private Enterprises in Rural China*; Susan Young,
"Policy, Practice"; and David Wank, "State Socialism to Community Capitalism."
78. Fu Gang, Xinhua, 12 November 1991, in *FBIS-CHI-91–221*, 15 November 1991,
p. 54. The rate of growth has been uneven. Shandong ranks among the top provinces in
terms of growth of the private sector. The top five provinces, Zhejiang, Liaoning, Hebei,
Shandong, and Guangdong, account for 54 percent of all private enterprises.
79. "Individual, Private Business Makes Big Strides," Xinhua, 19 August 1992, in
JPRS-CAR-92–064, 24 August 1992, p. 23.

rate of 42.81 percent between 1990 and 1995.[80] In 1996, in the country as a whole, private enterprises employing eight people or more had a total fixed-capital investment worth more than 105.48 billion yuan.[81]

The rapid growth of the private sector in the 1990s can be traced partly to a change in the allocation of resources from that which existed in the early to mid-1980s. Figure 8 shows that by the 1990s the savings of individuals had expanded considerably. Average savings went from almost nothing in 1979 to close to 600 yuan in 1994. This increase can be explained by the intervening period when individuals did well as small individual operators, whether in the service trades, construction, or small-scale production. In addition, some of those who had worked in nonagricultural labor, either in local firms or in more lucrative jobs elsewhere, returned home with large savings. This added up to a configuration of resources similar to that which existed at a much earlier date in places like Wenzhou and parts of Fujian. Today, individuals in an increasing number of areas, through one means or another, have sufficient start-up capital.

Preferential Policies Toward Private Business

Another reason for the rise of the private sector is that local governments over the course of the 1980s and into the 1990s began to change their attitudes and policies. Local officials, in an about-face, are now overtly promoting the private sector. In some cases, as I indicated earlier, county governments have even issued quotas to their townships on the number of new private firms to be established. As part of this new strategy, localities have instituted preferential policies for the private sector. Local governments especially want to develop large private firms.

Chapter 4 will detail the specific measures taken, but for now the change in attitude is easily conveyed by looking at the change in the amount of official bank credit going to the private sector after 1990. As table 3 shows, and as indicated earlier, the private (and joint) sector received only 2.8 billion yuan in 1985, but by 1990 it was receiving 11.7 billion yuan and by 1995 64.7 billion yuan. For the period 1990–1995, the average annual rate of increase was 40.78 percent. In comparison, the annual rate of growth of loans to the collective sectors declined during these same periods.

80. Nongyebu xiangzhen qiyesi jihua caiwuchu, *1995 nian quanguo xiangzhen qiye*, pp. 2–12.
81. Nongyebu xiangzhen qiyeju jihua caiwuchu, *Quanguo xiangzhen qiye*, p. 191.

State-Sponsored Privatization

The change in attitude toward the private sector is exemplified in *state-sponsored privatization*.[82] Aside from encouraging the adoption of new management forms in still collectively owned enterprises, some areas have decided to sell collectively owned firms at auction (*paimai*).[83] In a number of localities, those sold tend to be the problematic ones, often those that have been declared bankrupt (*pochan*). In some other instances, healthy firms are being sold. The variation is extensive. In one Shandong county, the auctioning of enterprises began in 1994 with the sale of a small township-owned factory. By the end of 1995, the township that had started the trend had sold a total of eight firms.[84] However, eight other townships have sold only one firm each. The township in which the county seat is located sold two.[85] So far, few village enterprises have been sold.[86]

These moves toward privatization raise a number of questions. Why would communist officials want to change ownership forms in a way that more closely approximates private ownership? Why promote the development of new large private enterprises? Why should local officials take actions that remove economic resources from their control?

RECALCULATING THE COSTS AND BENEFITS OF COLLECTIVE VERSUS PRIVATE OWNERSHIP

The decision to foster the development of township and village enterprises was based on political and economic expediency and feasibility, not the inherent efficiency of the collective form of ownership. Chang-

82. There are reports that in 1996 a directive was sent down from the Ministry of Agriculture ordering that all township- and village-owned enterprises under a certain value were to be sold. David Zweig, who has done fieldwork in Jiangsu, also reports that such a directive has been issued to the local levels, but, as usual, not all locations are heeding the policy. Nantong has begun to sell its township and collective enterprises, but Jiangjiagang has not; instead, it is forming conglomerates to try to remedy the problems of rural industry. Personal communication with Zweig, 18 June 1997.

83. The assessment of value is handled by an "asset assessment small group" under the industrial-commercial management bureau of the county. CI 24696.

84. According to county officials, the township had already leased out a number of its enterprises by 1994. The township decided to sell these enterprises after the township party secretary went on a study trip to the United States. Only five of the township's enterprises remain collectively owned. CI 24696.

85. CI 23696.

86. No sales have been officially registered. It was unclear to county authorities how many may have been sold informally.

ing economic and political conditions have necessitated an evolution of local state-led development in the 1990s. On the surface, the solutions that have been adopted in an increasing number of localities—the leasing or sale of former collectively owned enterprises and the active promotion of a large-scale private sector—seem to be in direct contradiction to the notion that officials in Leninist systems are unwilling to give up power. A closer look, however, shows that the logic of changing ownership forms in rural industry is still squarely rooted in a calculation of costs and benefits by local governments and by the officials who staff them in China's current economic and political environment. Again, there is a mixture of necessity, advantage, and feasibility. The strategy of the 1980s that centered on township- and village-owned enterprises was simply the one that best "satisfied" the different interests that needed to be met during that period. It was not cost-free. As competition has increased and profits have become more difficult to achieve, the weaknesses of collective ownership and the contracting system—issues of accountability and property rights—have come to the fore. The distinctive relations of county, township, and village to rural industry in the area of property rights have influenced how each level has reacted to these problems and have shaped the solutions that are now being tried in an effort to keep rural industry competitive.

County

The county has no property rights over the residual of township and village enterprises. It relies primarily on taxation from these enterprises. In the 1990s, counties have become less enthusiastic about township and village enterprises as costs have begun to outweigh benefits and as an increasing number of these enterprises have run into financial difficulty. As table 3 shows, losses in these enterprises are increasing. Between 1985 and 1990, the total deficits of township enterprises increased by 660 percent, from 500 million yuan to 3.8 billion yuan. The 1990 deficits of village-owned enterprises were much less, only 1.2 billion yuan, but still a big increase over the 1985 deficits of 300 million yuan. By 1995, the losses for village enterprises had risen to 4.2 billion yuan. During the same periods, as table 3 shows, the annual tax revenues from the private sector increased at a much higher rate than that from the collective sector.

Some enterprises have gone bankrupt or closed as a result of their losses. National statistics indicate that in 1995, eighty thousand township and village enterprises suffered losses (*kuisun*). The number was

approximately the same as in 1994, but the total amount of losses had
increased by 84.6 percent, which suggests that larger enterprises were
having difficulties. According to a Ministry of Agriculture study, the reasons include increases of over 30 percent in wages from 1994, raising average wages to 3,730 yuan per worker in these enterprises.[87]

The closures of some township and village enterprises have left county
banks holding substantial amounts of bad debt. This reflects poorly on
the counties at the higher levels and affects future investments. In 1996
approximately sixty township and village enterprises in one North China
county had outstanding loans totaling around 40 million yuan that local banks were dubious about ever recovering. Of the total amount, approximately 20 million yuan was owed by thirty enterprises that had already closed. Not surprisingly, government banks to which these loans
were owed were increasingly seeing township and village enterprises as
liabilities that needed to be restructured or closed. As early as 1992, following a number of failures in the previous year, the banks stopped giving financial ratings to township and village enterprises.[88] The Agricultural Bank in this county, the major lender for rural enterprises, became
highly concerned about debt repayment and became a strong advocate
of privatizing township and village enterprises. In the view of one leading bank official, too many loans to township and village enterprises
were improperly guaranteed, many by township economic commissions
rather than by economic entities. In the 1980s, particularly before the
1988 retrenchment and the downturn in the market, the collective
sources of revenue described earlier in this chapter had allowed township and village enterprises to develop rapidly. But in a prolonged economic downturn, when large numbers of factories incurred debt but
earned little or no profits, neither the factories nor their corporate par-
ents had sufficient funds to repay what they owed. The root of the problem, according to a local bank official, was in the collective ownership
of these firms and the way loans were guaranteed. He said, "This makes
it difficult to know who ultimately the bank should pursue for the repayment of these debts."[89] When banks are expressing such strong

87. Nongyebu xiangzhen qiyesi jihua caiwuchu, *1995 nian quanguo xiangzhen qiye*,
p. 27.
88. CI 21696.
89. When debts cannot be repaid and an enterprise closes, bankruptcy is declared.
Banks receive a portion of the proceeds once an enterprise declares bankruptcy, but they
are the last in line to receive payment. Consequently, banks recover only a portion of the
original loan. CI 21696.

reservations it is difficult for the county government, which previously had lobbied banks to provide collectively owned enterprises favorable loans, to continue on this course of development.

But the economic rationale has not always prevailed. Why should it now? Why would officials support a group that could undermine their power? Here one finds that the economic impetus for reform is reinforced by a political environment that is now much more hospitable to the private sector. There is some evidence to suggest that in some areas the movement to privatize has been driven by directives from the upper levels. It is the combination of economic and political pressures that has led counties to take steps to increase the efficiency of their remaining collectively owned enterprises and to support the private sector.

Townships and Villages

The attitudes of township and village officials are more ambivalent than those of county officials. Some have eagerly sold almost all of their enterprises, but others are more hesitant. There are signs of resentment on the part of some village officials who have had the tables turned on them. Instead of being favored, they are finding it increasingly difficult to get loans and other assistance, while the county is giving preferential treatment to the private sector. Interviews suggest that beneath the anger even these village party secretaries who have been successful at building up their village corporations have come to realize the need for change.

Villages and townships have begun to feel the costs of maintaining ownership and control of their collective enterprises. The less favorable economic conditions have necessitated reassessment and, in some cases, consolidation. But the need for change has also been prompted by success. Some thriving industrialized villages are now facing problems of overexpansion.[90] While the contracting system allowed villages broad intervention, it also required extensive monitoring and problem solving. In many successful industrialized villages, the party secretary took a hands-on attitude and was intimately familiar with each and every factory, in spite of the fact that they were all contracted to individuals for management. This continued economic and political control made the

---

90. It was their smaller size that allowed these publicly owned firms to escape the problems of the large state-owned enterprises. Andrew Walder, "Local Governments as Industrial Firms," discusses the differences in size and the effects on monitoring.

contracting system attractive to local officials, but it carried heavy costs, especially as these village cadres aged.[91]

Local officials have encountered other difficulties as rural enterprises have had to become more efficient in an increasingly competitive market. One is disciplining the local labor force, especially in village-owned enterprises. Wuxi, which has long used the collective model, is finding that local peasants, because they feel that they, too, are the owners of the village factory, tend to resist the strict labor discipline that village officials try to impose to improve efficiency. This has caused disagreements and bad feelings between local officials and the populace, leaving the factories with little prospect of improved economic performance.[92] The solution has been to sell some collective factories for private ownership. The reasoning is that if these factories are sold to individuals, the new private owners will not be bound by social obligations to keep excess laborers, nor will they face the same problems in disciplining the workforce. It is too early to know if the sale of these firms has produced the desired results.

There are also reports that officials are having difficulty maintaining high levels of loyalty and performance from factory managers. As successful factory managers gain experience and connections through years of managing collectively owned enterprises, they are becoming increasingly dissatisfied with the contracting system and resentful that the residual is taken out by local officials. They feel that they no longer need the connections and intervention of these officials. The relationship is not viewed as being as mutually beneficial as it was in the 1980s, when the cadres clearly had a monopoly on connections and information.[93] Some cadres have tried to come up with new management schemes that provide higher salaries for the managers.[94] In other instances, given the amount

91. I was impressed by the number of villages where the rise of rural industry seems to have been the work of one individual able to remain in office throughout most of the reform period. Some of these individuals were in power even before the reforms began. More than a few of them, including many village party secretaries, are nearing retirement; some have already retired. One question is whether similarly singleminded officials can be found to replace them. The central leadership is already concerned about this problem in poor areas, where there has been difficulty recruiting new leaders. I discuss this in "Economic Development."

92. James Kai-sing Kung, "Evolution of Property Rights."

93. Ibid.

94. One village is trying to increase enthusiasm by raising all pay levels and providing a floor below which salaries will not fall. The aim is to even out swings in managers' pay resulting from dips in the market. At the same time, however, the village is instituting strict accountability for managers and will fire them if they do not meet expectations. CI 23696.

of effort required from local officials and the problems that have emerged, village or township leaders have decided to rid themselves of some of their burden, particularly the unprofitable firms, to focus their energies and resources. At a minimum, they are more interested in leasing out enterprises that are problematic. Collective ownership seems to have reached a watershed that requires adaptation to new conditions both within the collective and in the broader market environment.

While some have considered sale, and more have taken leasing as the first step, others have allowed their firms to become shareholding co-operatives. Often this is done only to raise funds; the local officials retain the majority, controlling shares (*konggu*) for the collective. Successful villages with large numbers of enterprises are taking advantage of the opportunity to become corporations, or, in the case of the very large entities, to become conglomerates so that they can bolster their performance and image, thereby becoming more competitive in the national and international arenas. The result has been a rapid evolution of rural industry toward a mixed economy, with a still strong collective sector and an increasingly important private one.

CHANGING OWNERSHIP FORMS IN RURAL INDUSTRY

Local state-led development is not confined to one particular ownership form. The initial preference for collective ownership in China grew out of a particular set of circumstances; the growing diversity in ownership forms signals change in the broader economic and political context. Local development strategies have evolved within as well as across localities. Local economies are now qualitatively different from those of the 1980s. Counties, townships, and villages in China's countryside have shown an impressive flexibility and an ability to face problems and adopt timely development strategies that are suited to changing political and economic conditions.

China's rural growth in the 1980s was an evolutionary process that began with the development of publicly owned township and village enterprises using the collective structure that survived intact despite the decollectivization of agriculture. This was a public-sector strategy in which the mix of private and public enterprise, and the forms of governance of public enterprise, evolved gradually. Privatization began on a significant scale only after more than a decade of rapid public-sector growth. Even then, it proceeded only gradually, and its acceptance is still localized. Taken as a whole, China's rural development is illustrative of its gradual transition from a socialist system toward a mixed economy. Slow institutional change has occurred within a context of rapid economic growth.

The next chapter will examine the mechanisms that have propelled these different phases of China's local development and have served as instruments of growth. It will identify how local governments went about intervening in and assisting enterprises, both public and private. What will become clear is that when diversification and the promotion of the private sector were pursued in the 1990s, many of the characteristics of the 1980s local state-led growth were retained. Chapter 4 will further consider how local governments control the new economic elite (i.e., the private entrepreneurs).

Local State Corporatism

The Organization of
Rapid Economic Growth

Previous chapters have laid out the incentives and described the sequence of rural industrial development in China. The task of this chapter is to penetrate into the process by which rural enterprises, both collective and private, took off and grew. This will get at the heart of the question of how relatively small, out-of-the-way firms owned and operated by poorly educated peasants, either as individuals or as a collective, could operate outside the state plan, where they had to procure their own inputs and sell their own goods and where only the beginnings of a market were in place. The answers to these questions will illuminate the nature of the local state-led growth and the relationship between local government and firms of different ownership type during the reform period.

MAOIST LEGACY AS THE FOUNDATION

As surprising as it may seem given the problems of the Maoist system, it was the institutions inherited from the pre-reform period that provided local governments with the basic tools to foster the rapid growth of rural industry.[1] The Maoist system was plagued by economic inefficiency, but

---

1. An earlier version of this argument is presented in Jean C. Oi, "Role of the Local State." Steven M. Goldstein, "China in Transition," makes a parallel argument about the legacy of the Maoist system.

once modified to allow for local initiative—with the proper incentives introduced to channel talent toward economic development—this system became the basis of a new and effective form of local state-led development. It contained a political capacity and an array of policy instruments, some of them similar to those found in successful developmental states of East Asia,[2] that allowed post-Mao China to turn in short order into an economic dynamo.

Unlike late-industrializing countries of Africa or Latin America that are often plagued by bureaucracies lacking experience or organizational capacity,[3] the Maoist bureaucracy was an elaborate network that extended to all levels of society down to the neighborhood and work unit, and, by international standards, it exhibited a high degree of discipline.[4] Within each level there existed an impressive organizational apparatus that could effectively transmit the state's plans to producers by issuing quotas passed down step by step through several layers of government bureaucracy.

Unlike the Soviet Union, where the strong ministerial system bypassed local governments and transmitted plans directly to their enterprises, the Maoist system decentralized economic and administrative power to the localities. The extensive and still-functioning bureaucracy, presented with the new incentives and freed from constraints on economic activity, made local governments at the county, township, and village levels well situated to launch rapid economic development.

Working within a strong bureaucratic system, local government at the county, township, and village levels used its official position and administrative resources to foster the development of local enterprises, first collectively owned firms and eventually private ones as well. At the township and village levels, cadres used their administrative authority to mobilize resources within their communities to fund collectively owned rural industry directly, redistributing capital and pooling risks. When necessary, townships and villages could turn to the county for assistance, as they did in other policy areas.

2. The similarities are not precise. For a useful discussion of some key differences, see Margaret Pearson, *China's New Business Elite*, chap. 6.
3. On the importance of what is sometimes also called the maturity of a bureaucracy, see Dietrich Rueschemeyer and Peter Evans, "The State and Economic Transformation." A useful succinct statement on effective bureaucracy as key to capacity is Stephan Haggard and Robert Kaufman, "Market Oriented Reform."
4. See Martin Whyte and William Parish, *Urban Life;* and William Parish and Martin Whyte, *Village and Family.*

The Maoist legacy is the foundation for a distinctive form of state-led growth that I have termed *local state corporatism.*[5] It is a new form of development that is committed to growth and the market, but it is led by a party-state with roots in a Leninist system and with the Communist Party still at the helm. The Maoist legacy is the basis from which the local corporate state developed, along both corporate and corporatist lines.

For much of the 1980s, when the reforms were getting under way, officials, working largely within the confines of an economy still under local state government ownership, turned collective enterprises into quasi-corporate entities. Relying heavily on the existence of a collectively owned economic base and administrative power, local governments treated the enterprises within their administrative purview as components of a larger corporate whole. Local officials acted as the equivalent of a board of directors, with the locality's top official as the chief executive officer. At the helm of this quasi-corporate organization stood the local Communist Party secretary. Control was exercised through the monopoly of property rights that local government retained.

The flow of revenue from enterprises to township and village government, above and beyond standard tax assessments, is likely to be interpreted by outsiders as rent seeking. Even the official press criticizes local governments for taking too much from its enterprises.[6] While some governments do engage in predatory behavior, it is important to realize that often there is also a substantial flow of funds and support services from the local government to the enterprises.[7]

Unlike the rent-seeking situations that one finds in some developing countries, the relationship between local governments and their enterprises is not a zero-sum game. Redistribution can be either an inducement or a constraint of the corporatist system, depending on whether the en-

5. For my earlier writing on this, see "Fiscal Reform and Economic Foundations"; a preliminary formulation is in "Chinese Village, Inc."

6. National regulations have stipulated that the amounts taken by some economic commissions should be reduced. According to a county official of a rural enterprise management bureau, before 1985 the township economic commission took as much as 40–50 percent of total after-tax profits. CI 53188.

7. For example, in the late 1980s, a township economic commission outside Tianjin took 40 percent of the quota profit and 30 percent of the over-quota profit. Local officials acknowledged that this was a considerable extraction, but they also explained that the funds were used for the unified management of the enterprises as a whole, and eventually some of the money would be returned to the enterprises. CI 8688.

terprise receives or gives. Mutual dependence rather than predation is a more apt description of the relationship. This explains why large extractions of revenue have not negatively affected growth, as the rent-seeking literature shows occurring in other developing countries.[8]

The situation becomes clearer if one keeps in mind that these are collectively owned firms, not private firms or firms over which the manager has rights to the residual. As I stress in earlier chapters, contracting left the rights to the residual with the village or township government. The flow of funds from enterprises to township and village governments can be understood as a form of profit-taking to pay for collective expenditures and reinvestment.

Aside from being reinvested in industry, these funds are also used to pay for subsidies to the community and to cover corporate overhead, including the support of industries that are not profitable but provide jobs for the village's surplus labor. They may even be used to keep an enterprise open because it carries prestige and gives "face" to the village.[9]

Such practices can be criticized on a number of counts, including that of adding yet further to the "burden on the peasants." The collective financing and debt repayment system described in the last chapter also softens the budget constraints that firms would otherwise face—a cushioning that led to problems in the 1990s—but it is one reason township and village enterprises have been able to grow so rapidly with limited funding. New enterprises do not have to raise all the funds they need for their start-up operation—they can borrow funds from sister enterprises within the local corporate community. The fiscal health of an enterprise depends not only on its own internal sources of wealth and on the credit that it can mobilize, but also on the financial resources of the corporate state of which it is a part. Corporate financing was particularly useful and feasible in the 1980s, when many village and township enterprises started out on a relatively small scale and loans, especially for village enterprises, were extremely limited.

In the 1990s, the emergence of semiprivate and private ownership of rural industry has been accompanied by an evolution of local state corporatism. The local state has no rights to the residual from private enterprises, but, by the same token, private enterprises are not eligible to re-

8. For example, Krueger, "Political Economy."
9. See, for example, "Township Enterprises Should Also Implement Reform," *Jingji cankao*, 18 November 1987, p. 1, translated in *JPRS-CAR-88–005*, 18 February 1988, pp. 20–21.

ceive the corporate funds that township and village enterprises benefit from. Nonetheless, the rapid growth of the private sector cannot be fully accounted for without understanding the role played by the local corporate state. This growth has not been a manifestation of laissez-faire capitalism. As the last chapter already suggested, cadres did not simply step back and let the private sector grow. This chapter details how local governments, using a combination of inducements and administrative constraints characteristic of a state corporatist system, managed to promote the private sector while at the same time preventing it from becoming an economic elite over which they had little control.

The first part of the chapter, which discusses the corporate management of collective assets, will explain how collectively owned township and village enterprises grew so rapidly during the 1980s. The second part of the chapter will turn to the way the local corporate state has evolved to incorporate a dynamic private sector.

THE LOCAL CORPORATE STATE

Village, township, and county make up the local corporate state directly responsible for the dramatic growth of rural enterprises in China. Table 4 shows the leadership structures and organizations at the three levels. Each level has its own interests, resources, and accounting each level is in itself a corporate entity—but the levels are intimately connected. Hierarchy and obligations are explicit; those at the lower levels are subject to the directives of the higher levels; and those at the lower levels turn over to those at the higher levels a portion of their revenues. Control within the local corporate state involves constraints and inducements applied to each level of local government and to enterprises within each level. The distribution of resources follows the hierarchical nature of the state bureaucracy, and the availability of resources increases with the level of the bureaucracy.

While the initiative of each level is crucial, the rapid development of rural industry has been a multilevel process. Each level has had access to inputs for economic activity, but no one level has had sufficient access to all of the key inputs needed for the rapid economic development that has taken place in China during the period of reform. Each level has its own resources and strives to be self-sufficient, but it can appeal to the next higher level for assistance and intervention. Just as no collectively owned enterprise is limited to its own funds, no one level is dependent

TABLE 4. THREE LEVELS OF THE LOCAL CORPORATE STATE

	County	Township	Village
Leading Cadres	Party secretary	Party secretary	Party secretary
	County magistrate	Township head	Village committee chairman
	Party vice secretaries	Township Party vice secretaries	Enterprise management committee director (not in all villages)
	Vice magistrates	Township vice heads	
	General Office director		
Key Economic Commissions and Agencies	Banks		
	Economic commission	Auditing office	Enterprise management committee (not in all villages)
		Economic commission	
	Finance bureau	Finance office	
	Industrial-commercial management bureau		
	Planning commission	Grain station	Village committee
	Rural enterprise management bureau	Industrial-commercial management office	
	Tax bureau	Tax office	
Other Agencies	Administrative control bureau	Agricultural technology station	
	Agriculture, husbandry, and fisheries bureau	Birth planning office	
	Archives bureau	Health station	
	Audit bureau	Land management station	
	Bureau of appeals (letters and visits)		
	Bureau of mines	Rural economic work management station	
	Civil administration bureau	Security station	
	County research bureau		

(continued)

TABLE 4. *(continued)*

County	Township	Village
Culture bureau		
District division office		
Education bureau		
Environmental protection bureau		
Family planning commission		
Foreign affairs office		
Foreign trade company		
Forestry bureau		
Grain bureau		
History office		
Irrigation bureau		
Justice bureau		
Labor bureau		
Land management bureau		
Materials supply bureau		
Notary office		
Personnel bureau		
Place-name office		
Price bureau		
Public health bureau		
Public security bureau		
Science and technology commission		
Security office		
Sports commission		
Statistics bureau		
Technology control bureau		
Town and city construction commission		
Transportation bureau		

NOTE: This list is only a rough approximation of offices and organizations. The tax bureau, for example, as of 1994 divided into a national tax bureau and a local tax bureau. Moreover, the precise names may differ. This structure reflects the organization prior to the proposed elimination and merger of bureaus put forth at the 9th National People's Congress in March 1998.

only on its own resources. The rapid development of China's rural industry stems from the input of all three levels—county, township, and village.[10]

The local corporate state is akin to a large multilevel corporation. The county is at the top of the corporate hierarchy, corresponding to the corporate headquarters; the townships are the regional headquarters; and the villages are the companies within the larger corporation. Each level is the approximate equivalent of what is termed a "profit center" in decentralized management schemes used in business firms.[11] Each successive level of government is fiscally independent and is thus expected to maximize its economic performance. Like a profitable company or division within a large corporation, those townships and villages that succeed in becoming highly industrialized will command positive attention, will be listened to at corporate headquarters, and will have more leverage to be "innovative" in their implementation of rules and regulations. Their leaders will be promoted up the corporate hierarchy. In this sense, China is coming closer to the ideal of the NIC model of development, where subsidies are given to firms judged to have the best potential or are already the best in a particular field.

In contrast to any multinational corporation or East Asian NIC, however, the local Communist Party secretary plays a key role in economic decision making in the local corporate state. But this is not communist politics as usual. Subject to the same incentives as other local officials, Communist Party secretaries in industrially developed areas of the countryside are at the helm of economic development. How involved they are in the details of management varies with the level of government. The lower down the hierarchy, the more intimately cadres are involved. Most visible is the village party secretary, who can be found personally intervening in the economic decision making of the village's enterprises, often chairing the board of directors of the village enterprise management committee.

10. This view contrasts with that put forth by Yingyi Qian and Chenggang Xu, who stress the independence and self-sufficiency of townships and villages in the development of rural enterprises. They note that "each geographic region [in China] at each layer can be regarded as an operating unit. Each unit is divided along geographic lines and at the same time the unit controls its own enterprises along functional lines. Operating units (regional governments) are semi-autonomous and relatively self-sufficient in terms of functions and supplies in production." Yingyi Qian and Chenggang Xu, "Why China's Economic Reforms Differ."

11. See Harrison C. White, "Agency as Control."

CORPORATE HEADQUARTERS: THE COUNTY

Barnett noted thirty years ago that the county is the "most important administrative unit in rural China now, as in the past. . . . Most counties have tended to be relatively stable administrative units, because more often than not they have constituted natural centers of transportation, communications, industry, and commerce. Traditionally, the county seat has served not only as an administrative headquarters but also as the economic and social center of a fairly well-defined region."[12] This description remains apt today in many respects, with the exception that the county has now taken on a much more active role in fostering local economic development in response to the fiscal pressures and opportunities offered by the reforms.

The county government oversees, guides, and promotes the direction of growth, including that of its townships and villages. As county officials describe their own role, it is to coordinate (*xietiao*). Concretely, this is to arrange for the necessary inputs and bureaucratic services that allow local enterprises to prosper. Township and village officials appeal to the county for assistance if problems cannot be resolved with their own resources. Officials at the county level often are likely to have the broadest knowledge of developments outside their county and to have the widest network of personal and professional relationships. County officials go on fact-finding missions to developed areas to study advanced models; some even go abroad. They are the ones with whom foreign investors meet, and they guide such investors to particular sites within the county.

Leadership

The county party secretary (*xian dangwei shuji*) and the county magistrate (*xian zhang*) head the local corporate state. Like most leading local officials, magistrates and party secretaries are rotated from place to place, usually avoiding assignment to their home areas.[13] Their term of office varies. Some serve in a locality for less than a year. In one Shandong county from 1949 to 1989, the term of office for a party secretary

---

12. A. Doak Barnett, with Ezra Vogel, *Cadres, Bureaucracy, and Political Power,* p. 117.
13. There is no law of avoidance as in Qing China, but many of the county magistrates whom I interviewed did not serve in their home counties.

ranged from less than six months to over seven years; that of a county magistrate from a few months to over nine years. The average term of office in this one county for these top positions was only 2.5 years.[14] While such terms of office may be relatively short, officials may still become deeply immersed in local development. Anecdotal evidence suggests that those in counties that flourish are the ones most likely to be promoted up the bureaucratic ladder. Economic performance has become a key criterion for political promotion.

The duties and authority of the party secretary and the magistrate overlap in their oversight of the economy. The party secretary, as the ranking official in the county, is something akin to a "hands-on" chairman of the board, who sets policy direction, decides development strategy, and makes long-term plans. The county magistrate, more like a chief operating officer, is the head of the government, leads the bureaucracy to implement the broad development goals of the county, and handles immediate concerns of development and problems relating to the bureaucracy. The size and wide range of responsibilities facing both the party secretary and the county magistrate require that their involvement be limited to making the major decisions. The staff of the county magistrate and the county bureaucracy are the people intimately involved in economic work, attending to routine matters and details that affect development.[15] The key bureaucratic players involved with rural industry are the finance bureau, the tax bureau, the rural enterprise management bureau, and the banks (see table 4). In some counties, the foreign trade companies are assuming increasing importance. The functions that they each perform may be gauged from table 5.

Resources

County government facilitates development of rural enterprises through the provision of services and resources. The inputs that the county bureaucracy controls have changed as markets have matured. After almost two decades of reform, there is an increasing number of alternatives by which the lower levels can bypass the bureaucratic hierarchy for material inputs. An increasing concentration of resources is building up at the bottom levels of that hierarchy; this trend is changing the role of the

---

14. *Shandong Zouping*, pp. 337–38.
15. The staff consists of the General Office director and vice magistrates to whom the magistrate delegates responsibility for specific areas of decision making, such as rural industry.

TABLE 5. ECONOMIC DUTIES OF THE
LOCAL CORPORATE STATE

Economic Sector	County	Township	Village
Agriculture	Set production quotas	Issue grain contracts	Contract land
	Set purchase targets	Collect agricultural tax grain	Ensure tax payments
	Allocate procurement funds	Collect procurement quotas	Divide village procurement quotas among households
	Allocate credit	Distribute production inputs	
	Overall planning	Pay peasants for procurements	
Industry	Issue licenses	Issue credit and loans	Contract village-owned enterprises
	Determine tax breaks	Supply materials	
	Administer product certification	Manage investments	Make production decisions
	Grant loan deferments	Make production decisions	Manage investments
	Issue credit and loans	Contract township-owned enterprises	Procure production materials
	Supply materials	Act as liaison	Procure credit
	Manage investments	Conduct coordination work	Generate/procure capital
	Rate enterprises	Repay debts	Act as liaison
	Contract state-owned enterprises	Guarantee loans	Conduct coordination work
	Act as liaison		Repay debts
	Conduct coordination work		Grant permission for outside factory work
	Provide information and technology		
Private Business Sector	Oversee Individual Entrepreneurs Association	Oversee Individual Entrepreneurs Association	Provide reference letters
	Issue licenses	Collect taxes	Check applications
	Supply materials	Process license applications	
	Issue credit and loans		
	Regulation		

county. Table 6 shows the resources at each level of the bureaucracy. The dependence of the lower levels of government on higher levels for material production inputs is determined by the scarcity of the inputs, the quantity of goods needed, and the price the lower levels are willing to pay for them. Furthermore, this dependence is related to the existence of alternative channels that are not under state control. Where there are no alternative sources, and when sophisticated technology or scarce resources are needed, one must continue to go to the county or higher up the bureaucratic hierarchy to secure sufficient amounts.

One source of the county's power that is independent of market growth is its exclusive control of bureaucratic inputs. Some of these inputs (for example, licensing and product certification) are procedures to start up businesses. Others (for example, tax breaks and loan deferrals) provide economic advantages. County agencies critical to rural enterprises, such as the rural enterprise management bureau, spend large amounts of time and energy representing local industries at higher-level key agencies in efforts to acquire technology, materials, funding, and so on. Officials from these county agencies may personally accompany factory managers to the higher-level agencies. The daily routine of cadres at the county-level rural enterprise management bureau is filled with trips to the prefecture, even to Beijing, on behalf of specific enterprises. A diary of an official from a county rural enterprise management bureau shows that in May 1988 he made six business trips to the provincial capital, one to Beijing, three to other townships, and six to various villages. In contrast to political systems where such closeness between government and business would be viewed with suspicion, in China local officials see it as part of their duty to provide direct assistance to local firms, including intervention with higher levels on their behalf.

Moreover, a county government can mobilize not just one but all of its agencies and bureaus to nurture township and village enterprises. Some even provide services well outside their administrative domain. For example, the county tax bureau not only collects taxes and gives tax breaks, but also helps enterprises train accountants and find scarce technical personnel, a pressing problem for rural industry. One agency may use its connections to influence other agencies—for example, banks— to bend the rules in favor of a pet enterprise. Or an agency may use its bureaucratic power as a type of collateral to secure a loan for a favored firm. For example, before the practice was prohibited, the tax bureau would sometimes allow an enterprise to repay a bank loan before taxes were assessed (*shuiqian huankuan*) in order to win the bank's support for the loan.

Counties also have had funds that they could lend directly to enterprises through various bureaucratic agencies such as the tax bureau, the finance bureau, and the science and technology commission. Although banks were still the major sources of credit, local government bureaus in the 1980s could unilaterally provide no- or low-interest loans to help certain industries. These amounts were not large, but they could be significant, particularly if a factory needed circulation funds to purchase raw materials. Such sources of support and funding were critical when the upper levels of government tried to rein in growth by cutting credit, as they did in 1988–1989 (see chapter 6). Enterprises usually had one to two years to repay such a loan. If the loan was repaid on time, there was no interest, only a fee. A low interest rate was charged only if the repayment was delinquent.[16] Moreover, because the loans were transacted through the county branch of the Agricultural Bank, they qualified for the *shuiqian huankuan* provision that allowed enterprises to write off repayment before tax assessment.

REGIONAL HEADQUARTERS: THE TOWNSHIP

Township government, in its economic role, guides and promotes the direction of growth in the township and oversees development in its villages. In its administrative capacity, a township serves as the liaison between village and county, as the first formal rung in the local government hierarchy. Township government acts as the agent for the county, implementing county targets and plans. The township collects industrial taxes from enterprises and agricultural taxes from peasant households. It plays the middleman role but is no longer the gatekeeper through which all resources must pass. Township authorities may be bypassed when a village has the contacts to go directly to the county.

Township government, as an official fiscal unit, receives a portion of the taxes it collects. Its officials are considered state cadres, paid according to a standard scale, and they hold an urban, rather than a rural, household registration.[17] The financial wealth of a township depends on the

16. For agriculture, it was 2.5 percent; for animal husbandry 3.5 percent; and for industry 4.2 percent.
17. There are many advantages to urban household registration. One is grain supply. Before the dual-track price system for grain was abolished, only those with an urban

amount of rural industry. As I point out in chapter 2, townships not only can collect tax revenues from both township- and village-owned enterprises, but they can also extract substantial extrabudgetary revenues from township-owned firms (*xiangban qiye*). Most townships inherited an industrial base from the Maoist period and have used that as the foundation for their current firms.[18] Nationally, the number of township enterprises has grown more slowly than the number of village-owned enterprises.[19] This may be explained partly by the fact that townships have less strict budget constraints than villages. Remember that township government is provided a budget by the county to cover basic expenditures, and it is given a subsidy when tax receipts are insufficient (see chapter 2).

Leadership

The leading cadres at the township level are the township party secretary and the township head (*xiang [zhen] zhang*).[20] These officials, like those at the county level, are rotated. They have overall control of development, like their counterparts in the county, but they are more likely to participate in micro-level decisions affecting their enterprises. These might include obtaining loans or securing approvals for large development projects.

As table 5 shows, the economic work of the township encompasses a variety of tasks. To the extent that there is a division of labor, township party secretaries tend to be concerned with economic development, specifically industrial development, while township heads deal with civic matters. Regardless of who is most actively involved in the economy, at the township level as at the county level the bureaucracy manages day-to-day affairs. Subordinate offices (*suo*) of most county-level bureaus are at the township level. A special office, the township economic commis-

---

household registration were granted grain ration tickets that allowed the purchase of low-priced state grain. For details of the differences between urban and rural household registration, see Whyte and Parish, *Urban Life;* and Oi, *State and Peasant.*

18. In some counties, there seems to be little change in the overall number of township-level enterprises from the Maoist period, although some have changed products, expanded production, and undergone technological renovation. For example, in Zouping county, Shandong, there were 97 commune-level enterprises in 1978; in 1983 there were 110 township-level enterprises. Oi, "Evolution of Local State Corporatism."

19. Nongyebu xiangzhen qiyesi jihua caiwuchu, *1995 nian quanguo xiangzhen.*

20. If the township qualifies as a *zhen*, the government head is called a *zhen zhang.*

sion (*jingji weiyuan hui*),[21] working in conjunction with township leaders, manages industrial development.[22] This commission, a subordinate of the rural enterprise management bureau, has overall responsibility for township enterprises and has jurisdiction over village enterprises.

Resources

The township facilitates the provision of services and access to selected inputs that it controls, as well as to those that exist at higher levels. To obtain county-level agency loans, collective enterprises apply to their township finance office, which then passes the application on to county finance bureau officials. The licensing process is also started at the township level, even though the county makes the final decisions.

As table 6 shows, compared to the county, townships have relatively limited state-provided resources to help rural industry. Each township is provided with one official credit cooperative and a branch of the Agricultural Bank to serve its township and village enterprises. More recently, some townships have established semiprivate financial institutions to provide local enterprises with nonbank funding.

Because of increasing demand for credit in a time of frequently tight monetary policy, townships (and villages) have had to raise supplementary capital within their own corporate economy. Like a large corporation, each township pools its resources and risks, using the same strategies I describe for villages (see chapter 3). It can use the profits of its richer enterprises to see poorer enterprises through a downturn in the market or to start new enterprises.[23]

COMPANIES: THE VILLAGE

At the bottom of the local corporate state are villages. The village is distinctive in that its officials must act as the agents of the township and the county, but as I indicate in chapter 2, it is not accorded the status or the resources of an official level of government. Village officials have no formal bureaucratic positions (*bianzhi*) and receive no state subsidies;

---

21. The name of this office differs by locality. Sometimes it is known as the township industrial corporation.

22. A party vice secretary or township vice head is often the head of the township economic commission. He or she is frequently the only state cadre on the commission. The rest of the staff are considered local cadres and paid from extrabudgetary funds.

23. This only applies to collectively owned enterprises.

TABLE 6. RESOURCES AT THE THREE LEVELS
OF THE LOCAL CORPORATE STATE

Resource	County	Township	Village
Revenue	County-level state-owned enterprises County-level collectively owned enterprises Within-budget taxes Extrabudgetary revenues Subsidies and grants	Township-owned enterprises Enterprise profits Within-budget revenues Extrabudgetary revenues *Tongchou* and *Tilu* from villages Subsidies and grants	*Tilu* Village-owned enterprises Contract fees
Capital and Credit	Banks County government support funds Semiprivate credit associations	Savings and loan cooperative Business office of Agricultural Bank Workers Enterprises Semiprivate financial institutions Outside investments	Village government Workers Enterprises Villagers Within-village loans Outside investment Credit associations
Materials	Materials supply bureau Rural enterprise management bureau supply company Markets	Sales and marketing cooperative Markets	Village government procurements Markets

(continued)

TABLE 6. (continued)

Technology Information and Markets	Rural enterprise management bureau	Officials	Officials
	Science and technology commission	Economic commission	Factories
	Factories	Factories	Villagers
	Officials	Workers	
	Foreign trade companies		
Bureaucratic Services			
Tax Breaks	County government	Limited	None
Loan Deferrals	Finance bureau		
	Tax bureau		
Licenses	Industrial-commercial management bureau	Limited	None
Product Certification and Grading	Rural enterprise management bureau	Limited	None

their salaries come entirely from village revenues.[24] To reiterate an earlier point, village-owned enterprises (*cunban qiye*) pay taxes to the upper levels,[25] but villages have no right to keep any portion of those revenues. They have a hard budget constraint, but they also have an exclusive right over the residual after taxes. This helps explain why village enterprises have been among the fastest-growing sectors within rural industry.

Leadership

Like all levels of the bureaucracy, the village is headed by a party secretary and a government head. The government head, called the chairman of the village committee (*cunmin weiyuan hui zhuren*), was formerly known as the village head (*cun zhang*) (see table 4). Unlike county and township officials, village leaders are longtime village residents who have strong ties with those over whom they have administrative control. Because they are not rotated, their actions have long-term consequences for both their own positions and for the village's economic well-being. This makes the incentives for village-level officials more direct than those for officials at other levels of local government.

The bureaus at the county level have no representatives at the village level. The village bureaucracy is composed of a committee (*cunmin weiyuan hui*) of five to seven members, each of whom has specialized tasks. Since 1987 the members of this committee, including the chairman, are supposed to be elected directly by the members of the village. The election of these individuals has received attention as an important step in the democratization of village politics.[26] In practice, the committee's power is still limited and under the firm control of the party secretary, who is exempt from popular election.

The party at the village level, more than at any other level, is at the forefront of China's rural development effort. Where there is industry,

24. Village cadres have rural rather than urban household registrations. Up until 1993, when grain rationing was abolished, this meant that they had to grow their own grain rather than receive grain ration coupons that allowed access to low-priced grain sold by the state.
25. Village enterprises do not pay any fees to the township economic commission, even though they are nominally controlled by them.
26. See, for example, Tyrene White, "Reforming the Countryside"; Kevin O'Brien, "Implementing Political Reform"; Oi, "Economic Development"; Melanie Manion, "Electoral Connection." Daniel Kelliher, "Chinese Debate," provides a nice review of much of the writing on the subject.

the party secretary often personally makes key decisions regarding the operation and management of enterprises, sometimes temporarily taking charge of a factory. In more than a few villages, the party secretary is the chairman of the village enterprise management committee (see table 4). The government head, the chairman of the village committee, is left to tend to agricultural matters. But even there, if necessary, the party secretary will intervene when needed. The hands-on attitude of village party secretaries has led to authoritarian one-man rule in a number of highly industrialized, wealthy villages.

Whether a village economy is successful depends heavily on village leadership. The initiative, skill, and connections of the top officials determine whether the village can successfully mobilize needed resources, be it funds from inside the community or assistance from the upper levels. But these top officials are a different breed from the highly polished elite who have led development in the NICs or in Japan.[27] These individuals are usually not particularly well educated; many of the older leaders are lucky to have had even a primary school education.

While personal ties and political skills are obviously necessary, as the reforms have progressed proven economic performance has been a key to the successful development of rural industry. Sometimes this is difficult to disentangle from political status because of the close connection between the two, even during the Maoist period. For example, a prominent village party secretary who enjoyed privileged access to inputs needed by his village after decollectivization had also been named a model worker during the Maoist period and elected to the National People's Congress prior to the reforms. He had received honors for his good work as party secretary of a very successful brigade that sold large amounts of grain to the state. After decollectivization, he further enhanced his reputation by leading the village in the cultivation of exceptionally high-quality wheat that was sold to the local seed company, and by being among the first to develop village industry. His combination of skill, proven performance, and easy access to inputs brought the villagers among the highest incomes in the area.

But past credentials are not essential. Another highly successful village party secretary built up his reputation only over the course of the reforms. The reason he has become so powerful, not only in the township but even among county officials, is his leadership in developing his village's

27. For a more extensive discussion of this difference, see Pearson, *China's New Business Elite*.

enterprises after decollectivization. The village has become one of the richest and most industrialized in the entire county, with the villagers enjoying various subsidies as well as high incomes. This success has brought him numerous honors, including being named a "provincial-level entrepreneur." Eventually he was appointed to be a township party vice secretary (although he still spends most of his time managing the village). Because of his and the village's reputation, he managed to secure credit when others were having difficulty. For example, he was one of only a few able to secure substantial loans from a semiprivate credit institution outside the township when it first opened in 1988. During that difficult period of retrenchment, his village received a short-term loan from the county Agricultural Bank. Such loans were given only to those villages that were considered the most likely to be able to repay on time.[28]

The ultimate example of a powerful village leader is Yu Zuomin, the now deposed leader of Daqiuzhuang village outside Tianjin.[29] He rose to become a national model as central-level leaders visited him and praised his success in using the reforms to turn what had been an extremely poor village during the Maoist period into one of the richest villages in all of China during the 1980s.[30] Without a doubt, its model status brought the village preferential treatment in securing needed materials, contracts, and favors.

Resources

Part of the reason village leadership is so important is that villages have had to be the most self-reliant of the three levels of the local corporate state in the development of industry. Village industry has on the whole received fewer state-supplied resources than have township enterprises. This is especially true of credit. Banks hesitate to loan to most smaller-scale village enterprises. As indicated in chapter 3, table 3, bank credit for rural industry in the 1980s went primarily to township enterprises.

28. There are indications that some of these funds for loans were diverted from other sources, perhaps agricultural procurements, to tide over local enterprises during this period of crisis. Consequently, it was essential that the money be repaid on time. CI 52090.

29. He was sentenced in 1993 after harboring two village employees who had killed a worker. His power is reflected in the fact that he was able to hold off Tianjin officials who came to arrest his men. For a press report on this affair, see "CPC Politburo Meets on 'Manslaughter' Case," *Ming pao,* 7 March 1993, translated in *FBIS-CHI-93–044,* 9 March 1993, p. 19.

30. The walls of the reception room where I interviewed him were covered with pictures of him accompanied by various top central-level leaders. His own "collected works" had been published, as well as the story of the success of his village.

In one township in 1987, 30 percent of the loans made by the Agricultural Bank and credit cooperatives went to township enterprises. Only about 10 percent went to village enterprises.[31] This is where reputation and connections come into play. Officials who have shown themselves to be innovative and successful in developing their village economy are given preferential access to the limited resources.

The need to be self-reliant creates a certain level of ambivalence toward the upper levels, even among those who succeed in getting support. Some villages claim that the success of village industries is due entirely to their own efforts. Successful villages boast that they never sought outside loans to fund development. One village secretary bragged that the township had come to him for loans! While there is some truth to the claims of self-reliance, close questioning reveals that villages, like townships, would not have been able to succeed without assistance from higher levels. Funding alone does not determine whether village industry is successful or not. Licenses, technical assistance, and a slew of bureaucratic inputs are necessary. Furthermore, over time, as entry costs have risen, even once fiscally self-sufficient villages need assistance in procuring large base loans for expansion and technological renovation. Interviews suggest that the most highly industrialized and successful villages are those whose leaders have the best connections and have received the most support from higher levels of local government.

ADAPTING MAOIST INSTITUTIONS TO MARKET PRODUCTION

The Maoist legacy provided the political capacity for the local corporatist state, but the aims for which it is used and the way it is applied are significantly changed. This is not the same type of state-led growth practiced during the Mao period. Local governments have adapted the Maoist institutions to promote rapid economic development in an increasingly marketized environment.

FROM IDEOLOGICAL TO MARKET PLANNING

There continue to be plans, targets, and meetings, but they operate differently from those of the Maoist period. The closest thing to a central plan is what the Chinese now call an "industrial policy" (chanye

31. CI 22688.

zhengce), which targets specific sectors the government wants to pro-mote.[32] But this resembles Japan's industrial policy[33] more than the man-datory plans of the Maoist period. As in Japan, the targets are general and sectoral in nature.[34]

In practice, more important than national-level plans is local-level planning. Numerous plans and targets continue to be sent from one local level to another. For example, the county finance bureau sends revenue plans to each of its townships; the county economic commission sends plans to its county-owned industries; the county rural enterprise management bureau sends plans with detailed targets for total production value, tax payments, and income to each of its township economic commissions. Township economic commissions send similarly detailed plans to their township-owned enterprises. Sometimes villages also receive plans from the townships.

While there is planning and local government involvement, the plans are no longer mandatory (*zhilingxing jihua*). If a locality or an enterprise does not want to produce a certain product, the upper levels will not force the issue.

By the mid-1980s, most plans were "guidance plans" (*zhidaoxing ji-hua*).[35] Theoretically, the difference is that mandatory plans are fulfilled by administrative fiat, whereas guidance plans are fulfilled by the use of economic incentives. In practice, this distinction is ambiguous; "guid-

32. The degree to which there has been a movement away from central planning is suggested by the debate in Beijing about whether there should be even an industrial policy. According to a member of the State Planning Commission in Beijing, the issue, in part, is that some feel it might look too much like a plan and lead to too much government direction, resulting in the same problems that were experienced under central planning. CI 62094.

33. According to a State Planning Commission official, after 1984–1985 a group of students from Peking University strongly advocated that China adopt an industrial policy similar to those used in Taiwan, Korea, and Japan. CI 62094. According to one source, China has consulted with the Japanese on this subject.

34. Product preference lists are still sent to the provinces. It is understood that these are the products the center is interested in supporting. I was not able to ascertain how specific these lists are.

35. Few rural enterprises were ever subject to mandatory plans, but there were exceptions. In the mid-1980s, there were some rural enterprises that produced "key items" and acquired supplies from the government at state prices. Their production and sales plans were mandatory. An exhaust-fan factory outside Tianjin received 80 percent of its supplies from the state, specifically the Tianjin Planning Commission, so the majority of its production was dictated by the plan. The factory manager of this plant had no say in who was hired, and he was required to keep on the payroll many unneeded and unwanted personnel. When workers were needed, the township government apportioned jobs among the villages and village small groups (formerly production teams). The township was in charge of labor allocations and administered qualifying examinations to workers when necessary. CI 71886.

ance" plans seem to carry considerable weight. According to an interviewee, "Mandatory plans are like putting a ring through the nose of an ox and pulling it wherever you want it to go. Guidance plans are like letting the ox roam where it wants, but not feeding it if it refuses to go where you want it to go."

While factories need not adhere to their "guidance" production plans, those that do have the best chances for success. Local governments give such factories crucial assistance in the areas of loans, investment opportunities, and raw materials,[36] and arrange buyers for the finished goods.[37] Particularly during the early days of reform, when markets were just beginning to grow, the issue was not only price, but access and convenience. What was needed was proper connections (*guanxi*), which many firms lacked. For instance, a coveted and profitable arrangement for rural industry is a contract with an urban unit. This usually is an industrial unit, but it may also be a "scientific unit," such as a university or scientific lab developing new products. The urban and rural units form a "horizontal linkage" (*hengxiang lianbo*) in which the rural partner undertakes all or part of the production and assembly process. The urban partner is responsible for supplying the raw materials and for the marketing or purchasing of the output.[38] Local governments can be instrumental in finding such opportunities. On the outskirts of Tianjin in the 1980s, local officials arranged special tours of rural factories for prospective customers and investors. In Sichuan, near Chengdu, various government offices, including those at the county level, actively sought cooperative relationships for their rural industries.[39] Officials everywhere repeatedly said: "*Guanxi* is important for getting business. We have built up old connections and we now use them."

FROM EQUAL ALLOCATION TO PREFERENTIAL TREATMENT

The types of assistance that local governments provide may be reminiscent of central planning in the Maoist state, but a crucial difference be-

36. Some local governments, usually at the township level and above, assist by investing in factories that produce raw materials needed by their enterprises. This guarantees the needed supplies and provides local authorities with profits.

37. Byrd and Lin, *China's Rural Industry: Structure, Development, and Reform*, chaps. 15 and 16, also make this point.

38. There are exceptions, as in the case of the exhaust-fan factory mentioned earlier, where the factory itself sold its own products. This was not a problem because the demand for fans was high.

39. CI 81386.

tween local state corporatism and its Maoist antecedent is that the local corporate state selectively targets certain enterprises for development. Subsidies and assistance are no longer given equally or to all. In this sense, China has switched to a strategy similar to the industrial policies of the East Asian NICs. Local governments use the "carrot" characteristic of the administrative guidance found in Japan. Preferential allocations are given as an inducement.

Under local state corporatism, enterprises most likely to receive this assistance are those deemed most capable of contributing to the corporate good. What that means changes over time. The corporate good may be defined more broadly than in terms of mere economic interests and profits. During the 1980s, it included such social interests as the provision of employment. As profits have decreased in the 1990s, the emphasis has seemed to shift increasingly to profitability, competitiveness, and growth.

Local governments began relatively early, in the 1980s, to rank enterprises for the purpose of determining the level of services and assistance they would receive from the government and its affiliated institutions. The strategy was to concentrate the use of limited resources. The various bureaucratic funds held by the county bureaus were given to favored enterprises. Tax breaks were similarly concentrated. In one county, for example, in 1989 123 enterprises received tax breaks and exemptions totaling 2.42 million yuan, which equaled 6.07 percent of the total taxes paid by the village and township enterprises. However, closer inspection of the records shows that one enterprise alone received 800,000 yuan in tax breaks.[40]

There are two types of selective allocation. The first grew out of the remains of national planning that still existed when rural industry began its rapid growth in the mid-1980s. Favored enterprises were given privileged access to items that were rationed or were being sold at the low state-set prices. This included anything from steel to cement to lumber. The amounts of such inputs allocated to the rural areas under the plan were extremely restricted, if there were any at all. Localities made use of what remained of central allocations to help favored enterprises, but most of the time they had little discretion with regard to production materials, which were usually earmarked for specific enterprises that were producing for the national plan. By the late 1980s, this type of allocation was almost nonexistent. The most that a locality could hope for

40. CI 52290.

was access to state-supplied goods that were sold at higher than rationed prices but lower than market prices.

The second and more common type of selective allocation is privileged access to inputs that are not rationed but simply scarce. Over time, various items fell into this category. Fuel oil, electricity, and certain raw materials have topped the list. These allocations are similar to the allocations made under administrative guidance. However, whereas in places such as Japan the goods and resources are usually provided at below-market prices, in China they are secured and sold at market prices. Like the privileged access that came from using connections and "going through the back door" in the Maoist period, what is being given is not necessarily a cheaper price but the chance to be first in line to buy the best available items at the posted prices. In China's market context, preferential access means having the chance to buy the one ton of steel that the material supply bureau was able to procure at a favorable market price. It might also mean the opportunity to be hooked up to the special electric generator the county or township installed to provide its most important industries with uninterrupted power. As the market economy has developed, this type of selective allocation of raw materials has decreased in importance, but it may still make a difference in an enterprise's profit margin.

USING STATE-ALLOCATED CREDIT TO TARGET LOCAL GROWTH

Credit falls under the second type of selective allocation: scarce resources. As the literature on the state and economic development points out, credit control is one of the most important policy instruments a government can possess for shaping industrial growth.[41] China, like many of the East Asian NICs, is primarily a credit-based rather than a capital-based system, allowing for the coordinated intervention necessary for an effective industrial policy. During the Maoist period, private banks were prohibited. Firms did not sell stock to raise capital; in fact, all firms looked to the government for their capital, as well as for all of their operating budget. The state, through its allocation of credit and capital—as well as other production inputs—was the exclusive arbiter of devel-

41. See, for example, Zysman, *Governments, Markets, and Growth;* on the East Asian NICs, see the work of Robert Wade. One of his best short statements is "The Role of Government in Overcoming Market Failure: Taiwan, Republic of Korea and Japan."

opment. Government policy directly dictated bank activity. Banks in China were an administrative arm of the government, not commercial operations, as will be described further in chapter 6.

Control of bank credit by local governments has remained strong during the reform period. In the rural areas, the organization of the banking system corresponds roughly to the levels of bureaucratic administration. It is similarly hierarchical and is subject to the influence of officials at each level of government, even though bank officials are not directly appointed at the level at which they operate (e.g., the county Agricultural Bank officials are not appointed by the county government). In the 1980s, county officials could exempt certain enterprises from penalty interest payments, extend the payback period, or allow the use of tax payments for loan repayments. Village and township governments could intervene to grant subsidies so that their enterprises could pay interest on loans. The close relationships between banks, finance and tax offices, and local officials facilitated the rapid growth in the 1980s, but, as I describe in chapter 3, they are also the cause of the problems that have come to haunt banks in the 1990s as bad debt has mounted.[42]

The major bank serving peasants and rural enterprises at the county level is the Agricultural Bank (*nongye yinhang*).[43] Below the county, at the township level, are branches of that bank, known as business offices (*yingye suo*). There are also credit cooperatives (*xinyongshe*).[44] Officially

42. Some have criticized these relationships as too close. See, for example, "Township Enterprises Should Also Implement Reform," *Jingji cankao*, 18 November 1987, p. 1, translated in *JPRS-CAR-88-005*, 18 February 1988, pp. 20–21; also Xu Hao and Wang Qingshan, "China's Rural Financial Markets: Current Situation and Strategy," *Nongye jingji wenti*, 23 September 1987, no. 9, pp. 39–43, translated in *JPRS-CAR-88-002*, 5 February 1988, pp. 54–57.

43. The structure of the Agricultural Bank remains strikingly similar to what it was during the commune period, as described by Barnett and Vogel, except that what were formerly branches of the People's Bank are now township branches of the Agricultural Bank. Barnett with Vogel, *Cadres, Bureaucracy, and Political Power*, pp. 293–94.

44. The relationship between the Agricultural Bank and the credit cooperatives is ambiguous and complex. Both make loans, both accept savings deposits, and peasants and enterprises use both. The difference involves ownership and interest rates. The credit cooperative is a collectively owned institution. Each peasant is allowed to own one share and receives interest on savings and dividends from shares. The citizen management board (*minguan hui*), a committee of peasants, government leaders, bank officials, and entrepreneurs governs the credit cooperative. This committee receives an annual report, but it does not approve loans. Its members are elected by the stockholders of the cooperative. Each person with a share has a vote in the election of representatives, who then elect the citizen management board. The representatives are elected once every two years. Every ten agricultural households that hold shares are allotted one representative, but in some cases an entire village may be represented by one or two people. At the end of the year, the representatives meet and the bank makes its report. A subgroup of representatives is elected to deal with the bank. This working body consists of the township head, the head of the sales

the business offices of the Agricultural Bank and the credit cooperatives are separate organizations, but in practice their funds are linked. The difference is that funds in the branches of the Agricultural Bank are state funds. They are therefore loaned at lower interest rates, which is why they are preferred by local enterprises. The credit cooperative funds are from local savings. Below the township level are substations of the credit cooperative or of the Agricultural Bank, but these exist only in the larger villages.[45]

The approval process for loans also conforms to the bureaucratic structure. A graduated approval system sets limits on the size of loans that different levels of the banking system can approve and allows for county input into the investment process.[46] Local government control over credit and investment was further strengthened by a State Council requirement that all enterprise loans had to have guarantors to ensure repayment.[47] In practice, for much of the 1980s, the guarantors for loans were local government agencies such as the township economic commission.

To make maximum use of the limited funds available to develop rural industry, county officials began in the mid-1980s to provide annual ratings of enterprises, which determined how much fixed-capital credit and what level of financial services enterprises should be given by local banks and savings cooperatives.[48] In some counties, such ratings continued into the early 1990s, until many collectively owned enterprises started having difficulties (see chapter 3). This system identified for the banks those

---

and marketing cooperative, the head of the township economic commission, the head of the Agricultural Bank, and the head of the savings and loan cooperative; the rest are peasant representatives. CI 22688. The county Agricultural Bank takes a management fee from the credit cooperatives in the townships. This is not more than 1 percent of all income. In one county, the Agricultural Bank took only about .04 percent. CI 8991.

45. In one county, about 80 percent of the villages had substations.

46. The county branch of the Agricultural Bank must approve all loans above 10,000 yuan; townships have authority to approve loans under that amount.

47. This order came approximately at the same time that rural enterprises began to develop. Prior to this requirement, the enterprises would repay as much as possible whenever possible. The bank would try to get back whatever it could, and the county branch of the Agricultural Bank would make up for any shortfall. Previously, the amount that could be borrowed depended on the amount of circulating funds in the enterprise, which could not be less than 50 percent of the amount it wanted to borrow. The enterprise was entirely responsible for the loan; there was no guarantor requirement. CI 22688.

48. The rating committee was made up of members of the county Agricultural Bank, the township economic commission, the county rural enterprise management bureau, and the township branch of the Agricultural Bank. Ratings were set at the beginning of each year, based on fixed-capital assets, circulating funds, and the overall credit plan of the enterprise. A credit limit could not be more than 30–50 percent of an enterprise's circulating funds. In most cases, it was no more than 30 percent. CI 22688.

enterprises deemed important by the local government. For loans within their prescribed credit limit, enterprises with the highest rating were given automatic approval from the township savings and loan cooperative or the local branch of the Agricultural Bank; county approval was not required. Moreover, once an enterprise was designated important, local governments tried to ensure that it received credit, especially during periods of centrally mandated retrenchment when bank credit was greatly restricted.[49]

Even the rating system was selective; only enterprises that paid their debts each month received a rating.[50] Enterprises that were found to be in deficit (*kuisun*) were automatically disqualified.

Among those that did receive a rating, there were further distinctions, such as "special first class" and "first class." However, these were rarely awarded. For example, in 1991, of the seventy to eighty firms that were rated in one county, only two enterprises received the special-first-class rating and only ten the first-class rating. The previous year, no enterprise obtained the special-first ranking and only eight were ranked first class. Most of the ranked rural enterprises were at the township level; very few village enterprises were rated, although highly successful village enterprises were exceptions.

The differences in the service and credit accorded each rating were almost imperceptible, but in times of tight credit, they were significant. For example, those enterprises that had a first-class rating received almost the same benefits as the special-first enterprises, but the latter had priority in getting what limited credit was available at the best interest rate, and as long as they stayed within their assigned limit they did not need to obtain a guarantor. Enterprises with special-first ratings could exceed their credit limits for large projects.[51]

49. CI 22688.

50. In one county, only 70 to 80 of 119 township enterprises were rated. In one township, the number of enterprises that received a rating and the amounts of their preapproved credit were as follows: in 1987, five enterprises, 580,000 yuan; in 1988, three enterprises, 460,000 yuan. The number decreased in 1988 because two of the five enterprises went under. In 1988 the credit limits were raised for the three remaining enterprises. An agricultural tool factory had its limit raised from 310,000 yuan to 320,000 yuan; a construction company went from 40,000 yuan to 70,000 yuan; and a fertilizer company from 60,000 yuan to 70,000 yuan. The head of the township Agricultural Bank said the large increase for the construction company was due in part to the fact that it was repaving the roads. CI 22688.

51. In those cases, they had to go through the regular application process and secure a guarantor. The guarantor had to have average deposits equal to the amount of the loan; otherwise there were no other restrictions. The guarantor did not have to be the township

THE BUREAUCRACY AS A SOURCE OF
INFORMATION AND TECHNOLOGY

The bureaucracy is often identified as a source of red tape, but it has also proven to be a valuable resource in providing assistance to local enterprises. Local officials have turned the bureaucracy into a channel for information and resources that facilitate market production. Many of the institutional supports it has provided fledging firms have allowed them to succeed in China's transitional economy.

Using information and contacts gained through their routine conduct of administrative work, local officials provide an array of essential services and information about new products, technology, and markets for finished goods. The degree to which officials get involved in product development, market research, and the acquisition of technology suggests that this is not the usual provision of bureaucratic services but the activity of an entrepreneurial developmental state.

The cadre networks are among the most important personal connections through which firms gain access to information, technology, and business. This was particularly the case in the early days of rural industrialization. In many cases, the cadre network was the means for obtaining sales or processing contracts with large state enterprises, and for making contacts that eventually led to the establishment of joint ventures and export orders. Individual enterprises are free to do their own market research and product development, but cadre networks and government are there for factories that do not themselves have the resources for product development and market research. Such help has been particularly useful as these firms try to enter the more competitive international market.[52] Here one sees how having a developed and experienced bureaucracy works to China's advantage.

The bureaucracy is an information grid where government officials are the primary nodes in the network that provides information to local enterprises. The precise form of the information grid may vary from locality to locality, but much of the flow of information follows the contours of the administrative bureaucracy. It passes through routine channels of communication within and between levels of government, from

---

economic commission. A number of enterprises could act as a joint guarantor to spread the risk. CI 22688.

52. See Jean C. Oi, "Cadre Networks," for more details about these networks and how they provide information to local enterprises.

the village to the township to the county, and then on to the prefecture, the province, and finally to Beijing.

Not all officials are equally plugged into each level, nor do all officials have a direct line to all nodes. As I suggest in the discussion of village leaders, the success of local economic development is dependent on how well local decision makers are connected into this network and how far up and across they can operate. The normal order of communication is to pass information through the successive levels of the bureaucratic hierarchy, but those who are well connected, such as those successful village leaders who have established personal ties with county officials, can bypass certain levels and go directly to higher levels.

The branches of this network multiply as one goes higher in the bureaucracy. In the rural areas, the county has the widest network of personal and professional relationships along with the broadest knowledge of developments outside the county. When a village needs help, the township is the first stop in the search for information. If the township is unable to help, the village can go to the county, either directly or through township officials. Enterprises are the ultimate consumers and beneficiaries in this information hierarchy. Regardless of the type of ownership— state, collective, or private—all enterprises have the potential to benefit from information that flows from the cadre networks. The amount of help that is provided to the different types of enterprises has varied over the course of the reforms as local development strategies have evolved. As detailed in chapter 3, the collective sector received most of the attention during the 1980s.

The diffusion of information and technology takes place through various channels. Some are new, but a significant number are adaptations of Maoist modes of bureaucratic operation.

Meetings

Official meetings, the staple of any bureaucratic system, have been adapted to provide market and technological information. When a locality wants to develop local industry, it can call rural enterprise development meetings. These may be countywide, or they may be more localized, with only selected townships and villages invited. Township and village officials have recounted meetings in which the county has suggested specific products and enterprises for its different townships. Such practices were common in the 1980s, when enterprises were most in need of market information and collectively owned enterprises were at their strongest. For example, it was at a three-day rural enterprise development meeting in 1984 that a Shandong county worked out plans to have one of its townships start a tire factory, which has since grown to be the largest business in the township. The meeting was for all thirty-five townships in the county. During part of the meeting, the townships were divided into small groups, led by county officials. These groups met for about half a day to solve concrete problems of individual townships.

A number of examples suggest that entrepreneurial initiative on the part of the county is sometimes in response to lower-level concerns and sometimes to specific inquiries. In the example above, the township tapped to started the tire factory had previously consulted county officials about the need to convert an unprofitable machine factory into a more profitable product line. The county rural enterprise management bureau had discussed the matter with the township heads and with the economic commission, which manages all township-owned enterprises. The vice head of the township economic commission initiated the idea of a tire factory, after noticing a shortage of tires in Qingdao and seeing a very successful tire factory in Shantou. After the county and township decided that this was the route to take, the vice head of the township economic commission used personal and professional connections to secure the needed technology. A key contact was an old classmate who was working in Qingdao but who had maintained good connections with his hometown of Shantou. It was through this classmate that the township eventually secured the needed technology from Shantou.[53]

In another example, the county rural enterprise management bureau organized a meeting to promote the production of chemical products, which it thought would be profitable and suited to local conditions. The county convened the meeting in one of its townships and had a township official chair it. Notices had been sent to the villages, and the meeting was attended both by those that already had chemical plants as well as by those that had an interest in starting such ventures. The same county held similar meetings to promote rug making; again, these were held at the township level. The idea of producing rugs stemmed from a township that had been subcontracting production for a Tianjin carpet company since 1986. Once the township began making rugs, a number of private entrepreneurs started to subcontract for the township-owned carpet factory. One of the county's townships now exports rugs to the United States.[54]

53. CI 62694.   54. CI 62294.

Assistance

In other instances, a township or a village comes up with an idea for an enterprise or product and then seeks the help of county officials to carry out the project. Aside from shepherding the project through the bureaucratic process of licensing and approvals, county officials can provide technical assistance. For complex projects, they will help seek outside expertise. For example, a Shandong village cornstarch factory came across a highly marketable type of cornstarch byproduct in a trade magazine, but its managers knew nothing about the technology involved. At a provincial people's congress meeting, the village party secretary discovered that the developer of this product was the Wuxi Light Industrial Research Institute.[55] He followed up by pursuing his connections in the county and enlisting the support of various county officials, including the county magistrate. The project was turned over to the county rural enterprise management bureau. One of the bureau vice heads, who often took the lead in searching out relevant technology, knew about the product and had good connections in Wuxi, having gone there a number of times on official business. He took the village official with him to Wuxi to negotiate with the research institute. Together they succeeded in convincing the institute that the village, with the help of the county, would be capable of producing the product. A deal was concluded in which the village paid the institute 520,000 yuan in technical fees for training, resident experts, and equipment.[56]

Visits to Models and Study Tours

The old Maoist practice of visiting model units has been adapted to gain firsthand technical and market information. Many local officials, particularly those at the county level, take factory managers and township or village leaders to the most industrially developed areas, such as Jiangsu and Guangdong, and to nationally famous models like Daqiuzhuang village outside Tianjin to study management techniques and to see what

55. The acquisition of technical assistance has become much more feasible for local levels in recent years as specialized research units have been established, often by professors linked to universities or academies. These units may provide both expertise and specialized equipment. In some cases, research units seek out local enterprises to produce items that they have designed for profit-making purposes.

56. CI 62494.

products can be made. Once they find a product, they use connections to learn how to copy or adapt the item for local production.

In recent years, local officials have expanded upon the traditional study tours to go abroad to gain contracts, buy machinery, and search for products. Heads of successful factories are sometimes included in delegations. Foreign companies trying to sell technology to China have also invited important prospective buyers to visit their countries to see their equipment in operation. Some county-level factory managers, even in interior provinces such as Henan, have taken advantage of such opportunities.

Regardless of whether a factory manager goes along, local government officials who take these tours are well versed in the production processes and technological needs of their key industries.[57] While abroad, officials scour the stores in search of products that their localities can produce or export. They take products back to be studied, modified, and reproduced. This practice of copying foreign products seems to be particularly widespread in provinces close to Hong Kong. Officials in Guangdong, including managers of large enterprises, have special visas that allow them easily and regularly to go to Hong Kong to do market research.[58]

Equipment Supply Corporations

In addition to long-established bureaucratic channels, local governments have established new instruments in response to current market conditions. Some provinces have set up companies such as the Guangdong Engineering and Equipment Supply Company that provide complete machinery systems, including technical assistance. The provision of such services is available to all types of enterprises, private as well as state and collective. The supply company researches and procures the equipment and charges a percentage of the total cost of the package as its commission.[59]

---

57. The degree of attention local officials pay to their important industries was evident in the barrage of technical questions that a county magistrate asked when touring the Sam Adams Brewery in Boston. This is not surprising given the concentration of investment by the county in its local brewery, which was the top revenue earner for the county. Andrew Walder, "County Government."

58. Others have to go through a long, complicated process that allows them only a single entry.

59. CI 7394.

ADAPTING LOCAL STATE CORPORATISM TO PRIVATE ENTERPRISE

The increasingly profit-oriented calculations of local governments, particularly at the county level, are reflected in the decisions described in the last chapter to rethink their development strategies and broaden their industrial base to encourage other forms of ownership in rural industry in the 1990s. Chapter 3 describes three of the most prominent: (1) adopting new management schemes; (2) selling problematic enterprises; and (3) encouraging the growth of large new private enterprises as sources of revenue and employment growth. The result has been the emergence of a mixed economy in which private enterprise now plays an increasingly important role.

The task here is to examine how the local corporate state has adapted itself to these new ownership forms and especially to the increased importance of private firms. What is the relationship between these new firms and local government? Another question to be considered is why local officials would risk the emergence of a strong private sector. We will examine how the local state has been able to manage what in other settings is an independent economic elite—private businesspeople. Here one sees how communist officials are now using corporatist mechanisms to deal with a sector that the government does not own and therefore cannot control through manipulation of contracting arrangements or distribution of property rights.

ADMINISTRATIVE CONTROLS

Local officials continue to fall back on Maoist practice and use administrative measures to facilitate control of the private sector.

Licensing

The granting of permits is universally used to prevent undesirable firms and individuals from legally operating within society. In market economies, licenses are granted on the basis of the service and honesty of those operating the enterprises. Quotas sometimes exist to limit the number of vendors or operators, and sometimes there is corruption involved in the allocation of such licenses—as is the case with coveted taxi medallions in large American cities—but few ideological or political criteria apply. In China, licensing is a regulatory mechanism that screens applicants and either encourages or discourages certain activities according to prevailing political winds or economic advantage.

The process of licensing in China reflects the corporatist nature of the relationship between private business and the state. All three levels of local government from the county to the village can affect whether a license is granted. To apply for a business license, a peasant first needs certification (*zhengming*) from his or her village party cell (*dangzhibu*) testifying to residency and good standing in the community. With certification in hand, he or she must then apply to the branch office of the industrial-commercial management bureau at the township level. This application requires bank verification of sufficient funds to cover a minimum amount of fixed capital (*guding zijin*) and circulation capital (*liudong zijin*). The amount required depends on the business and potential for credit. There must also be verification of the ability to procure raw materials.[60] The industrial-commercial management office or its agent conducts an investigation. Only after approval is given at the township level can the peasant go to the county-level industrial-commercial management bureau, which decides whether or not to issue the license.

The licensing process concurrently provides local authorities with detailed records regarding the entrepreneur, the number of people to be employed, the scope of the business, the amount of fixed capital, the amount of circulation capital, the equipment to be installed, and the location where the business is to be conducted. Such information can be used for regulation during periods when the private sector comes under attack. During the 1988–1989 retrenchment period, for example, licenses for new enterprises in certain categories were forbidden, and some existing enterprises were closed down and their licenses revoked.

State-Created Interest Groups

Licensed individual entrepreneurs have their own special interest group called the Individual Entrepreneurs Association (*geti xiehui*).[61] Officially, this is a mass organization representing the interests of the private sector. In reality, it is, at best, a semi-autonomous organization. It pro-

---

60. In some cases, the village must verify that the peasant will be able to secure the raw materials to operate the factory. It is unclear, however, how a village can vouch for such material supplies. CI 23688.

61. There is also an organization for larger private businesses: the All-China Federation of Industry and Commerce (*quanguo gongshang lianhui*). It is discussed in Pearson, *China's New Business Elite*, chap. 5.

vides some services to members, but it also is a form of administrative control. Membership is automatic with licensing, and dues are taken with licensing fees.

The dual nature of this organization is suggested by the official positions of its leaders. The offices of the association are often located within the industrial-commercial management bureau, and the cadres who work in the association are paid by the county government. In one county, the head of the association, who originally was an individual entrepreneur, is now a full-time cadre, with the equivalent status and pay of a bureau vice head.[62] However, unlike most bureau heads, he is not a party member.[63]

The work of the association is described by officials as including (1) oversight to ensure that individuals conform to rules, such as the one requiring them to stay in their proper stalls at the markets; (2) policy education for entrepreneurs; and (3) assistance with member problems such as harassment, unfair surcharges, and disputes. These functions are further facilitated by the existence of branch suborganizations at the township level.[64] Under the branch associations are professional trade groups (hangye xiaozu) with designated group leaders.

The semipublic nature of these organizations is further reflected in the fact that the president of the National Union of Associations of Independents,[65] the parent organization of the associations, is also the head of the State Administration for Industry and Commerce; its secre-

62. This private entrepreneur was the first person in the county to be licensed. He operated a repair shop and did well. He claimed he did not want the job as head of the association; he even stayed away from home to avoid the officials' approaches. He dreaded getting involved in politics, and he was afraid the position would interfere with his moneymaking. In the end, probably because of a combination of political pressure and inducements from local officials, he agreed to serve, with the understanding that the work would not take up too much time. The government compensated him for his time with 20–30 yuan per month. In 1987 he retired from his own work to head the association full-time. He then received a cadre's salary. As of 1996, he was still serving in this position. CI 81291; CI 24696.

63. This particular entrepreneur had wanted to join the party but was told in 1984–1985 by the local political consultative conference that it would be better if he were not a party member. In 1986 he decided to apply for party membership anyway, but he withdrew his application when it became apparent that the conference standing committee would oppose his application.

64. Some township associations may employ more than one full-time official. In one Shandong county, there is a total of twenty-six full-time personnel for the seventeen townships. Most townships have at least one, three of the larger ones have two, and the county office has five. This county is in a somewhat unusual situation: one of its townships is the product of a merger but there still are two offices for the association.

65. This organization was founded in 1986; it is also known as the National Association of Individual Entrepreneurs.

tary general concurrently serves as head of the department for individual business of this same administration.[66]

While control is a defining feature of the relationship between the private sector and the local state, it is only half the story. The local state offers inducements as well as using constraints, as is typical of a corporatist system. Both the collective and the private sectors benefit from and have reason to maintain the corporatist relationship with the local state. As with the extraction of revenues from the collective sector, the relationship between the private sector and local officials is not a zero-sum game.

INDUCEMENTS FOR PRIVATE ENTERPRISE

By the mid-1990s, many local governments had altered their initial development strategies and adapted to encompass the private sector. Yet the activist role of local governments remains; most of the types of assistance that were formerly provided to collectively owned township and village enterprises have been adapted or extended to the private sector, with a few exceptions.

Credit

Townships or villages are unlikely to provide private enterprises with the same type of corporate funding through the redistribution of government funds. But counties have increasingly provided credit assistance to the private sector. The dramatic increases in the amount of bank credit received by the private sector, described in the last chapter, would not have been possible without the support of county and township officials.

Some counties have reduced the bureaucratic loans to collectively owned enterprises from the finance and tax offices and enlarged the number and types of credit associations to serve a more diversified development strategy that encompasses a growing private sector. Some counties have created their own credit companies, under the name "county finance investment companies" (caizheng touzi gongsi), to which all types of enterprises may apply. At the township level, semiprivate credit associations (jijin hui), many of which are indirectly or directly supported by township governments, proliferated by the mid-1990s to serve all types of

66. Kraus, *Private Business in China*, pp. 92–93. There is also a China Association of Private Laborers,. In 1991 Bo Yibo was honorary president. "Bo Yibo Praises Private Sector," Xinhua, 15 April 1991, in *SWB FE/1048*, 17 April 1991, p. B2/4.

clients. Some counties have such associations in each of their townships. There also are credit associations, such as the Individual Entrepreneurs and Private Business Economic Fund (*geti siying jingji jijin hui*), that exclusively serve private enterprise.

These local credit associations directly compete with the state-created credit cooperatives in each township. Money from these associations costs the borrower more than that from either banks or credit cooperatives, but the new institutions give local enterprises access to easier credit, especially for smaller, short-term, circulation-capital loans. Deposits are attracted by offering higher interest rates than those given by the state banks or credit cooperatives. Initial reports suggest that the local credit associations are doing well. For example, in one county, the township in which the county seat resides established a credit association in 1992 with an initial fund of approximately 100,000 yuan, half of which came from the township government. By 1993 its funds had increased to 5 million yuan, by 1994 to 15 million yuan, and by 1995 to 20 million yuan.[67]

Market and Technology Information

Equally if not more important, local governments are in a good position to extend to the private sector technical advice and market information—a relatively costless service that the county can provide as part of its bureaucratic duties to any enterprise likely to bring in new revenue. Technical assistance is important for private firms in the early stages of their business when their resources are limited, as it was for collectively owned township and village enterprises at the same stage.

For example, a tilemaker could turn to steelmaking because he could call upon the county rural enterprise management bureau for technical assistance. He approached the county, and local officials helped him contact consultants in Shanghai.[68] A scrap metal collector was able to start his own factory with assistance from county and township officials. In this case, the entrepreneur was from an area that had a long tradition of making small metal tools, but he needed help from county officials in securing land and the necessary licenses, as well as technical personnel to bring his products up to acceptable standards.

The promotion of the private sector in the 1990s represents a shift

---

67. CI 21696.
68. This private tilemaker had previously developed close ties with the rural enterprise management bureau when he managed a township-owned tile factory. CI 62294.

from China's original development strategy, but it is not a renunciation of its earlier course. In most counties since at least the mid-1980s, there have been large numbers of legally registered small individual entrepreneurs. What the localities did in the mid-1990s was simply to provide this sector with preferential access to resources that would allow the best firms to grow and help new ones to become established, just as the counties had helped the collective sector in the 1980s.

Beginning in the mid-1990s, in order to encourage the development of large private firms (*siying qiye*), local officials promised to provide assistance in a number of ways, from facilitating approvals and the granting of licenses to helping with markets.[69] In one county, to spur interest, private businesspeople who paid over 10,000 yuan in taxes were allowed to change their household status from rural to urban and were exempt from such rural household obligations as performing corvée labor (*yiwu gong*) and paying fees to their village. If the taxes paid by a private businessperson were sufficiently high, the exemptions and change in household registration could be extended to an entire family.[70] The sector responded positively. The number of large private firms grew from 69 in 1990 to 528 in 1995.

Previous works on the private sector in Wenzhou and parts of Fujian have described the phenomenon of "fake collectives," where private enterprises sought the protection of a "red umbrella" and the associated benefits of the collective label.[71] Such a practice has spread to counties like the one just cited. Areas that were once staunchly collective in orientation have since allowed privately owned firms to take full and direct advantage of the preferential taxes and credit policies that have been available to collectively owned enterprises.[72] According to one county official, approximately 10–20 percent of the enterprises officially registered as "collective" in his county in the mid-1990s were, in fact, private.[73] Moreover, as the reforms have matured and the political context become more relaxed, the private sector has increasingly come to enjoy openly advantageous access to goods and inputs that were earlier re-

69. CI 23696.
70. In 1994 four private businessmen in this county changed their household status under this provision. CI 24696.
71. Susan Young, "Wealth but Not Security"; and Liu, "Reform from Below."
72. In addition, the collective label also allows companies to acquire land more easily, which in the current context may be one of the most important benefits once a private company reaches sufficient size to secure its own loans. CI 7794.
73. CI 24696.

served exclusively for collective enterprises. A close business relationship has developed between private entrepreneurs and the public sector—both state and collectively owned enterprises. The state and the collective sectors have become sources of wealth for the private sector.[74]

THE PRIVATE-PUBLIC SYMBIOSIS:
THE INTERPLAY OF STATE AND MARKET

The fact that the growth of the private sector was spurred by local state intervention—in some cases by outright state-sponsored privatization of formerly collectively owned enterprises—has implications for the relationship between the private sector and local government. It diminishes the chances that a growing private industrial sector will emerge as an independent economic elite capable of usurping the power of local officials. On the contrary, the relationship between the local state and the private sector has become increasingly symbiotic.[75]

Production contracts, a long-practiced tradition in China, have reappeared to provide connections and opportunities for private business-people. "Horizontal linkages" (*hengxiang lianhe*) form between large state and collective factories (at the county level or above) and rural enterprises. In the 1980s, these occurred primarily with township- or village-owned firms. In the 1990s, similar arrangements are being made with private firms.

Even in places like Wenzhou, which is noted for its private enterprises, individual entrepreneurs are often part of an assembly-line operation, where an entire village contracts to make certain items and individual households perform specialized tasks necessary to produce the finished product. Instead of directly participating in the market as individuals, the village contracts with larger corporate organizations. Either the village or smaller subgroups handle the marketing. The various trade associations are another mechanism through which the difficulties of operating in a market context of limited information and skills are reduced for small producers. Associations find markets and sometimes help with the procurement of materials.[76]

Where "market" activity relies on contracts involving state or collec-

74. I present preliminary versions of this argument in "Private and Local State Entrepreneurship" and "Rational Choices."
75. David Wank, "Bureaucratic Patronage and Private Business"; and "State Socialism to Community Capitalism."
76. Parris, "Local Initiative and National Reform," also refers to this as corporate activity.

tively owned firms, the implications for the distribution of power are very different from those in situations where entrepreneurs do not rely on official intervention. In rural areas, where private entrepreneurs have become part of, and in some cases rely on, the state and collective sectors in order to reduce risks while pursuing their economic interests, the relationship between the local state and the private sector is no longer likely to be adversarial. Local governments have used their control of these contracts and resources to bring the private sector into the corporatist fold.

Private business in China is often closer to that found in the developmental states of the East Asian NICs than to the models described in neoclassical economic theories. Some successful private entrepreneurs in China seldom venture into the open market, either for the procurement of production materials or for the sale of their products. Instead, they produce as individual firms but sell their products to large collective or state enterprises on contract.[77] The state enterprises to whom they sell their goods often supply them with basic raw materials and design options. The role of the individual entrepreneur is in processing, as in the putting out system in traditional China.

The operation of a private rural sofa-frame factory illustrates how the system works. In 1990 this factory had a production output of over 3 million yuan and employed over fifty workers. The private entrepreneur who owned the factory did not have to worry about supplies, designs, or the retailing of his products.[78] He simply produced the sofa frames and delivered them to a nearby large collective enterprise, with which he had contracted to make the frames. The physical plant, workers, hours, conditions, and wages were his responsibility.[79] But the price of the goods, the provision of materials, and the amounts to be produced were determined beforehand by the terms of his contract with the collective factory.[80]

The interplay of plan and market, the resilience of old patterns of behavior, and the importance of personal relations are aptly captured by

77. Young, "Wealth but Not Security," reports that larger private businesses, too, sell to collective or state enterprises. The point is not the establishment of contract sales but the fact that those with whom the contracts are made are part of the state.

78. As his business grew and became more secure, and as he accumulated more capital, he found it more profitable to procure some of his own materials.

79. Eighty percent of the workers were from the village. They were paid on a piece-rate basis. Their average wage was about 270 yuan per month, but they sometimes earned as much as 500 yuan per month. Work hours were from 7:30 A.M. to 11:00 A.M. and from 3:00 P.M. to 7:30 P.M., with fifteen days off to plant wheat.

80. CI 81191.

Solinger in her description of trading in the urban state industrial sector.[81] Building on the work of Oliver Williamson, she highlights the prevalence of relational contracting in reforming socialist systems. She describes the "sticky" pattern of behavior displayed by firms in a reform environment: though free from the constraints of mandatory planning, they continue to rely on previous relationships and on trust and familiarity developed during the period when the state arranged trading partners. She notes that "the pathways [of the planning system] . . . continue to bring the old partners together—this time, however, as a matter of *choice*" (emphasis added).[82] The importance of established personal connections is also seen in the market behavior of private entrepreneurs. But the contractual partnerships in the rural private sector do not stem directly from the pre-reform planning system, although some contacts were developed from jobs held in the state or collective sectors.

Private entrepreneurs, like their urban counterparts in the state industrial sector, build on previous relationships or cultivate new contacts with large state and collective firms. The goal is to build trust and familiarity to maximize their economic interests in what might otherwise appear to be an impersonal market context.[83] Just like those in the state sector, private entrepreneurs try to minimize risks, reduce transaction costs, and engage in relationships that "offer a premium of trust, predictability, and security of supply, and which cut down on information-search costs."[84] It is here that the role of local governments and the publicly owned sectors becomes significant for private firms.

In the above example, the sofa-frame maker secured his contract through his personal connections with the local government—in this case, a large urban, collectively owned factory. He had been a cart driver before 1980, and in 1982 he started a family enterprise, employing two or three relatives. Around 1984 he expanded his business and changed his product line from end tables (which he sold to a collective factory) to sofa frames. This change, which set him on the road to success, was somewhat fortuitous. He happened to be at a large collective factory on other business when he heard that the factory desperately needed fuel. Through his various contacts, he managed to secure a large supply of

81. Solinger, "Urban Reform in Post-Mao China."
82. Ibid., p. 118.
83. See David Wank, "Bureaucratic Patronage and Private Business"; Margaret Pearson also focuses on the role that clientelism has played in fostering the success of the private sector in China. See *China's New Business Elite.*
84. Solinger, "Urban Reform in Post-Mao China," p. 106.

fuel for the factory. The factory manager was so grateful and impressed with this man's resourcefulness that he decided to help him and gave him a contract to supply sofa frames. A personal relationship with the collective factory thus developed into a profitable business.

As the sofa maker became more successful, the smaller producers in the village became his subcontractors. He provided his neighbors with the market and the expertise needed to break into a rather profitable profession. He described this as a process in which "he carried them along." By 1991 there was a total of ten household factories in the village— three large ones (each employing over thirty people) and seven smaller ones—producing sofa frames. The original sofa-frame maker collected the frames made by his neighbors and sold them, along with his own frames, to the collective in the nearby large city.[85] The ability of this entrepreneur to help his neighbors was enhanced by the fact that he also happened to be a village official; he was a group head (*zu zhang*), with 210 members of the village under his jurisdiction.

A successful private shoemaker similarly produced for the market with minimal risk by taking orders from the large collective or state-owned department stores in the area. The materials and styles were provided by the stores; he merely produced according to specification.

The Individual Entrepreneurs Association, of which both the shoemaker and the sofa-frame maker were members, reported that most larger private businesses sold on consignment (*daixiao*) to either state-owned or collective enterprises rather than directly participating in the market. The majority of smaller individual entrepreneurs also sold to factories, with only about 10 percent of them actually selling to the public.[86] These symbiotic relations between private and public enterprises, coupled with the assistance provided by the local corporate state, have kept the private sector within the corporatist fold.

THE EVOLUTION OF LOCAL STATE-LED DEVELOPMENT

With decollectivization and fiscal reform, local officials at the county, township, and village levels were given incentives to generate new sources of revenue. Resources and local conditions determined how they would choose to respond to these incentives. Some chose to support the private

85. CI 81191.
86. In some places, the *geti* are not paid until the products are sold. CI 81291.

sector from an early date. Most chose to build on existing strength and take the route of least political change and resistance by first developing collectively owned township and village enterprises; only gradually did they allow the private sector to grow. Contrary to the worst predictions of those familiar with the Soviet system, China's local officials succeeded in generating dynamic growth in rural enterprises. The speed of growth is impressive, but what is perhaps even more noteworthy is the flexibility these officials have exhibited in adapting to changing political and economic conditions while at the same time keeping at least indirect control of the development process.

Local governments have used a combination of inducements and constraints to fashion a local corporatist system that melds the entrepreneurial and governmental roles of local governments, keeping intact the fusion of economic and political power characteristic of Leninist systems. Rather than casting aside the Maoist system to achieve revolutionary change, local officials adopted a much more evolutionary approach and turned this system to their advantage. This chapter has shown how communist officials used the mechanisms of a centrally planned economy as policy instruments to foster rapid economic growth and to maintain their own political power, even as the private sector began to grow. These were the institutional supports that kept many of China's rural industries from drowning during the early stages of economic takeoff.

At the same time, this type of positive intervention allowed local cadres significant influence over the speed with which particular sectors and enterprises developed. This leeway provides some insight into the significant variation that one finds in different localities within China. It has been up to local officials to decide how much local enterprise, and what types, will in practice be supported.

But the power of local officials to direct the local economy and the close relationships that they have developed with both collective and private firms carry with them significant costs for central-local relations. The following chapters examine these consequences of local state corporatism.

CHAPTER 5

Principals and Agents

Central Regulation or Local Control

The Chinese state, like all organizations, faces the problem of moral hazard: local agents always have an advantage over the principal in their knowledge of the true level of implementation and performance of policies at the local levels, and they may use that information to further their own rather than the principal's interests.[1] The Maoist system was already inherently weak in its regulatory power because the regulators were also the implementers.[2] The reforms and the emergence of local state corporatism further intensified the moral hazard problem because they increased the need of agents to protect first the locality and only second the center.

The crucial determinants of whether a local government will effectively implement central regulations are the degree to which the policy is compatible with local interests and the degree to which the upper levels are watching. During the Mao period, the center had to rely on the commune and the county to keep those interests in check, but local officials had divided loyalties. The interests of cadres at the team and brigade levels were tied to local economic conditions—the amount of grain left with the team. These officials were always in a situation where they engaged in various cat-and-mouse games with the center, maintaining a "facade

---

1. On moral hazard, see Stephen Ross, "Economic Theory of Agency"; Michael Spence and Richard Zeckhauser, "Insurance, Information, and Individual Action"; Michael Jensen and William Meckling, "Theory of the Firm"; and Michael Jensen, "Organization Theory and Methodology."
2. See Oi, *State and Peasant*, on this problem.

of compliance" to avoid detection by the upper levels while trying to satisfy local interests.[3]

In the post-Mao period, the rationale that drove team and brigade cadres to shortchange the central state has spread to those at the township and county levels. The personal and administrative well-being of those at the township and county levels now rests with "what is left" in their locality. With the fiscal reforms and the transfer to the localities of the rights to the residual, county officials have an increasing need to look out first for local rather than central interests.

The degree to which local officials are able to serve local interests varies with time and with level of administration. The political climate has always affected the amount of leeway that officials have had to serve their interests. In the Maoist period, full compliance was the best strategy during a campaign, when all levels were under increased pressure to ensure the correct implementation of policy. But significant latitude exists when the center is not focusing its regulatory attention on any particular official or level. The trick has been for local officials not to disobey openly or to attract attention to their activities. A big difference exists between minimal and full compliance.

At the subprovincial levels, monitoring is particularly difficult in the policy area of taxes and revenues—unlike capital spending at the provincial level,[4] which is more susceptible to close scrutiny and detection. Tax evasion and illegal retention of revenues by county, township, and village officials are activities at least two levels removed from the center, involving resources that can be much more easily hidden or explained away than is a major investment project. The 1994 decision to readjust taxes to give the center more direct control over extrabudgetary funds is an indication that the center's regulation of revenues at the local levels was ineffective.

At the same time, it would be a mistake to think that central control has disintegrated because localities now have increasing resources, just as it would be incorrect to think that the Maoist system was weak because peasants were able to engage in evasion. Local economic activity in China's countryside is still subject to extensive regulation, much of it centrally mandated. As the following sections elaborate, local officials still carry out central-level directives regarding the types of investigation to be undertaken, and they carefully follow centrally stipulated procedures.

3. See Oi, *State and Peasant,* chap. 6.
4. See Huang, *Inflation and Investment Controls.*

The issue is what happens after the investigations. Effectiveness in ferreting out problems does not necessarily translate into the center's interests being served.

The reality is that regulation at the local levels continues to exhibit two faces—minimum compliance and protection of local interests. This chapter examines why this duality remains and how the two faces coexist.

OVERLAPPING LINES OF AUTHORITY

During the Maoist period, the Chinese communist state relied on intersecting lines of authority to act as checks for the center. First, there was horizontal (*kuai*) rule. Local bureaucrats were led by their territorial administrative leader, be it the county magistrate or the commune head. These officials in turn were under the supervision and regulation of superiors at the next level of the government hierarchy. Second, each bureaucratic agency was subject to vertical (*tiao*) ministerial rule, which constituted "a distinct chain of command organized on a nationwide basis and reaching from the central authorities through individual ministries to the local levels."[5] Third, overseeing both the territorial and the ministerial rule was the Chinese Communist Party, which exercised control over all administrative officials within each locality through a hierarchy parallel to that of the government. Long ago Barnett noted: "Party membership in itself confers great prestige and authority, and special political status . . . not infrequently, relatively low-ranking Party members are recognized as having greater political authority on many matters than higher-ranking non-Party cadres."[6]

These three lines of authority remain in force today. The party still holds power at the local levels, each level is still subject to control by its superiors at the next level, and ministerial control continues to check the behavior of subordinates in successive levels of the government bureaucracy.

This system is designed to provide multiple checks at each level, but in practice it has suffered from multiple points of weakness. Observers have long noted the problem of conflicting commands coming from different lines of authority, leaving local cadres caught in the middle.[7] In

5. Barnett and Vogel identify horizontal and vertical rule in pointing to the importance of functional "systems" (*xitong*). *Cadres, Bureaucracy, and Political Power*, p. 6.
6. Ibid., p. 37.
7. See Jonathan Unger, "Struggle to Dictate China's Administration."

the past, local officials were able to use the existence of different directives to serve their own interests. In the countryside during the Cultural Revolution, they could selectively implement directives that suited their purposes.[8]

Some evidence also raises questions about how effectively the center's interests are protected by having a separate party hierarchy at each level. It was assumed that there would be a difference in orientation between party members and nonmembers. It was further assumed that this would facilitate the use of the party as a monitoring device to detect activity against the party-state. A final assumption was that the interests of party members were consistent with those of the central party leadership. The first two assumptions may be valid, but the third is problematic.

First, almost all the government officials whom the party oversees are themselves also party members. Second, those in government positions sometimes also hold party posts. For example, the district magistrate is often not only a party member but also the party vice secretary of the county. Third, the party secretary and the county magistrate are sometimes one and the same individual. In one county, between 1949 and 1989, of the fourteen individuals who served as county party secretary, eight had also served at one time as county magistrate.

Similar overlap exists at the township and village levels, although it is sometimes disguised. Some officials make special efforts to maintain the appearance of a division between party and state. If they hold both government and party positions, they may use two sets of name cards, designed for different occasions. For example, a village party secretary who was also head of the village enterprise management committee said that when he handled economic matters, it was appropriate that he be known only as an administrative leader, so he had a special card for that purpose that identified him as the chairman of the board of the village corporation.[9] But the fact remains that he also spoke for the party.

Cases that strongly suggest sharp distinctions between party secretaries and the administrative officials under their supervision come from factories where party secretaries with little or no technical knowledge have overruled competent factory managers. In such situations, there may be a qualitative difference in the expertise of the two individuals. But there are also instances of former factory managers becoming party

8. See Oi, *State and Peasant,* chap. 6.
9. CI 72188.

secretaries. In those situations, conflict may stem from rivalry between the two people, both of whom supposedly hold decision-making power, rather than from ideological differences related to their government and party affiliations.[10]

To the extent that ideological conflicts between party and government heads occurred during the Maoist period, they were likely due to ideological prohibitions on economic rewards and to the responsibility of the party secretary to enforce those prohibitions. But after the reforms, most such prohibitions were removed, and any that remained were minor. The interests of both party and government heads are now increasingly centered on the economic situation of the locality for which both have responsibility. Local Communist Party officials are as much judged by economic results as are local administrators. Party secretaries take an active part, and in some cases play a pivotal role, in the economic development of a locality. It is no longer the case, if it ever was, that local party officials will safeguard the interests of the center before taking care of the locality.

The effectiveness of central regulations depends on who the regulatory agents are, on their ability to carry out their tasks, and most important, on whose interests are affected when they process the information they unearth.

LOCAL REGULATORY AGENTS

Beijing retains a powerful tool for the control of lower-level agents: the *nomenklatura* system.[11] Annual cadre evaluations can effectively weed out elements likely to cause problems.[12] The personnel system does prevent most officials from overtly defying stated rules and regulations. Local officials are careful to follow central regulations about inspections, both in form and in timing. But as in the Maoist period, the regulatory agents are local officials who have divided loyalties.

---

10. A vivid example of this is found in Anita Chan, Richard Madsen, and Jonathan Unger, *Chen Village.*
11. This argument is made by Huang, who describes the effectiveness of central control over provincial appointments in managing investment and inflation. *Inflation and Investment Controls.*
12. Huang compares such evaluations to the security checks on potential employees conducted by government agencies in the United States. *Inflation and Investment Controls,* p. 93.

Unlike the U.S. Internal Revenue Service employees, who are agents of the federal government, regulators responsible for overseeing tax collection in China are part of *local* government. They are charged with policing themselves. Many have dual roles as both administrators and regulators; few have responsibility only to regulate. In either case, the level they are supposed to oversee pays their salaries and bonuses.

China's local regulatory agencies include the tax, finance, and audit bureaus. Officials of the tax and finance bureaus are both administrators and regulators. They are the major agents for county fiscal control, responsible for tax assessment, collection, budget allocations, and regulation.[13] The county-level tax bureau assesses and collects taxes from industrial enterprises, handles the deposits of these funds at the local People's Bank of China,[14] and conducts investigations to ensure that enterprises pay their taxes. Township-level tax offices have similar responsibilities.[15]

The finance bureau is the center of overall fiscal planning and management. Each county finance bureau has the primary responsibility for the county's within-budget funds, allocates the budgeted funds for all the state agencies within the county,[16] supervises the fiscal affairs of all enterprises and administrative units, receives daily reports of tax collections, and oversees extrabudgetary funds (see chapter 2).[17]

The regulatory work of the tax and finance bureaus is carried out by special units that exist at the county and township levels. The county tax

13. The tax and finance bureaus divide the administration of taxes by type: the tax bureau controls the industrial-commercial taxes (*gongshang shui*), while the finance bureau controls the agricultural taxes. The finance bureau also controls land use, the orchard and forest products tax, and the house sales tax.

14. This is also the depository for the local finance bureau.

15. CI 8791. The township tax office decides which of its enterprises are to be checked, but the powers of the office are limited. It has no power to fine; this requires the approval of the county, which is often overwhelmed with cases. In one township, no one has ever been fined. Township officials complained that private businesses went without paying taxes for half a year while the township waited for the county to decide these cases. CI 24688.

16. The budget-making process is complex. The budget form (*yusuan biao*), which covers within-budget revenues and expenditures, is completed by February. The numbers are gathered from other, more specialized, sections of the finance bureau, such as the administrative finance (*xingcai*) section, the agricultural finance (*nongcai*) section for the agricultural tax, and the enterprise finance (*qicai*) section for enterprise income. The budget section then sends the preliminary budget back to the more specialized sections, each of which then produces a more detailed budget for its sector. The final budgets are then distributed to the various institutions and agencies.

17. CI 8791.

bureau, for example, has an investigative team (*jicha dui*);[18] within the township tax office, there is an "investigative group" (*jicha zu*).[19]

In contrast to the responsibilities of the tax and finance bureaus, which include both administration and regulation, the sole duty of the audit bureau (*shenjiju*) is to regulate. In the 1980s, the central authorities created this specialized agency to bolster their ability to monitor economic activity in a growing and increasingly complex system.[20] The rationale for the establishment of a separate investigative body was to allow specialized, "high-level supervision" (*gaozeng jiandu*) that would investigate the fiscal affairs of enterprises, government agencies, and institutions.[21] The bureau determines whether there has been a violation of law (*weifa*) or an infraction of a regulation (*weiji*).[22] The staff of county-level audit bureaus includes specialists and nonspecialists, but most have accounting backgrounds.

Interviews suggest that local-level audit bureaus have slowly had their resources increased. One county audit bureau originally was given only six official slots (*bianzhi*); the number increased to eleven in 1986, and to twenty-one by 1991. Of these, three had the rank of auditor (*shenjishi*), six were assistant auditors (*juli shenjishi*), and a number were audit clerks (*shenjiyuan*).[23] Similarly, for the first five years, the audit bureau was located in the offices of the county government, but in 1990 it was given a new building of its own. Suboffices of the audit bureau (*shenjisuo*) were established to further facilitate oversight below the county level.[24]

18. In one county, the team consisted of five people.

19. The group consists of two or three people who specialize in investigations on a year-round basis.

20. For an explanation of the center's aims in establishing of this regulatory body, see Huang, *Inflation and Investment Controls*, chap. 4.

21. The audit bureau is one level above the tax and finance bureaus in its power to supervise and regulate. But while it has an advantage over those offices, its independence of the level that it is charged with regulating is still limited. The heads of the audit bureau are still subordinate to local government and party leaders. Their individual bonuses and the extrabudgetary funds available to their bureau hinge on the health of the local treasury.

22. There are other local agencies that deal with economic crime. Which agency is involved depends on the crime and on what type of funds have been misused. CI 81291.

23. CI 8991.

24. Establishment of the audit bureau system in China was relatively recent: the regulation to establish county-level offices was passed in 1981. Many counties had offices by 1983. Even though this county audit bureau was established in 1984, three out of the seventeen townships in the county were still without suboffices in 1991. Each suboffice was allocated three to five official positions, only two of which were specialized full-time posts (*zhuan bianzhi*) for audit work; the others fell into the special administrative category of "concurrent positions" (*jian bianzhi*). In 1990, there were forty people working in the

SCHEDULED INVESTIGATIONS

The process by which investigations and audits are undertaken is strictly regulated and depends heavily on a preset schedule. The first, "propaganda," stage of an investigation involves alerting units that they may be examined. The second stage allows the units to check themselves (*danwei sicha*) and clear up any mistakes by paying the taxes owed. If they take advantage of this opportunity and come clean, they are not fined. Only at the third stage are work teams sent to selected units to investigate and examine the books.

There is a division of investigative targets among the three bureaus. The county tax and finance bureaus are responsible for state, collective, and private enterprises in the county seat.[25] Their subordinates at the township level investigate the collectively owned township and village enterprises and private enterprises at the township and village levels, although county officials may personally visit the largest of these as well. The audit bureau's original mission excluded rural enterprises in its scope of responsibilities, but over time, and in response to changing conditions, such enterprises have come within its purview. Also now part of its routine work is the monitoring of the collection of the village-retained funds (*tiliu*) and collective reserves (*gonggong jilei*).[26]

The investigations conducted by the audit bureau are subject to a plan issued by the province and relayed by the prefecture. Early every year the prefecture meets with its county audit bureaus to draw up its plan (*shenji jihua*), which specifies the minimum number of audits to be conducted and the types of enterprises in which "systems" will be audited. In one county, the overall objective of the plan was to audit all units in the county within three years.[27] The actual number of audits may be more than is stipulated in the plan. In 1990 one county audit bureau received a plan from the prefecture that called for a minimum of thirty-six audits. By the end of the year, the county had audited seventy-four units, including ad hoc cases that it had selected itself.[28]

In addition to scheduled investigations, the audit bureau in each locality conducts ad hoc investigations based on information from various

---

fourteen suboffices, more than the number of positions the county had originally allowed. CI 8991.
    25. CI 23688.
    26. This expansion of responsibilities occurred in the late 1980s.
    27. CI 8991.
    28. Of these, thirty-eight were administrative units.

sources, including citizen tips. A designated person in the county audit bureau examines letters from citizens reporting on tax or economic crimes. According to local auditors, every complaint that comes to the audit bureau must be investigated, even though most of these inquiries do not turn up anything illegal. Sometimes the audit bureau acts "like the security (*gongan*) bureau and investigates to get a general sense of the situation."[29] Sometimes it receives voluntary confessions of wrongdoings.

The investigative work of the tax and finance bureaus is not dictated by quotas, but investigations must follow a set schedule. A 1985 State Council regulation requires county and township tax and finance bureaus to carry out a "major investigation on taxes, finances, and prices" (*shuiwu caizheng wujia dajiancha*) every September and October. County finance bureaus have a "major investigation office" (*dajiancha bangongshi*) that coordinates work teams assembled from the finance, tax, price, and audit bureaus.[30] In 1990 one county had seventy teams of three persons each. Eighty members were from the tax bureau, sixty from the price bureau, twenty from the audit bureau, and fifty from the substations of the finance bureau at the township level. The investigations were organized by the township, all of whose leading personnel were mobilized to form a "township leading group" (*xiang lingdao xiaozu*). This group was led by the tax office and included a township vice head and the heads of the finance office, the industrial-commercial management office, and the economic commission. Units with large incomes were the primary targets of investigation.[31]

Like the audit bureau, the tax and finance bureaus do ad hoc checks, and their targets are similarly easy to predict. Again the most likely candidates for investigation are those enterprises that have substantial income. Each year county tax officials go to all of the major firms, designated as *key-point enterprises*.[32] State-owned enterprises and county-level collectives are checked at least annually. Tax officials investigate private enterprises at least twice a year.[33] Commercial enterprises, such as retail stores, are also examined—as are government agencies—to deter-

29. CI 81391.   30. CI 8891.
31. CI 24688. There are no reliable numbers indicating how many units were involved in the investigation, but one finance bureau official estimated that 20–30 percent of the county's governmental and collective units were examined. The investigation did not include private businesses, because independent investigations by the tax bureau had already been conducted. CI 8891.
32. CI 81391.   33. CI 24688.

mine whether spending is in accordance with regulations and whether there is any misappropriation of funds.

In one county, the number of ad hoc checks by the tax office ranged from thirty to fifty per year. In 1990, about 30 percent of the units investigated were found to have problems. Three collectively owned county-level enterprises were fined a total of 7,000 yuan for tax evasion.[34] These enterprises had written off costs illegally and distributed the extra profits within the factory. Some private businesses (*siying*) were also guilty of tax fraud.[35]

ANNOUNCED AUDITS

Like investigations, audits are subject to strict regulations imposed on the audit team and the unit audited. The bureau is required to send notification three days in advance of an audit with information about what is to be audited along with the names of those conducting the audit. This advance notice is intended to allow the unit to assemble its materials, but it also no doubt gives the unit an opportunity to correct or juggle its books.

The auditing team usually consists of three people—five for important and complex audits. Not all members of the team need be from the audit bureau; only the head of the team must be a bureau member. The audit process follows a set routine, though the time a team spends in a factory or unit depends on its size.[36] When the audit team arrives, the responsible person of the unit being audited is required to present a report. The team then examines all relevant documents—most importantly the unit's books, receipts (*piaozheng*), and reports—as well as the physical stocks and/or funds (*kucun xianjin*), which must match the account records. If problems are found, the team will determine who is responsible. That person must either write a certification (*zhengming*) in which he or she takes responsibility for the document in question or sign each document (*zhengming cailiao*) that the audit team has found problematic. If necessary, more than one person will take responsibility. For example, if there is a problem with the account books, both the accountant and the factory manager must write a declaration. This signed ma-

34. The amount of fraud involved was fairly small, but the fine was five times the tax owed.
35. CI 81391.
36. In one county, it was usually five to seven days.

terial is used as evidence of wrongdoing. The audit team writes a three-part report covering the basic conditions of the unit, the problems found, and the recommendation of the team for handling the problems (*chuli yijian*). The report is shown to the audited unit, which can either sign it, agreeing that it is accurate, or reject and contest it. Either way, the report is taken back to the audit bureau.

The county audit bureau makes a final judgment on the unit in a meeting (*juwu huiyi*) led by the bureau head and attended by the audit team members. Cases are considered in batches or individually. At this meeting, the county bureau puts forth its opinion on each report in an "audit decision" (*shenji jueding*), which may or may not endorse the recommendations of the audit team. This final decision, along with the original report, is sent to the audited unit. If the unit wishes to contest the county bureau opinion, it has fifteen days to appeal to the prefectural audit bureau for a further investigation. The prefecture then has thirty days to conduct its audit.[37]

UNCOVERING MISCONDUCT

Even though the annual investigations by the tax, finance, and audit bureaus are routine and generally known about in advance, local regulatory agents do detect cases of evasion and other misconduct. The tax and finance bureaus have found a wide range of problems relating to tax, fiscal, and pricing matters, including incorrect calculation of enterprise income tax and inappropriate expense claims.[38] They are particularly vigilant in regard to the private sector. This is understandable, because local governments have no direct way to intervene in the affairs of private businesses, and such enterprises often fail to keep standard account books.[39]

The number of problems discovered by the various bureaus in any given year may be considerable. In one county in 1990, about 30 per-

37. Audited units do contest decisions. In 1990 the service company of a county material supply bureau refused to accept the audit bureau's findings that it had illegally divided its profits with its township office before paying taxes and had spent the extra revenue on cars and entertainment. In the end, the prefecture agreed with the conclusion of the county audit bureau. The unit had to pay 296,000 yuan in additional income tax. Two cars purchased with the illegal profits were given to the finance bureau because the service company had insufficient funds to pay the taxes it owed. CI 81291.

38. CI 8891.

39. This is the explanation for why some private businesses are assigned a set amount of tax (*dingshui*) rather than being assessed at standard rates. CI 81391.

cent of all enterprises admitted to problems during the self-examination (*sicha*) stage. In the same year, audit teams discovered problems in about 10 percent of the units they investigated and recovered 500,000–600,000 yuan. Some cases—for example, peasants illegally selling fertilizer without paying tax—were relatively minor; others involved substantial amounts of money. In 1987 a township tax office recovered over 20,000 yuan from a single private firm.[40] One suspects that the number of problems discovered and reported varies with the political climate and the amount of pressure or direct supervision from the upper levels, as in all types of policy regulation. The greater the pressure, the higher the number of problems likely to be found.

The audit bureau, as the specialized economic investigation unit, boasts a particularly impressive record in catching problems, some of which are missed by the tax and finance bureaus. For example, the audit bureau found that two township-level factories had underpaid taxes, one by 120,000 yuan, the other by 190,000 yuan. The township tax office had missed both of these cases.[41] The audit bureau's annual checks of all key-point units, enterprises, and institutions are designed to catch such slip-ups. It watches for underreporting of profits (and overreporting— see below), illegal spending, individual corruption, and hidden funds. It is particularly vigilant about construction and investment.[42] In one case, the bureau discovered that a company had illegally used 500,000 yuan of its circulation funds to construct a building.[43] The scope of the bureau's authority also includes oversight of the use of special project funds, such as those for developing coal, cotton, grain, or irrigation.

The audit bureau even inspects county government expenses once a year. Banks also fall under its authority, but the scope of the bank audits is limited: the bureau checks only that interest rates are appropriate and makes sure that specified funds have been used for the procurement of grain and cotton, not for the granting of loans. In one 1990 case, a county-level Agricultural Bank was found to have illegally used its cotton pro-

40. CI 24688.

41. When the audit bureau was asked why these cases had slipped past the tax office, the response was that the office was understaffed. Moreover, in one instance, the personnel in the township tax office had just arrived and were unfamiliar with the situation. CI 24688; CI 8991.

42. According to Huang, investment control is one of the two central areas of concern assigned to the General Auditing Administration. The other is fiscal matters. *Inflation and Investment Controls*, p. 106.

43. CI 8991.

curement funds for other purposes.[44] In the mid-1980s, the audit bureau was called in when a local cotton procurement station that was short of funds deducted illegal fees from the amount it paid peasants for their cotton.[45]

The following is a partial list of practices that come under the jurisdiction of the audit bureau.

Underreporting (*Shaobao*) Profits

Some enterprises underreport their profits because they want to pay less income tax; others do so to pay less rent to the county or to the township government in contract fees. Much like team leaders in the Maoist period, factory managers who contract do not want higher profit quotas to be imposed for the following year; such managers may also fear rent increases. In 1990, for example, the audit bureau found that a county beer factory had reported only 11.2 million yuan in profits instead of its actual profits of 13 million yuan.[46]

Illegal distribution of profits and expenditures is another aspect of the underreporting problem. Because central authorities want to prevent factories from haphazardly giving out bonuses and gifts (*luanfa jiangjin luanfa shiwu*), including clothes and food, national regulations specify that bonuses should not exceed preset amounts unless a bonus tax is levied, nor should they be deducted as expenses. Both practices would reduce the income tax base. These are, nonetheless, common problems. In one county, over twenty industrial-commercial enterprises were found to have engaged in such illegal practices. Enterprises preferred to provide extras to their workers than to pay higher taxes because the latter would effectively have raised their profit quotas for the following year.

Individual Corruption (*Tanwu*) and the Misappropriation of Public Funds (*Nuoyong Gongkuan*)

Corruption cases routinely fall under the jurisdiction of these bureaus in their regulatory capacity. For example, the audit bureau in 1988 found

44. This county did not give IOUs for grain, but did for cotton in 1984, 1985, and 1986. CI 81291.
45. This deduction was charged as additional *tiliu*. The *tiliu* rate is supposed to be monitored by the county People's Congress. The incident was reported to the congress, but was later assigned to the county audit bureau.
46. CI 8991.

that an accountant of the forestry bureau had engaged in corruption involving 30,000 yuan. There are also related offenses known generically as "misappropriation of funds" (*nuoyong*). The latter is defined as taking public funds and using them for oneself or for others; such misuse may include unauthorized public expenditure. Either an individual (*siren nuoyong*) or a public institution (*gongjia nuoyong*) may be guilty of such an offense. The penalties are different in the two cases, but in both, the embezzled or illegally used funds must be repaid.[47] Included in this category are the illegal use of procurement funds, instanced above, and the destruction of public property (*langfei sunshi*). In one case in which a liquor factory let its grain rot, the warehouse management was held responsible. In cases of corruption or misappropriation of funds, depending on the amount involved and the seriousness of the crime, the problems may be reported to other legal and judicial agencies within the county.

Unreported Funds

The failure to report funds is colloquially referred to as keeping "small treasure chests" (*xiaojin ku*). The sources of these funds vary: a factory may rent space to a private entrepreneur and fail to report the rent, or a factory may sell scrap (*feijin*) and not report the proceeds.[48] Although it is difficult to discover such income, and local officials claim the amounts are small, audit bureau cadres openly acknowledge that such problems exist.[49] One strategy that the audit bureau uses to detect such hidden funds is to look at the unit's entertainment accounts. In 1988 a county audit bureau investigated the entertainment fund of a construction materials company and found 4,000–5,000 yuan in unreported funds. All discovered "treasure chests" are confiscated and turned over to the county finance bureau.[50]

THE CORPORATE NATURE OF LOCAL REGULATION

The previous sections have shown that local regulatory agents are careful to follow upper-level directives and that they can uncover cases of malfeasance and recover funds. The centralized appointment system is effective enough to prompt this type of compliance. A remaining ques-

47. CI 8991.   48. CI 8991.
49. Between 1988 and 1991, one county audit bureau reported that it found only ten units that had hidden funds.
50. CI 8991.

tion is how local regulatory agents use the information gathered. Do they punish the offenders? Do they relay all information to the upper levels, thereby serving the best interests of the center—the principal— or do they keep some information within the bounds of the locality to protect local interests?

All principal-agent relationships face the problem of asymmetrical knowledge. The agent always has the upper hand with regard to information. The trick is for the principal to devise sufficient incentives so that the agent will find it to be in his or her interests to serve the principal's needs. The problem for China is that at the county level and below, the central state's incentives are overshadowed by those provided by the more immediate principal—the local corporate state.

The agency problems at the county level and below derive from the "nested principal-agent model" where there are many different principals and agents.[51] The interests of the regulatory agents are only partially tied to the principal mandating the investigations—that is, the central state. Their positions are dependent on the goodwill of the central state through the *nomenklatura* system, but their salaries and general economic well-being depend on those whom they are investigating within the county. For tax, finance, and audit bureau officials, the principals who count are the county leaders: the party secretary and the county magistrate. Though auditors pay careful attention to form and schedule to please the center, the center's interests will not necessarily be served by the information gathered in the investigations within the county. Effective monitoring by a central state depends on the independence of the regulatory agents from those they are charged with overseeing. In creating the residual, the center motivated economic growth, but granting property rights to the localities over this residual undermined the center's role as the principal most able to affect the well-being of its agents.

Monitoring can be used by the local corporate state to safeguard local interests. As examples will show, sometimes local government officials have condoned behavior that violates central rules and regulations in order to help their various enterprises.

CURE THE OFFENSE TO SAVE THE ENTERPRISE

Officials of the county audit bureau took pride in describing to me the skills and effectiveness of their specialized staff, but they also revealed an

51. J. Mirrlees, "Optimal Structure of Incentives."

attitude toward offenders that makes it clear that local rather than central state interests were being protected. Sanctions have become very much a family matter; if the "children" admit their mistakes and, most important, show a repentant attitude, they will be forgiven and treated leniently.[52] The annual investigations uncover numerous problems, but one of their main purposes seems to be to scare businesses into correcting their mistakes during the self-examination stage.

In its adjudications of cases of underpayment, the audit bureau distinguishes clearly between intentional tax violations and those arising from ignorance or oversight. Many problems are attributed by local officials to low standards in enterprise accounting work, sometimes stemming from unfamiliarity with regulations or from incorrect accounting procedures.[53] If the failure to pay taxes (*loushui*) is unintentional, the unit simply pays the amount due; only intentional underpayment (*toushui*) is fined, the amount depending on the size of the indiscretion.

This forgiving attitude toward offenders was evident in the records of a county audit bureau. In the course of one year in that county, of seventy-four units audited 60 percent were found to have committed infractions; 1.36 million yuan was recovered in taxes, but not one enterprise was fined for breaking administrative rules. The head of the audit bureau rationalized this record by explaining that it is very difficult to prove something is done on purpose. Errors may be attributed to merely a lack of skills or to ignorance of regulations.

Others have commented, "We can't punish (*chuli*) everyone; there are just too many offenders!"[54] Only in the most severe cases of personal corruption is there harsh treatment, and even then, once the offender has served his time, he may return to his former unit, albeit in a lower position. For example, in 1985 the head of a branch office of a county electrical bureau was found guilty of embezzling fees and taking bribes totaling over 4,000 yuan. After serving three years in prison, he was released and given a job as a temporary worker (*linshi gong*) at the bureau.

As in the Maoist period, the treatment of guilty parties depends on their attitude (*biaoxian*).[55] The consequences are less severe, for example, if the enterprise itself reports the error. As the head of a county audit bureau explained, if an enterprise has a good attitude, admits its

---

52. According to one source, there is a 1990 People's Congress document stating that if the offender confesses and pays, he will not be fined for corruption. CI 81291.
53. CI 24688.   54. CI 8991.
55. See Oi, *State and Peasant;* and Walder, *Communist Neo-Traditionalism.*

mistakes, and pays the delinquent taxes, no fines are levied. Audit officials are especially prone to take this lenient stance toward state-owned enterprises in which the county has a direct stake. When a state-owned enterprise is found to have underpaid taxes but confesses to the problem, the county will allow the enterprise simply to repay the tax owed as part of its regular responsibility contract payment (*chengbao renwu*) to the county government. No penalty is imposed in such cases.[56]

To the extent possible, the local government will try to keep the information gathered from investigations and audits for internal use. The task of local regulators, including the audit bureau, is similar to that of internal auditors within a large business corporation. Internal auditors try to ensure that the parent corporation stays within the guidelines specified by the national authorities (to protect it from outside legal entanglements with the tax authority). This helps to guard against external audits and penalties. The degree to which local agents are able to do this depends on whether the center is employing its own elite force of regulators, work teams composed of people from outside the locality who report directly to the center; such teams were dispatched by then vice premier Zhu Rongji in 1993 in his attempt to regain control of the economy.[57] This is, however, a measure of last resort. The limited staffing of these teams makes it impossible for them to go to more than a few of the most serious trouble spots, as was also the case in the Maoist period.

As in the past, localities try to avoid attracting undue attention so that they do not become targets for inspection by outside work teams.[58] The internal audits and inspections conducted by the finance, tax, and audit bureaus help maintain the impression that the locality is faithfully complying with upper-level directives. For example, when the tax bureau finds that an enterprise has underpaid taxes, it will discreetly collect the taxes owed but not report the matter.[59] This is technically illegal. Local audit bureau officials say they know about this practice but do not report the infraction because doing so would be harmful to the county. They further imply that officials at the prefectural level have a similar lenient philosophy. It is the same with the province. As long as the locali-

56. If the enterprise does not correct its mistakes and they are discovered by the work teams during an annual investigation, it must pay the finance bureau the amount owed and a fine. CI 8891.

57. "Banks Send Teams to Branches to Enforce Policy," *China Daily (Business Weekly)*, 1–7 August 1993, p. 3, in *FBIS-CHI-93–147*, 3 August 1993, p. 23.

58. For a discussion of the hierarchy of control mechanisms and the effectiveness of outside work teams during the Maoist period, see Oi, *State and Peasant*, chap. 4.

59. Sometimes these taxes are reported as part of the collection in the following year.

ties can discipline their own members, they may treat their problems as internal family matters.

Internal resolution is particularly easy when the problem is over-reporting and no tax is owed by a firm. As one county official openly stated, "If these enterprises are fined, it would not be good for the enterprise." In this county, when the audit bureau encounters overreporting, it prepares a report, orders the factory to clean up its accounts, and forces it to admit its problems. The factory manager may be asked to step down, but there is no fine. Usually even the accountant is not removed.

Evidence suggests that audit bureaus have been sympathetic to the plight of local enterprises that are caught in an increasingly tight fiscal situation. The 1980s rating system provided higher credit limits and other preferential access to key-point enterprises (see chapter 4). But this same system made everyone sensitive to the need for enterprises to maintain good ratings. Regulators knew that if enterprises revealed that they were in the red (*kuisun*), they would lose their privileged status. Such motivations are apparent in the case of false reporting of profits by a county cement factory that failed to report 350,000 yuan in expenses.[60] Had it been officially determined to be in deficit, it would have lost its credit privileges, and the limit on its circulating funds from the bank would have been reduced. Thus, to protect itself, it reported an over-fulfillment of production and profit targets. This ensured sufficient funds for worker bonuses and other preferential opportunities. As a result, the factory was able to continue to obtain credit. For this particular factory, solvency was particularly important because it had obtained the distinguished ranking of a "prefectural advanced enterprise" and all the advantages that went with that designation. No one at the county level wanted to see the enterprise lose its title.

Another reason audit bureaus are lenient toward those found guilty of infringing regulations is that local government officials may have sanctioned the actions under investigation. For example, a county liquor factory had contracted with the county to pay a lump sum in product taxes (*chanpin shui*) rather than to pay at the standard rate in proportion to total income. The arrangement resulted in a surplus for the factory, and the county had allowed the factory to keep the surplus. Later this was judged

60. CI 8991.

to be illegal by the prefecture.[61] The case was a complicated one; when local officials recounted it to me, they were still debating who was right.

The difficulty was that the county had approved the deal to give the tax break to the liquor factory and therefore was ultimately responsible.[62] The head of the county economic reform committee (*jingji tizhi gaige weiyuan hui*) had proposed the tax contract, and the county magistrate had approved it. The committee included representatives of the tax, finance, audit, price, personnel, and labor bureaus, as well as the economic commission. These are the key agents on whom the center depends for regulation and prevention of such actions, but they are also people who want to promote local development. All knew that the legality of such a measure was questionable, but they agreed to allow it because it helped to develop the local economy. Local authorities tried to justify their actions by arguing that the 1988 State Council directive that made such practices illegal had not been received when the contract arrangement became effective.[63]

PROTECTING INVESTMENTS

The practice of handling problems "within the family" is also driven by the desire of local governments to protect their investments. They have a stake in protecting those enterprises to which they have extended credit. This was evident in the reaction of county officials to a corruption case involving a small but highly successful village that had developed many village-owned enterprises. The village had become something of a model for the county, a place that was shown off to foreign visitors.[64] In the late 1980s, the village was exposed for corruption and other transgressions, including setting up fake companies (*pibao gongsi*), illegally selling transport space on railways, and amassing a large debt. Some accounts suggested that the death of a former village party secretary in an automobile

61. An audit by the prefecture found that (1) the county had overextended its authority to give tax exemptions; (2) the county had paid taxes to the prefecture when it should have paid the central state; and (3) money had been put into extrabudgetary funds when it should have been placed in the within-budget account.
62. In another example, the county allowed a sales and marketing cooperative to contract for a lump-sum income tax. Although common, the practice is technically illegal. The county magistrate had to take ultimate responsibility for this. He had to report his mistake and promise to pay more attention to such problems in the future.
63. CI 8991.
64. I interviewed in this village a year or so before the scandal broke. It was clearly a favorite of county officials.

crash opened the village to decline; others suggested that problems had existed already.[65] Regardless of what caused the problems, the important issue for the purposes of this discussion is the involvement and reaction of county officials and of the Agricultural Bank.[66]

Instead of confiscating the village's property when the corruption was exposed, the Agricultural Bank intervened to help the village. When asked why, one bank official said, "This is a socialist bank, so our first step is to help." Upon further questioning, it became apparent that the bank took a special interest in the village because of the size of its outstanding loans.[67] The village had borrowed between 5 and 6 million yuan from the Agricultural Bank before the problems came to light. The case was complicated by the discovery of abuse of power and corruption on the part of officials of the county Agricultural Bank itself.[68] As one government official bluntly said, it was the special connections of the village that had enabled it to take out such large loans in the first place. The loans never should have been made. The village cadres were simply not up to their jobs; they had mismanaged the village and overinvested.

The situation began to unravel when inspection of monthly reports revealed that three of the village enterprises were losing money.[69] The township government initially tried to resolve the debt problem, in part because the township economic commission was the guarantor of the loans. When the severity of the problems became evident, the township sought help from the county rural enterprise management bureau. Eventually, the county government sent to the village a work team consisting of seven people from the Agricultural Bank and a vice head of the rural enterprise management bureau. The following year, the bank sent another work team consisting of a vice head of the Agricultural Bank, someone from the agricultural credit section (*nongye xindai ke*), and someone from the bursary section (*chuna ke*). These county officials used their connections and expertise to raise the quality of the village's products and to obtain market information to help the village enterprises reform their management and sell their products. Punishment for the offenders

65. Most acknowledged that the problems would never have been allowed to get out of hand if the old party secretary had not died. One observer commented that the party boss already had encountered problems in 1984, but had he lived these problems would have been solved quickly because he had lots of contacts.

66. CI 81391.

67. About 60 percent of the village's loans were from the credit cooperative and 40 percent were from the Agricultural Bank. CI 8991.

68. CI 81391.

69. Up to that point, the village had managed to make its interest payments on time.

was relatively mild, except for one Agricultural Bank official who was convicted and sent to prison.[70]

Some might view the response of the county officials as stemming from their familiarity with those whom they were charged to regulate. Personal relations no doubt played a role, but so did self-interest. The county had fiscal revenues to consider. The stakes for the Agricultural Bank were quite obvious. The county intervened to protect its corporate investment by salvaging whatever it could and helping the village get back on the road to development and growth. This same principle of local corporate interest underlies the lenient attitude of the audit bureau with regard to errant tax payments. The taxes may be minor compared to other consequences for the interests of the local corporate state. If a unit is ineligible for a rating because of indiscretions, it may be denied valued privileges, as the example of the county cement factory suggests. Public disclosure of financial mismanagement may remove an enterprise's favorable ranking. The same logic applies to administrative units; they either become ineligible for the rating competition (*pingbi*) or have their rating removed, both of which lead to reductions in cadre bonuses.[71]

The localities have an interest in knowing which factories are in deficit and which are performing well. They want, if possible, to relieve factories of financial difficulties, but they want to do so without having them lose their preferential access. The concern of the localities is to prevent such problems from disrupting the economic well-being of the larger corporate economy.

LOCAL APPROPRIATION OF CENTRAL CONTROLS

March and Olsen have noted in regard to other contexts that "political institutions not only respond to their environment but create those environments at the same time."[72] The fiscal reforms in China have done just that. They have created effective incentives to prompt local officials eagerly to pursue the center's goal of revitalizing the local economy. However, they have also induced a separate set of incentives that leads these same officials to provide minimum rather than maximum compliance in

70. At least one other county-level official was involved, and he was also convicted. It is unclear whether the village leadership was eventually charged with a criminal offense. At the time of my interview, the party secretary had merely been transferred to a new position outside the village.

71. CI 8891.

72. James March and Johan Olsen, *Rediscovering Institutions*, p. 162.

other areas of policy implementation—primarily the assessment and collection of national taxes—that affect local economic growth and the revenues generated at the local levels. The emergence of local state corporatism has intensified the moral hazard problem in central-local relations by encouraging local officials to try to protect first the locality and only second the center when implementing central tax laws.

The central state still possesses the ultimate weapon of dismissal, but that is a credible threat only if officials cross the line into illicit behavior. Generally, officials are careful not to cross that line. For the most part, they carry out their assigned investigations faithfully and effectively. But carrying out state-mandated investigations is not necessarily incompatible with trying to maximize local interests. There is ample leeway, short of maximum compliance, to serve both the interests of the center and those of the locality. The *nomenklatura* controls have always been less effective in microregulation once officials have been screened and have assumed office.

Rather than think that, because of the appointment system, local officials are primarily motivated by fear of losing their positions, one must consider that with the institutional reforms described in chapter 2, the behavior of local officials as agents may now also be swayed by the lure of the residual.[73] My findings question the effectiveness of the norms and socialization that Huang and others say the system can fall back on.[74] Local pressures cause otherwise loyal and competent local officials at least to try to protect local interests.

The next chapter will further examine local compliance with central directives. It will focus on the period when central retrenchment policies designed to cut back the growth of rural enterprises directly threatened the interests of the local corporate state.

---

73. Huang assumes there is no such slack. *Inflation and Investment Controls,* p. 183.
74. Huang, *Inflation and Investment Controls.*

From Agents to Principals

*Increasing Resource Endowments
and Local Control*

China's reform leadership has tried to restrict reforms to the economic realm, but the dramatic economic growth that has come about has also brought political change. As others have observed more generally, "[I]nstitutions . . . influence subsequent actions. They may be created for economic reasons; or they may have been founded so as to enhance the fortunes of particular economic interests. But, once created, they generate positions of political power and systems of political incentives. They define strategic possibilities and impose constraints." [1]

After more than a decade of reform, local officials in China have gradually modified their role as agents to become more like principals as they have gained rights to the resources that once served as the basis of central-state control. [2] Over ten years of increased tax revenues and extrabudgetary funds have allowed localities to move beyond the strategies of passive resistance that were characteristic of the Maoist period to the active pursuit of their interests. Instead of simple resort to diversion of state-allocated resources, localities can now circumvent central restrictions on economic activity by using locally owned resources beyond the net of central regulation. [3] A shift in the resource endowments has upset the relationship between Beijing and its agents at the local levels.

1. Bates, *Beyond the Miracle*, pp. 151–52.
2. On agents becoming principals, see White, "Agency as Control."
3. Oi, *State and Peasant*, chap. 5.

Maoist control centered on the use of ideology and organization to cope with the problem of monitoring.[4] The task of control was made manageable by dividing the population into hierarchical organizations. The behavior of unit leaders and of those they governed was circumscribed by the issuing of plans, targets, and quotas, and the use of reports and inspections to ensure that behavior conformed to the directives and goals issued from above. The viability of the Maoist control system was rooted in the prohibition of alternatives to the official state-sanctioned channels—whether in the supply of food, housing, and employment opportunities for individuals or in the provision of materials, credit, and investment funds for industry.[5] This ensured at least a minimum of compliance and created a dependent relationship between the state and its agents. The question is whether the methods developed during the Maoist period are still viable in the reform context. If not, have new methods of control been introduced?

The last chapter examined the inherent weaknesses of central monitoring and the institutional reasons for selective local compliance. This chapter examines how corporate control, in conjunction with increasing local fiscal resources, was mobilized to resist the central retrenchment policies of 1988–1989 that clearly went against the interests of the local corporate state. But before we turn to that case study, the following section will detail the center's attempts to regulate local extrabudgetary funds and explain why these efforts failed. This provides further insight into why the center undertook the 1994 fiscal reforms.

REGULATION OF EXTRABUDGETARY FUNDS

Prior to the 1994 fiscal reforms, the bulk of the increasing extrabudgetary funds remained at the local levels, and the central state relied on administrative regulation to try to limit or at least channel the use of these funds. However, the regulations on extrabudgetary funds were imprecise and open to local interpretation. Rules were slow to evolve and varied by locality. Initially, each unit was simply required to produce an annual fiscal plan for its extrabudgetary revenues. The plan was submitted to the unit's supervisory agency, which then made a report to the local

4. For the classic statement, see Franz Schurmann, *Ideology and Organization in China.*
5. See Oi, *State and Peasant;* and Walder, *Communist Neo-Traditionalism.*

finance bureau; there the plan was examined prior to implementation. The finance bureau was instructed to use economic measures to "guide" the use of extrabudgetary funds for urgent national construction projects and technical renovation projects.[6] Later, regulations were set forth that required all units to provide an accounting of actual extrabudgetary expenditures and to show that proper accounting procedures were followed in the handling of these accounts.[7]

Beginning in 1985, more paperwork was required. Each prefecture, bureau, and agency was required to submit a midyear report in addition to a fiscal-year and year-end accounting. Finance bureaus at all levels had to establish the necessary organizational unit and allocate personnel to manage the extrabudgetary funds appropriately so that their use was consistent with the goals of national development.[8] The Finance Ministry set the regulations, issued official receipt forms, and devised the account categories (*kemu*); it also issued the required final accounting forms. Each basic-level unit was required to draw up an extrabudgetary revenue expenditure plan and submit it to its supervisory agency, which collected the data and sent it to the finance bureau for inspection. The finance bureau at each level assembled the reports and those of its subordinate levels and sent them to be audited, while also sending a report to superiors within the finance system at the next upper level. At the national level, the Finance Ministry collected extrabudgetary revenue expenditure reports and sent them to the State Council for review.[9]

In the latter part of the 1980s, a stricter method was promoted, which attempted to facilitate oversight by taking the funds out of the hands of the individual units.[10] Funds were centralized in a special local bank account of the finance bureau (*caizheng zhuanhu chucun*).[11] The finance bureau managed the funds for the units and paid interest on the account

6. This arrangement is known as the Changzhou method, which was introduced in 1981.

7. A February 1983 document, "On Experimental Methods for the Management of Extrabudgetary Revenues," issued by the Finance Ministry, standardized and systematized the management of these revenues. Caizhengbu, *Caishui gaige shinian*, pp. 324–25. This document defined the character, scope, and use of extrabudgetary revenues, providing collection schedules and retention ratios. It stipulated that localities, departments, and units had no power to define new items as extrabudgetary revenue.

8. Caizhengbu, *Caishui gaige shinian*, pp. 324–28.

9. Caizhengbu, *Caishui gaige shinian*, p. 326.

10. This was known as the Guangzhou method.

11. Caizhengbu, *Caishui gaige shinian*, p. 329. It is unclear whether the finance bureau could mandate spending for certain projects or whether it had the right to veto use of these funds.

according to bank regulations. Regulation of extrabudgetary revenues and expenditures was tightened.[12] With only a few exceptions, the finance bureau of each province, autonomous region, and municipality established a "consolidated planning office" (*zonghe jihuachu*) or an "extrabudgetary fund management office" (*yusuanwai zijin guanlichu*). At the prefecture, city, and county levels, special personnel were assigned to control these funds. Each unit had to use the funds in accordance with its income conditions and subject to an annual fiscal plan and a seasonal expense plan. The finance bureau checked and approved the project and then issued the funds monthly. A special fund could be drawn on for the purchase of property or for use in urgent situations. Using planned management, the finance bureau gave approval while the local bank held and disbursed the funds. This method was designed to control inflation by regulating self-financed investments that were made with extrabudgetary revenues.[13]

The following is an example of how extrabudgetary funds were controlled in one county that had approximately 48 million yuan in extrabudgetary funds in 1990.[14] These funds were owned by various units, including the county government itself, state-owned enterprises, and government departments, but all were managed by the finance bureau. The accounting department within the county finance bureau divided extrabudgetary funds into three categories: (1) local finance (*difang caizheng*); (2) state enterprise finance (*guoying caizheng*); and (3) finance of administrative institutional units (*xingzheng shiye danwei caizheng*). Management for each of these categories was different.

The money that belonged to the county finance bureau itself was controlled internally by two separate sections: the budget section (*yusuan gu*) and the extrabudgetary section (*yusuanwai gu*). The former prepared the extrabudgetary expenditure records (*yusuanwai shouzhibiao*), while the latter handled the analyses, bookkeeping, and oversight (*fenxi, tongji, jiandu*) of the extrabudgetary funds.

Each state enterprise submitted quarterly reports to the finance bureau on its extrabudgetary funds, and the records were examined to see if the money had been used properly. The reports were in addition to the

12. In April 1986, the State Council (Guowuyuan) issued "Guowuyuan guanyu jiaqiang yusuan zijin guanli de tongzhi" (Notice on Strengthening the Management of Extrabudgetary Revenues).
13. Caizhengbu, *Caishui gaige shinian*, pp. 327–29.
14. Unless otherwise noted, this section is based on CI 8891.

annual budget for the use of these funds and had to be submitted to the extrabudgetary section of the finance bureau. Before these reports were sent to the finance bureau, they first went to the county economic commission for approval. The enterprise had the right to use the funds within a set period, but use had to conform with certain regulations. Additional personnel could be hired only if the labor bureau gave approval. The plan determined how the funds were to be used for the year. Once the plan was set, the enterprise could not on its own decide to use the funds for some other purpose.

The funds owned by the various administrative departments and agencies were kept by the finance bureau in a special savings account. The money was owned by the unit and used at its discretion, but the account was managed by the finance bureau. Such management, however, differed from the management of an enterprise's extrabudgetary funds. Every three months, each unit submitted a report regarding the unit's plan (*bianbiao*) to the extrabudgetary section of the finance bureau. After it was approved, the bureau would allocate the money to the unit. It did not need approval from the economic commission. Units could change the amounts and use, but before doing so, they had to submit a revised plan for the extrabudgetary section's approval.

Expenditure of extrabudgetary funds was divided into six types.[15] Within these categories, some products, including cars and color televisions, were specially regulated. When a unit wanted to buy a car or some other strictly regulated item, it had to submit an application, but again it was to a special office in the budget section (*yusuan gu*) of the county finance bureau. Once approval was obtained, a separate section of the finance bureau (*xingcai gu*) allocated the money. Requests for funds for basic construction were also handled differently. They had to go to the county planning commission for approval. If approval was granted, an allocation slip (*bokuandan*) was sent to the unit. The unit then took this slip to its bank to get the money.

While there was a lot of bureaucratic paperwork, the biggest difficulty with all the methods for control of extrabudgetary funds was that the funds remained at the local level. Even when the moneys were under integrated control by a single agency, effectiveness in monitoring hinged on how strict local finance bureaus were in approving requests for the

---

15. (1) Basic construction expenses; (2) renovation expenses; (3) institutional expenses; (4) administrative expenses; (5) welfare expenses; and (6) other expenses.

use of the funds. No upper-level approval was necessary after 1980. With the interests of the county-level agents charged with control of these funds increasingly shaped by the local state, most requests for the use of extrabudgetary funds were approved.

ECONOMIC RETRENCHMENT
AND A TEST OF CENTRAL CONTROL

The issue of central control took on urgency in the late 1980s as double-digit inflation gripped China's economy and as state-owned enterprises had to compete with the rapidly growing rural industrial sector. Monitoring became a pressing concern for the central leadership when agents began to respond too enthusiastically to the incentives for local economic growth that the center had unleashed.

The solution was a centrally mandated clampdown on the growth of the rural industrial sector from 1988 to 1989. Rural industry was accused of overheating the economy, creating useless duplication, and wasting valuable and scarce resources that could be better utilized by the larger state-owned enterprises.[16] The rural industrial sector was to be cut back to restore the health of the larger economy. To accomplish this task, the central state used macroeconomic mechanisms to close down enterprises rather than relying on coercion or administrative measures.[17] Some categories of enterprises were prohibited, and others closed of their own accord because of increased costs and reduced profits.

The main mechanism employed to dampen growth was a severe restriction of credit to rural industry. During the retrenchment effort, banks were told to control loans, reduce credit limits, and generally tighten access and speed up repayment.[18] In 1988 interest rates were set as high as 21 percent for collective enterprises borrowing from credit cooperatives.

16. Rural industry was always in a very precarious position, even during the Maoist era. See, for example, Carl Riskin, "China's Rural Industries." This was not the first time rural industry was criticized after the reforms began; such criticism began in the early 1980s. For some examples, see Zhou, *How the Farmers Changed China*. See also Anthony J. Ody, *Rural Enterprise Development;* and Ji You, "Zhao Ziyang."

17. A similar view is expressed in Ody, *Rural Enterprise Development*.

18. According to the guidelines, the reduction in loans to rural industrial enterprises was to be only 3 percent. The state, however, cut term loans by 5 percent and reduced the credit quota of financially weak enterprises by 20 percent. In addition, it vigorously pursued overdue loans in agriculture, commerce, and transport, succeeding in reducing these by 30 percent, and forced the repayment of 20 percent of the loans that had been classified as "bad debts." *Zhongguo nongye nianjian, 1989*, p. 228.

Interest rates set by the central People's Bank for loans from the Agricultural Bank were lower, but they too increased.[19]

In addition, a number of preferential policies and lucrative tax breaks—described in earlier chapters—were abolished during this period. As of January 1989 the arrangement that allowed a factory to deduct loan repayments before taxes were assessed (thus reducing income tax) was eliminated for all new loans.[20] In one county, collected income tax increased by 1 million yuan after this policy change, although local officials conceded that it was difficult to say that the increase was attributable entirely to one cause.[21] Cuts were also ordered in the low- or no-interest loans from the local tax and finance bureaus to collectively owned rural enterprises. Although loans could still be given, few or no new funds were to be added; this decision effectively reduced the number of enterprises that could receive such assistance.

The outcome of the retrenchment policies was mixed. On the one hand, the center showed that it still held significant policy levers with which it could control inflation, and, as Huang has shown, large-scale investment was decreased.[22] On the other hand, in-depth investigation of local conditions and a disaggregation of local statistics show that state controls were only partially effective in curbing the growth of rural industry.

The effect of central retrenchment policies on rural industry was felt only selectively. Local governments were able to adopt calculated responses to central directives. Development was slower, but it was not brought to a halt. Rural industry was able to grow at a not insignificant rate. The minister of agriculture, He Kang, announced in the spring of 1990 that the output value from rural enterprises had increased

19. In one county, interest rates for circulation fund loans to rural enterprises from the Agricultural Bank in the period 1987 to 1990 ranged from a low of 8.64 percent in 1987 to a high of 11.34 percent in February 1989. The rates for fixed capital loans from the Agricultural Bank depended on the duration of the loan; for one-year loans, the rates for 1987–1990 ranged from 7.92 percent in 1987 to 11.34 percent in February 1989; for loans over five years the rate ranged from 10.08 percent in 1987 to 19.26 percent in February 1989. CI 8991. The interest rates of the credit cooperatives were more flexible, but they were always higher than those of the Agricultural Bank—for circulation fund loans, they were as much as 50 percent higher.

20. The arrangement was still available for state-owned enterprises.

21. The exceptions to these measures limited their effectiveness. For example, at the same time, the central authorities encouraged the export sector, allowing rural enterprises and joint ventures preferential tax breaks for exports. Not surprisingly, local enterprises began to promote exports. CI 6490.

22. Huang, *Inflation and Investment Controls*.

15.9 percent during the retrenchment period.[23] This announcement preceded the decision by the central state to reverse its retrenchment policy and again encourage the growth of rural industry.[24]

Although differences of opinion among top leaders led to inconsistent policies,[25] the mixed impact of the retrenchment polices resulted from a much more important feature of central control in the era of reform: by the late 1980s, there was an ambiguous balance of local and central power. The central state was able to control certain aspects of the economy but not others.

SLOWING RURAL GROWTH

National aggregate statistics show that the central Chinese state in the late 1980s had enough control over the costs of inputs to affect enterprise performance and profits. Higher production costs and a depressed market led to a dramatic drop in the profitability of township-owned enterprises. Nationally, profits for township and village enterprises decreased 7.34 percent.[26] Interview data further confirm the effect of the macroeconomic controls. Statistics for 1988–1989 from county, township, and village governments show that high interest rates effectively cut the profits of rural enterprises, causing many to fail to meet planned production targets and leading some to close. In one village, interest costs increased about 40 percent, rising to almost 700,000 yuan.[27] Local government officials could intervene to extend the repayment time or to negotiate favorable terms, but the bottom line was that the interest had to be paid by the enterprises or borne by the local governments that were dependent on these enterprises for their income. Unlike state industry, collectively owned rural enterprises lacked powerful ministries that could bear these costs. Both enterprises and local governments had to face much harder budget constraints.

The five-point credit-rating system described in chapter 4 further limited access to loans for all but the best enterprises. If an enterprise's rat-

23. During the same period, the rest of the economy was declining or stagnating. He Kang, quoted in James L. Tyson, "China to Boost," *Christian Science Monitor*, 26 March 1990.

24. See Ody, *Rural Enterprise Development*, for a discussion of various statements in the official press.

25. Yang, *Calamity and Reform in China*, chap. 8, provides a good description of the differences of opinion on rural industry between Zhao Ziyang and Li Peng.

26. *Zhongguo xiangzhen qiye nianjian, 1991*, p. 133.

27. CI 52090.

ing was below grade three, which was the average, the firm would almost automatically be excluded from consideration for a capital expenditure loan.[28] For example, in 1990, 297 of one county's 381 enterprises received a grade-three rating or below and were therefore ineligible to take out loans either from banks or credit cooperatives.[29] The number of ineligible enterprises increased after 1989. One enterprise that had had a "special first-class" rating lost its status in 1990 because of poor sales in 1989.[30]

Expensive credit was accompanied by increases in the costs of other production inputs, which dramatically decreased profits. In one county, total profits for collectively owned township and village enterprises decreased 5.87 million yuan between 1988 and 1989. In a single village within the county, there was a decrease in profits of 1.6 million yuan during the same period.[31] One factory lost more than half a million yuan in profits. The party secretary of a village explained that "increased expenses were the biggest impact of the center's retrenchment policies." He complained that the cost of electricity rose 20 percent from 1987 to 1988 and increased another 20 percent in the following year.[32] Between 1987 and 1988, the costs of wood, steel, and coal increased by 50 percent.[33]

The effects of increased costs were compounded by a sluggish market. For example, from September to December 1989 in one area of Shandong, the market price for one ton of cotton dropped about 10 percent.[34] These poor market conditions had already resulted in the stockpiling of goods, which caused cash-flow problems for enterprises. The combination of poor market conditions, stockpiling of goods, and decreased credit created cycles of bad debt in which everyone was a debtor to everyone else—a phenomenon that has come to be known as "triangular debt." One village at the height of the problems at the end of 1989

28. Enterprises were assigned a quota for circulation loans, which was separate from that for fixed capital.
29. There were some exceptions for those ranked grade three. For instance, a 50,000-yuan loan for a new machine was made to a shoe factory with a grade-three ranking.
30. This enterprise was primarily producing for export. Its loss of status was blamed on the international situation after Tiananmen. The local official recounted that in his county some factories had sent goods to Qingdao to be exported, but they had been returned. CI 6590.
31. In 1988 total industrial profits in this village was 3.32 million yuan.
32. It is worth noting that it was not the rates per unit of electricity that increased but rather the surcharges (*fujia fei*), of which there were five. CI 52090.
33. CI 52090.
34. There was no change in the plan price. CI 52090.

was owed 2.96 million yuan.[35] This cycle of bad debt further weakened an already depressed market, resulting in even more profit declines and more enterprises in deficit. Some firms were not able to survive; others suffered long-term consequences that eventually led to the general weakening of the collective sector in the 1990s that is described in chapter 3.

SELECTIVE COMPLIANCE

The retrenchment policies took their toll on rural enterprises, but when the statistics are disaggregated, a number of anomalies are revealed. One of the most significant is the unevenly distributed decline in the numbers of the three types of firms—township-owned, village-owned, and individually or jointly owned. The retrenchment policy was least effective in cutting the number of collectively owned enterprises, even though these were precisely the enterprises that consumed the most resources and were the biggest competitors to state-owned enterprises.[36] And within the collectively owned sector, township enterprises suffered less than village-owned enterprises. Individual entrepreneurs (*geti*) were the hardest hit. In one Shandong county, five thousand enterprises were closed, most of them private; no township-owned enterprises were closed.[37] In another county, the total number of closures (1,685) represented a 23.5 percent drop between 1988 and 1989, but in this same period the number of township enterprises remained unchanged. The number of village-owned enterprises dropped, but the percentage decline was smaller than that of privately owned enterprises.

More often than not, collective factories were merged (*jianbing*) rather than closed (*daobi*). This throws into question the significance of aggregate statistics, which suggest that factories were dissolved. A financially healthy factory would take over the debts of an insolvent factory along with its workers and equipment. The fiscal problems of the economically troubled factory would thus be remedied, at least temporarily, and the workers would remain employed. In the county with five thousand

35. The debtors were large enterprises. Many state-owned firms also faced problems of stockpiling and bad debt cycles. CI 52090.

36. The World Bank suggests that even in cases of enterprises that were considered "high polluters," there were few closures if the enterprises were collectively owned. See Ody, *Rural Enterprise Development*.

37. It is unclear how many of the five thousand may have been village-owned enterprises, but the comments of one official indicate that they were a minority. CI 6490.

closures, fifty collectively owned enterprises were merged.[38] In another example, three such mergers took place in a township with fourteen collectively owned factories.[39] In other cases, ailing collectively owned enterprises, both village and township, changed product lines rather than close.[40]

The continued existence of troubled enterprises in one form or another is further evidenced by the relative stability, and in some cases increases, in the number of workers employed in them. In one county, the number of workers increased by one thousand, even though the number of collectively owned enterprises decreased by two. If these local statistics are representative, few if any workers in township and village enterprises were actually laid off.

The rationale for local governments to keep open financially weak factories needs explication. One reason stems from the political reality described in chapter 3—the "iron rice bowl" has not been entirely eliminated from China's countryside, even though the communes have been disbanded. In some villages in 1988–1989, party secretaries gave the workers raises even though their villages had suffered huge declines in profits.[41]

Another reason stems from a calculation of costs. Some village party secretaries decided that in some cases the long-run costs of closing a factory with a deficit were higher than the costs of keeping it open. One party secretary explained that aside from the costs of unemployment for the villagers, the sunk costs were too high to forgo, at least in the short run. Such villages struggled to find ways to weather the retrenchment while hoping for an upturn in the market.[42]

For counties and townships, a factory in short-term difficulty could still provide lucrative revenues. Regardless of whether local collective factories made profits, local governments were able to benefit from sales and product taxes, as well as from nontax revenues in the form of rents and fees. As I explain in chapter 2, these taxes were not tied to profits. In 1988 almost three-quarters of the taxes from township and village en-

38. CI 6490.   39. CI 6790.
40. CI 52090.
41. One village party secretary explained that this was needed to keep up with increases in the cost of living. The village cotton mill that benefited from the raises employed 523 people; the average wage was about 2,300 yuan per year, including about 30 percent in bonuses. CI 52090.
42. CI 52090.

terprises nationwide were circulation or industrial-commercial taxes; the income tax accounted for only 25.3 percent of total taxes from such enterprises during this period.[43] The same pattern is reflected in my field data. For example, one large village factory had profits for the fiscal year 1987–1988 of 376,000 yuan. It paid 146,000 yuan in taxes, or 38.8 percent of its profits. But of this amount, only 36,000 yuan was paid as income tax; the remaining 110,000 yuan, or 75.3 percent, was paid as sales or other taxes.[44]

The protective attitude of localities toward their enterprises is evident in the measured rate of decrease in the availability of credit at local banks. In practice, the curbs on credit were less severe than the retrenchment policies explicitly called for.[45] In Shandong as a whole, for example, loans for rural enterprises increased 19.7 percent from 1987 to 1988.[46] But in some Shandong counties, such loans increased much more than that.[47] One bank official explained that had it not been for upper-level restrictions, his bank would have loaned out even more to rural industry in 1989.[48]

That localities resisted and tried to protect key enterprises was to be expected. What needs explanation is why the seemingly restrictive retrenchment policies were only partially effective.

THE EROSION OF CREDIT CONTROLS

Control of credit through the banking system was the centerpiece of the austerity program for slowing down rural industrial growth.[49] This strategy was premised on the notions that the central state still held a monopoly on key production inputs and that banks and credit cooperatives

43. *China Statistical Yearbook, 1989*, p. 240.
44. CI 6688.
45. Banks did not entirely cut off loans to rural industry. The guidelines set forth by the Agricultural Bank of China were much less drastic than the often-heard term *zero credit* would imply. Ody, *Rural Enterprise Development*, pp. 97–98, comes to a similar conclusion.
46. *Zhongguo nongye nianjian, 1989*, p. 58.
47. In one county, they increased 23.8 percent from 1987 to 1988 and 31.14 percent from 1988 to 1989; the increase was similarly large in another county. CI 52190; CI 6590. This contrasts sharply with Yang's finding of an 8.8 percent decrease in the national total of loans from the Agricultural Bank and from rural credit cooperatives to rural enterprises. *Calamity and Reform in China*, p. 220.
48. CI 6590.
49. I refer here specifically to the retrenchment effort in 1988 to 1989, but this comment also applies to the retrenchment effort instituted by Zhu Rongji in 1993. Many of the same methods were used to solve similar problems.

would be effective agents of the central state. Neither of these assumptions, however, reflected the reality that had emerged in China's countryside after a decade of reform.

The People's Bank, as the central administrative bank, regulated credit and made macroeconomic policy. At the local levels, down to the county, branches of the People's Bank still acted as the central regulatory bank for their administrative level. Through this bureaucratic structure, the central state instituted a credit freeze in 1988 and 1989 that overrode all other regulations on the amounts that banks could issue in loans. Interest rates were raised to the point that the costs of credit negatively affected the profits of enterprises. Yet the administrative measures designed to control economic performance through the careful division of economic activities were being undermined even as they were being implemented.[50]

COMMERCIALIZATION OF BANKS

Local banks remained the pivotal agents of the central state in credit control, but by the late 1980s, banks had become economic institutions whose interests coincided increasingly with those of the localities.[51] Originally, banks were simply an arm of the state fiscal system, charged with issuing grants to those projects designated in the state plan. They were not concerned with profits or repayments. Before 1978 the People's Bank was an administrative organ subordinate to the Ministry of Finance. The head of one of the specialized county-level banks explained the problems of the unreformed banking system by saying that whereas banks in the West are businesses, banks in China had been primarily tools to control enterprises and only secondarily businesses. Enterprise loans were granted according to policy.[52] The reforms elevated the People's Bank to ministerial rank equal to that of the Ministry of Finance and slowly transformed banks into economic enterprises. After 1979 three specialized banks that had been abolished during the Mao period—the Agricultural Bank, the Construction Bank, and the Industrial Commercial Bank (*gongshang yinhang*)—were restored.

50. For a more in-depth and technical discussion of the problems with banks as regulators during the retrenchment period, see Carsten Holz, "Contractionary Macroeconomic Policy."

51. For an extremely useful and detailed study of the role and operation of banks during the reform period, see Holz, *Role of Central Banking*. On bank reforms, see also Tam, "Prospects for Reforming China's Financial System."

52. CI 81391.

Banks first began to take on a business character in the 1980s. Grants (*bokuan*) to designated enterprises and projects under the plan were changed to low-interest loans (*daikuan*). Second, local branches of the specialized banks, such as the Agricultural Bank, were allowed for the first time to use their own deposits to make loans. However, they had only limited autonomy. During the early 1980s, banks remained bound by the system of unified management (*tongyi guanli*), the credit plan,[53] and reserve requirements.[54] As one bank official explained, "The size of the savings deposits was taken into consideration when the upper levels made the plan, but there was no guarantee that even if a county branch of the Agricultural Bank attracted a lot of savings, it would be allowed to grant a correspondingly large amount in loans."[55]

A similar transformation was beginning to occur in the credit co-operatives at the township level, where loans became partly tied to deposits. Full autonomy in the use of their funds was granted only when the ratio management (*bili guanli*) system was instituted in 1991, allowing them to lend 75 percent of their deposits.[56] These institutional reforms, even though limited, pushed banks, along with credit cooperatives, to behave more like economic entities.

What finally convinced local banks to become entrepreneurial and to worry about loan repayments was the action of the central bank itself. The reforms called for the central People's Bank of China to continue to provide funds in the form of loans to each of the specialized banks.[57] But local banks could no longer count on the upper levels to supply them

53. The credit plan (societal plan) consisted of four parts, dealing with the control, respectively, of banks, urban and rural credit cooperatives, various types of trusts and investment institutions, and the total volume of credit activities such as the sale of bonds and stocks and the collection of funds. See Financial Structural Reform Department of the People's Bank of China, "Survey of Reform"; also Holz, *Role of Central Banking,* for details of the different types of credit plans.

54. Beginning in 1985, the central bank stipulated the minimum amount that each bank had to deposit with the local People's Bank, thus dictating the percentage of the banks' deposits that could be used for loans.

55. CI 8991.

56. Thirteen percent of their deposits were turned over to the Agricultural Bank as a reserve (*cunkuan zhuan beijin*), but these funds were then given to the People's Bank. Seven percent of the credit cooperatives' deposits were kept at the cooperatives as reserve funds (*duifujin*), and the remaining 5 percent in a discretionary fund (*jidong zijin*) that could also be drawn on if the reserve fund was insufficient. Unlike the specialized banks, credit cooperatives originally were required to maintain their reserves at the Agricultural Bank; the amount of such reserves, ranging from 15 to 30 percent of total deposits, was determined by the Agricultural Bank at the provincial level. Holz, *Role of Central Banking,* p. 78. Beginning in 1991, each credit cooperative became responsible for its own profits and losses. CI 8991.

57. This was part of the "People's Bank of China Refinancing Plan."

with the funds allotted in the credit plan. The central People's Bank forwarded "credit notifications" to its provincial branches that specified the amounts that could be lent to the provincial branches of the specialized banks.[58] However, these notifications were not a guarantee that the People's Bank would provide those sums; they simply stipulated the *maximum* credit the central state would extend to a specialized bank.[59]

It became increasingly necessary for banks to go outside the state supply channels to attract deposits, because they could no longer rely on the upper levels to provide them with sufficient funds. The experience of one county Agricultural Bank suggests that banks were receiving increasingly smaller portions of their funds from the People's Bank. In 1985–1986, 25 percent of its funds came from the prefecture or the province. Beginning in 1987, the amount from the upper levels decreased to 15–20 percent; the rest came from deposits from the local areas.

By the second half of the 1980s, a much more direct relationship began to emerge between deposits and loans.[60] As one local bank official explained, beginning in 1985, banks had more leeway to determine how much they lent. The plan and the funds were separated; loans became increasingly tied to deposits. Nineteen eighty-six was a transition year. By 1988 it was clearly a situation of "more deposits, more loans." Those local banks that did not have enough funds simply had to stop giving loans. Local banks lost a degree of security, but they gained autonomy. In one county that succeeded in increasing loans by more than 30 percent during the retrenchment, only 15–20 percent of the money loaned was from the central plan; the rest was from local savings deposits.[61]

A corollary of this new concern for funds was that banks became more calculating in their loan decisions. In the past, when most loans were policy loans dictated by a plan and funds were supplied by the upper levels, banks had been relatively lax about repayment. But when they began to lend their own deposits, they were much more careful. As the

58. Holz, *Role of Central Banking*, p. 45.

59. As Holz explains, "While planning is still centralized, the funds are now divided in that each specialized bank head office has a certain amount of funds at its disposal and loans can be obtained (in accordance with the plan) at the local levels from the PBoC [People's Bank of China]." Ibid., p. 45.

60. A 1984 reform, "Unified planning, division of funds, deposits of credit funds, and mutual money flow" (*tongyi jihua, huafen zijin, shidai shicun, xianghu rongtong*), was instituted to allow branches of the specialized banks to pool deposits and make loans, as well as to strengthen the capacity of the central bank to regulate the money supply. Sheng Hua, Xuejun Zhang, and Xiaopeng Luo, *China*, provides a detailed explanation of this reform; see pp. 84–85 and footnote 40 on p. 215.

61. CI 5290.

head of a county Construction Bank explained, many rural enterprises came to the bank for loans, but not all were successful. Most of the loans to rural enterprises went to township-owned firms; only a few village-owned enterprises qualified. Whether an applicant received a loan depended on the bank's feasibility study of the proposed project and the bank's financial situation.

The economic character of banks grew in 1988 with the institution of a bank "money market" (*zijin shichang*), whereby banks from one locality could borrow funds from banks of another locality. Usually, the larger urban banks would borrow, typically from the provinces, and then lend to banks at the lower levels. This allowed the market and the banks themselves to determine the distribution of credit, undermining the central credit plans.[62]

INTERBANK COMPETITION

The competition for deposits that emerged among state banks as a result of the reforms further weakened central credit controls. Originally, central authorities had assigned different sectors of the economy to specialized banks in an attempt to regulate investments and credit for the multitude of enterprises in China's countryside. Neither individuals nor enterprises had the right to choose the specialized banks at which they made deposits or obtained loans. Rural enterprises were assigned to the Agricultural Bank and the credit cooperatives. Commercial concerns, such as the sales and marketing cooperatives, had to have their accounts at the Industrial Commercial Bank. To keep a tight rein on capital construction, the central state mandated that all construction companies and all funds for construction projects be handled by the Construction Bank.[63] Each specialized bank was thus charged with monitoring and regulating the financial activities of a different sector of the economy.

By the late 1980s, this highly segmented and regulated system of credit was no longer strictly followed. Enterprises were taking advantage of the emergence of interbank competition, dealing with financial institutions other than those to which central regulations had assigned them, depositing funds wherever they could obtain loans, and seeking the best service and terms. For example, in 1990 one county Construction Bank gave about 15 percent of its loans to rural enterprises, even though these

62. CI 8688.   63. CI 81391.

firms had not been assigned to work with it.[64] The largest of these loans, 3 million yuan granted to a village, clearly contradicted the official assignment of accounts.[65] Private entrepreneurs also began to enjoy flexibility and choice, going outside the Agricultural Bank to other specialized state banks, including the Construction Bank, for both fixed-capital loans and circulation fund loans.[66]

County-level state and large collective enterprises were also participating in this loosening of the credit system. For example, a county-level beer factory moved its major account from the Industrial Commercial Bank to the Construction Bank when it needed a large loan to expand production. According to regulation, this factory should have borrowed from the Industrial Commercial Bank. That bank was sympathetic but could give the factory only a portion of its needed circulation funds. In the new economic environment, the factory turned to the Construction Bank, which extended a larger loan.[67]

By the time of the centrally mandated retrenchment effort of 1988–1989, banks were still partially bound by the plan and received regulated deposits, but they were no longer mere administrative agents. The specialized banks all competed with one another for business, taking in whatever funds they could. Depositors were promised preferential services and interest rates as well as quick approval for loan applications.[68] A county Construction Bank, for example, continued to rely on state-mandated accounts, holding the funds that enterprises were required to deposit before construction projects could be approved.[69] But the majority of this bank's funds came from savings, which constituted about 50 percent of its deposits. To secure further funds, the bank sold interest-bearing bonds.[70]

64. This Construction Bank was established in 1979, but only after 1985 did it accept savings and make loans. Prior to that, it was simply a bank of the finance bureau that made grants to designated projects. CI 81391.

65. In one instance, circumvention of the rules was accomplished by the village taking out a loan in the name of the village construction company, but in fact it was for the use of the village textile factory. The Construction Bank was well aware of this. CI 81391.

66. Unlike collective enterprises, private businesses do not need guarantors, but they must provide collateral.

67. This was done in part to protect an earlier investment in the factory by the Construction Bank.

68. In August 1991, the Construction Bank lowered interest rates for preferred customers from 10.34 percent to 8.64 percent. CI 81391.

69. These construction accounts represented about 40 percent of its funds. They included self-raised funds for construction, which accounted for about 30 percent of enterprise deposits.

70. In August of 1991, bank officials reported that the state had supplied the bank with 100,000 yuan, but the bank had 70 million yuan of its own funds. CI 81391.

LOCAL CORPORATE INTERESTS AND COLLUSION

The loosening of the credit system ultimately hinged on the cooperation of local officials. The transfer of accounts from one financial institution to another required the approval of the local branch of the People's Bank. It is here that local corporate interests come into play. As I suggest in the last chapter, when local officials are forced to choose between protecting local interests and adhering strictly to central policies, the choice is clear. As the head of a Construction Bank explained: "The [local] People's Bank approves most requests for an enterprise to change banks because if it does not, the enterprise will fail. *What is most important is to support the enterprise. So the People's Bank has no choice but to approve* [emphasis added]. As Marx said, one must proceed according to conditions." [71]

However, given the prudent nature of local officials, those who make lending decisions at a bank—like others at the local levels who want to retain their positions and possibly be promoted up the bureaucratic ladder—are careful not to flout central regulations. [72] An effort is made at least to adhere to regulations, but as was pointed out in the last chapter with regard to taxes, this does not mean that in the end rules are not circumvented. For example, when enterprises took advantage of the new opportunities provided by interbank competition, they kept an account at their original bank but then opened another account at a second bank, from which they obtained the needed funds. [73] This is what the county-level beer factory did in the example cited above. The factory transferred its major account to the Construction Bank but kept an account at the Industrial Commercial Bank. [74] In other instances, regulations had loopholes. The land management bureau (*tudi guanli ju*), for example, should have had its account at the Agricultural Bank, but it could legitimately do business at the Construction Bank because the bureau handled projects in basic construction.

Local bank officials, along with county officials, have considerable discretionary power to decide how efficiently and strictly the rules and reg-

71. CI 81391.
72. Huang, *Inflation and Investment Controls*, is correct on this point.
73. A county-level Agricultural Bank official acknowledged that rural enterprises can shop for banks, even though according to the regulations they should have an account at only one bank. This is known as the basic account (*jiben zhanghu*). However, an enterprise can open a secondary or supplementary account (*fuzhu zhanghu*) at another bank for special projects. CI 8991.
74. CI 81391.

ulations will be followed. To a certain degree, the upper levels have allowed this leeway as long as it has promoted economic development. Local officials are quite aware of the personal nature of their power and the value that the upper levels place on their economic success. The head of a county Construction Bank attributed his bank's success to his ability to make quick decisions and give approval for large loans.[75] According to this official, his bank had flexibility (*linghuo*) because the province trusted his judgment and therefore gave him more autonomy.[76] But it also should be noted that the bank had expanded rapidly after he took over in 1987. In that year, it had only 3 million yuan in savings; by 1991 it had amassed 70 million yuan.[77]

MANIPULATION OF FUNDS

The dual role of banks as an administrative arm of the state and as economic entities allowed local officials considerable leeway in manipulating the use of state-supplied funds. There is evidence that some banks diverted funds earmarked for grain or cotton procurement to other purposes. Certainly there are examples of personal corruption, but in more than a few cases, the manipulation of funds (*nuoyong*) stemmed from the need to provide loans to other sectors of the local economy—most notably, during the retrenchment period, to rural enterprises.

The fiscal imperative facing the local corporate state put increasing pressure on the banks to direct funds to projects that would be more profitable to the localities. Such pressure was magnified during periods of retrenchment, when credit was cut. Given that the returns from investment in industry were clearly higher than those from agriculture, it is not surprising that local governments, through the local banks, channeled available resources to support industry, regardless of their officially designated purposes. Local governments attempted to protect community industry and cope with tight credit by "bending the rules" and diverting state funds. These strategies were similar to the Maoist-period practices of illegally keeping grain within the production team and diverting state funds to industry.[78] In the retrenchment context, diversion

75. In 1988, for example, he had authority to approve individual loans of up to 1 million yuan. CI 81391.
76. He assumed that this was due to his technical skills: he had the title of "high-level economist" (*gaoji jingjishi*).
77. CI 81391.
78. For details of the former, see Oi, *State and Peasant*; for a discussion of diversion of funds to county-level local industry, see Christine Wong, "Maoism and Development";

of funds took a number of different forms, involving local officials at the county or township level. In one 1988 case, when local banks did not have sufficient funds for a loan needed by a tobacco company to procure its supply of tobacco, the tax office allowed the company to delay its payment of the tobacco tax by one year.[79] This effectively allowed the company to use tax moneys to procure raw materials.

The problem with diverting funds to maximize the use of limited capital is that the sector that was originally earmarked to receive the funds is deprived. Unfortunately, one of the most serious problems stemming from the manipulation of state funds is the lack of money to pay peasants when they deliver their harvest for sale to the state—the notorious "IOU problem."

This problem came about in various ways, and not all were due to the diversion of funds by the county Agricultural Bank. That bank itself could fail to receive money for procurements. Procurement funds came from two sources: the central People's Bank and local savings deposits. The latter were composed largely of the funds of the local credit cooperatives, where peasants deposited their money.[80] According to county officials, by the late 1980s local Agricultural Banks became increasingly dependent on money held by the credit cooperatives.[81] The problem was that the credit cooperatives were themselves trying to maximize what little funds they had and were trying to play the game of rotational use. They would risk making short-term loans to their township and village rural enterprises under the assumption that the loans could be recalled before they had to send money to the Agricultural Bank. But in a period of fiscal austerity when the money supply was very tight, some of the loans made by the credit cooperatives could not be recalled. This reduced the funds available to the county Agricultural Bank, which consequently was unable to lend the granaries the amounts they had been allocated by the finance bureau for procurement. The granaries were thus without funds to pay the peasants for their grain and were forced to issue IOUs.

In a second scenario, the county Agricultural Bank received the procurement funds but decided to use them for other purposes, and was

---

also Vivienne Shue, "Beyond the Budget"; and Barry Naughton, "Decline of Central Control."

79. CI 6490.

80. As explained earlier, although officially these banks and cooperatives were two separate institutions, in reality they had one ledger book and were under single management at the county level.

81. CI 6690.

then unable to recover them in time to pay for the procurements. Again, it was a game of rotational use. A village party secretary who was fortunate enough to receive one of these loans explained how the process worked. The county Agricultural Bank took part of its procurement allocations and loaned it to the village as circulation capital to get through the fiscal crisis of 1990. To help the village even further, the loan was given at the same low interest rate that the bank was paying for this money.[82] Under the terms of the loan, the village was to repay it by harvest time: half by June, the other half by September.[83] Through this arrangement, the village received 5.35 million yuan in circulation funds to buy cotton for a new mill.[84]

CREATIVE ACCOUNTING

Retrenchment pressures also forced localities to engage in creative accounting that freed up funds and allowed enterprises maximum financial latitude to get through the period of fiscal austerity. One common method was for banks to permit enterprises to defer repayment of loans without penalty. Some local authorities solved the fiscal problems of their enterprises by simply erasing their debts. For example, in spring 1989, county officials who were working with one of their township economic commissions simply wrote off the old debts of some of the township-owned enterprises. Ten million yuan of debt was erased in this manner. The enterprises to which the debt was due were allowed to deduct the amount of the debt from their payments of fees and profits to the township economic commission. This worked because the debtor and creditor enterprises were in the same township. In other cases, officials allowed enterprises with ten- to twenty-year-old debts simply to write them off as costs, which reduced the amount of income taxes owed.

Officials regarded these procedures matter-of-factly. They explained that it was quite unlikely that ten- to twenty-year-old debts would ever be repaid. As one local official explained, erasing the debts simply "allows enterprise accounts to reflect reality."[85] What they did not say was that erasing the debts also made the local officials look good at the higher levels. It appeared that they were in fact implementing the re-

82. CI 8991.
83. The village received the money in March.
84. CI 52090. I do not know if the village repaid the loan on time.
85. CI 6490.

trenchment policy to reduce bad debts. Erasing the debts made the bottom line look better for everyone involved.

NONBANK SOURCES OF CAPITAL

The erosion of central control over local banks is in itself insufficient to explain the ability of the localities to continue to grow during the period of retrenchment. The diversion of funds was similar to the evasive strategies that local officials used during the Maoist period. They could frustrate the center's attempts at control, but the diversion of such resources was not sufficient to make up for the cutbacks. Localities survived the retrenchment period because they also had locally owned funds.

Chapter 4 outlines various support loans and unofficial credit that counties, townships, and villages were able to provide rural enterprises. Those funds existed because of the property rights that local governments had over a portion of the tax revenues and, most important, the rights to extrabudgetary funds that were exempt from revenue sharing, as well as to funds raised at the township and village levels. The substantial amount of these funds played a crucial role in allowing township and village enterprises to survive the retrenchment. In the longer term, they have dramatically affected the balance of resources between the center and the localities.[86]

ALTERNATIVE CREDIT INSTITUTIONS

In the latter part of the 1980s localities established local savings and loan institutions outside the central banking system.[87] A township official proudly stated that his township had been able to survive the tight credit policies because it had set up a financial service center (*jinrong fuwu suo*) to accumulate funds for use in the development of rural enterprises and agriculture.[88] He carefully pointed out that this money was not spent for education or health, only for economic development. He went on to explain that the service center had been set up in response to the

86. Chinese analysis strongly echoes this view. See, for example, Yu Jinman and Weng Xing'ou, "A Humble Opinion about Current Problems in Macroeconomic Management and How to Deal With Them," *Zhongguo jingji wenti*, 20 March 1990, no. 2, pp. 16–19, translated in *JPRS-CAR-90–049*, 11 July 1990, pp. 36–39.
87. The importance of these channels is also noted by Hua, Zhang, and Luo, *China*.
88. Unless otherwise noted, the information in this section is from CI 52490.

difficulties and the red tape involved in securing loans at the local credit cooperative. The financial service center made credit available to collective enterprises and private entrepreneurs. It was set up in 1988, and by May 1990 it had granted three hundred loans. The application procedure was fairly simple. For loans over 20,000 yuan, approval had to be obtained from a financial service center management committee (*jinrong fuwu suo guanli weiyuan hui*).

It is apparent that the financial service center was set up by local officials to circumvent the regulations that constrained funds held at local banks and credit cooperatives. Top local officials usually did not serve on the boards of these financial centers, but their tacit support was evident. In the above case, two of the nine board members held minor government positions.[89] One-quarter of the funds of the financial service center came from the county Agricultural Bank.[90] The largest percentage of its funds—more than 60 percent—came from the local peasant population. The rest of the money came from local enterprises themselves, which deposited their funds here rather than in the banks or savings and loan cooperatives.

Such semiprivate credit institutions were unlike the official savings and loan cooperatives. Most important, these institutions were outside the credit restrictions imposed by the retrenchment policies. In the case just described, the township's ten enterprises had all borrowed from the financial service center. The biggest borrower was a construction materials company that obtained 600,000 yuan in a number of small loans in February 1990. Moreover, because there was no residence requirement for those who used the service center, villages from other townships could also borrow from the institution. In fact, one of the largest loans given by the financial service center was to a village from a nearby township. In March 1990, this village borrowed 1.8 million yuan for use in a textile factory. The village was charged an interest rate of 15.8 percent and was given one year to repay.

It is difficult to determine how widespread such institutions were during the 1988–1990 period. Statistical information about them is not included in the various yearbooks. Similar organizations, some privately operated, have been reported in areas such as Wenzhou. The local offi-

89. One was a member of the town government and the other a head of one of the township administrative offices.
90. At the end of 1989, the service center received from the Agricultural Bank 2 million yuan in loans, which were repayable with interest.

cials who spoke about the financial service center cited above boasted that theirs was the only such organization in their prefecture. By the mid-1990s, however, as I indicate in chapter 4, there was an explosion of such private or semiprivate financial institutions. Some counties had one in each township. They ranged from village-level credit cooperatives that rivaled the township credit cooperatives to pawn shops.[91] All had the implicit, if not explicit, support of the localities.

COUNTY SUPPORT FUNDS

Retrenchment policies called for localities to stop adding funds to the pots of the various government agencies that provided low- or no-interest loans to local enterprises. Some localities may have followed this instruction, but some agencies already had sufficient funds to continue offering loans to selected enterprises by the time the cuts were mandated. The increase in extrabudgetary funds at the county level undermined the effectiveness of the center's attempts to cut off sources of credit. Moreover, there is evidence that during the retrenchment period, the funds were not summarily cut off. The money for these pots continued to be provided by local governments, from the province on down, during the retrenchment. Local governments at all levels tried to help their localities weather the tight money situation by directly granting economic assistance to enterprises through low-cost agency loans from their own funds.

Detailed county-level data reveal the resources potentially available through local government channels. The finance bureau in one North China county had various forms of support that it doled out on a case-by-case basis. There was a "develop agriculture" fund (*nongye fazhan zijin*) that was established as a result of a provincial-level directive. In 1990 this account contained 3 million yuan.[92] There was also a special extrabudgetary fund known as the "support agriculture" fund (*zhinong zhouzhuanjin*), which in 1990 totaled 2.365 million yuan.[93] Within this fund, there was a "finance support fund" (*caizheng fuchi zijin*) designated specifically for the support of collective enterprises; in 1988 it

91. See, for example, "Credit Cooperatives Help Rural Economic Growth," *China Daily*, 7 November 1992, p. 1, in *FBIS-CHI-92–217*, 9 November 1992, pp. 50–51; "Lun nongcun xinyongsuode"; *Zhongguo nongcun jingji*; "Diandang ye yingyou mingquede jingying guifan" (Pawnshops Should Have Well-Defined Operational Rules), *Guangming ribao*, 11 August 1993, p. 3.
92. CI 8891.
93. CI 8791.

TABLE 7.   SOURCES OF FUNDING FOR A
NORTH CHINA COUNTY'S FINANCE BUREAU
LOANS, 1984–1990 (UNIT-10,000 YUAN)

	Province	Prefecture	County	Total
1984	24	22	13	59
1985	30	9	17	55
1986	20	15	20	55
1987	50	18	19	87
1988	45	20	94	159
1989	165	62	70	297
1990	n.a.	n.a.	35	35

SOURCE: CI 52290
NOTES: Entries for 1990 are available for the first five months only.

TABLE 8.   A NORTH CHINA COUNTY'S
TAX BUREAU LOANS, 1988–1991

	Total Amount (10,000 yuan)	No. of Enterprises
1988	30	14
1989	47	20
1990	51	25
1991	75	n.a.

SOURCE: CI 81391
NOTES: Entries for 1988 and 1989 are approximations.
The amount for 1991 was given as 700,000–800,000 yuan.

amounted to 640,000 yuan. Between 1981 and 1987, a total of 2.03 million yuan was lent from this fund. The county government determined the amount to be put into the fund, which included repayments as well as new allocations.[94] Table 7 illustrates the amounts provided by the province, the prefecture, and the county as supplements to the finance bureau loans. The county gave less in 1989 than in 1988, but the funds from the province and the prefecture increased significantly in 1989, despite the retrenchment.

A similar situation existed with regard to the county tax bureau loans, as table 8 shows. Total funds lent to more than sixty enterprises between 1984 and 1987 amounted to 400,000 yuan. After 1988, there were yearly increases, from 300,000 yuan in 1988 to more than double that amount by 1991. In 1989 the tax bureau handed out 470,000 yuan in

94. CI 6288.

loans to about twenty enterprises.[95] Interviews with tax officials reveal that for this bureau, at least, the sources of funding were relatively secure and substantial by the time of the retrenchment. The funds the county tax bureau used for enterprise loans were drawn from a number of local sources. One source was taxes on the private sector. The bureau was allowed to keep slightly more than 2 percent of these.[96] In addition to tax moneys, supplementary amounts came from surplus allocations in the tax bureau budget granted by the county finance bureau.[97] The tax bureau was able to retain 20,000 yuan from these allocations. In addition, a temporary sales tax (*linshi jingyingshui*) was levied on traders (*fanmaizhe*) at a rate of 5–8 percent, depending on the prices of the goods sold. This tax amounted to about 500,000 yuan in 1987.[98]

Funds from county science and technology commissions were particularly valuable because enterprises had to repay only 70 percent of such loans.[99] When local sources were insufficient, the county science and technology commission could request project loans from the prefecture or the province. Projects to be aided could be designated at the province, prefecture, or county level. The level that designated the project provided the funding, and the loan was repaid to that level. In the case of money provided by the county, it was up to the county science and technology commission to decide how much had to be repaid. In 1988 one county gave its science and technology commission 200,000 yuan; the province gave 220,000 yuan; and the prefecture gave 80,000 yuan.[100] The science and technology commission, like the tax bureau, could also go to a local bank to secure loans for an enterprise. The commission might make

95. CI 52290.
96. According to local officials, this was a uniform rate for Shandong province, decided upon by the provincial tax office. CI 52290.
97. The surplus allocations stemmed from the slack in the budget provided by the prefectural tax office to the county tax bureau.
98. Of this amount, 30 percent was kept by the county and 70 percent went to the prefecture. The temporary sales tax was instituted in 1984, the year that local governments started actively to promote enterprises. CI 62288.
99. No interest was charged. Moreover, if a project was selected by the science and technology commission for aid, the enterprise would be guaranteed a set amount of materials at low within-plan (*jihua nei*) prices. CI 71888.
100. The total amount was a huge increase from 1987, when the commission had only 50,000 yuan, which was loaned to twenty applicants, five of which were rural enterprises. The largest loan was 15,000 yuan for a provincial-level apple production project. CI 71888. Within the county, the county finance bureau made an allocation to the science and technology commission in the form of a technology development fund (*keji fazhan jijin*). The bureau was not concerned with how the money was doled out. Beginning in 1986, the commission kept any loan money that was repaid.

the loan proposal more acceptable to the bank by agreeing to pay part of the interest on behalf of the enterprise.[101]

TOWNSHIP, VILLAGE, AND INTRA-ENTERPRISE FUNDS

Probably the single most important source of financing that allowed township and village enterprises to survive the retrenchment was collective funds. The ways in which these were used are described in chapter 3. It is not that collectives had an abundance of funds. Rather, the township or, particularly, the village could mobilize funds from within the community when necessary.

Economists using fieldwork survey data have gathered evidence showing that the dependence of villages on outside loans for industrial expansion decreased significantly over the decade of reform.[102] This is consistent with the decrease in credit provided by the state banks to village enterprises that is detailed in chapter 3. My own fieldwork confirms this trend. Well-off villages could generate their own funds, both from existing rural enterprises and, in some cases, from successful agricultural endeavors. A World Bank report also points to the prevalence of such redistribution and self-raised funds as sources for investment in fixed assets in rural collective industry, at least since 1985.[103] The relevant point for this discussion is that these funds fall outside the scope of central extractions through taxes and outside the net of central controls operating at the local levels.

Intravillage Funds

Villages as well as townships used the system of redistribution (described in chapter 3), in which one factory borrowed from more financially healthy factories within the village or township to deal with the fiscal austerity. For example, in one highly industrialized and wealthy village in August 1989, a new cotton mill borrowed 1 million yuan from other village factories, including 250,000 yuan from a forging factory.

As noted in chapter 3, finding the funds was not easy, especially when everyone was short. In the above case the party secretary realized that

101. The commission's resources come from its technology development fund.
102. See Scott Rozelle, "Principals and Agents."
103. Ody, *Rural Enterprise Development.*

each factory wanted to protect its own resources, especially during the retrenchment, even if all were part of the same family. The forging plant had tried to resist (the factory had "its own opinions" [*yijian*], as the Chinese say), but in the end was "persuaded" (*shuofu*) to make the loan. The plant manager knew that at some time in the future, it might need to be on the receiving end. In this particular case, the request was much more difficult to turn down because the village party secretary who was trying to negotiate the loan also personally ran the cotton mill. To make the transaction as palatable as possible, the village party secretary promised to repay the loan within three years, at 15 percent annual interest.[104]

Funds were also raised within enterprises from the deposits paid by their new workers. This practice had been in use for a number of years, but did not yield large sums of money. It was of limited effectiveness during periods of fiscal austerity, when factories generally did not hire new workers. The job bonding discussed in chapter 3 was more lucrative. This practice was resorted to in one Shandong county in 1989 when the local bank and savings and loan cooperatives gave out almost no money in loans.[105]

If village government failed to raise sufficient capital from its enterprises, it could borrow from villagers, usually from those who work in the enterprises. Fairly large sums were raised in this way during the retrenchment period. For example, in 1989 an industrialized village needed circulation funds to buy materials so that a factory could continue to operate. The village decided to have all of its factories sell shares[106] to their workers. Each worker contributed a lump sum of 5,000–10,000 yuan.[107] In return, the village paid each shareholder interest, at a rate higher than that of the bank. Workers could take out their money at any time. During the first half of 1989, the village amassed 700,000 yuan through these sales.[108]

Such methods became institutionalized and continued to be used after the retrenchment period. For example, in 1991, approximately

104. CI 52090.
105. CI 6490.
106. This system should not be confused with the shareholding system described earlier. Here, what was sold were simply shares in a cooperative savings scheme.
107. When asked if 5,000–10,000 yuan was a large amount for peasants, the village party secretary replied that it was no problem because each family had large savings. He said that those village workers who did not have enough funds were not required to buy shares. CI 52090. This village was particularly rich; in other villages, the amounts were more modest, only 300–500 yuan per worker.
108. CI 52090.

80 percent of the enterprises in the village cited above were still engaging in various forms of fund-raising (*jizi*). In that year, the village mobilized approximately 3 million yuan. In 1995, when the village had eighteen village enterprises, with total annual profits of more than 5 million yuan, it was still raising approximately 2 million yuan per year from its savings schemes.[109]

THE LIMITS OF CENTRAL CONTROL
IN A CHANGING ECONOMIC CONTEXT

The retrenchment policies failed to touch the all-important extrabudgetary funds and community-raised funds that were used to help enterprises weather the fiscal constraints imposed by the center.

For the first time, local governments could legitimately keep the fiscal resources that they generated and use them as they saw fit. They have been able to go beyond the previous passive strategies of resistance. Their resources have enabled them to take positive action to counter directly the policies of the center and to pursue their own local economic interests. Political actors at the lower levels of government, particularly at the township and village levels, can now adopt strategies that are beyond the legal and economic control of the central state. The strengthened ability of the localities to protect their local interests, evident in the response of local governments to the fiscal austerity measures instituted in 1988–1989, suggests that local governments have entered a new phase in their struggle with the center over the pursuit of local economic interests.

Without question, there were holes in the Maoist system of control. However, the Maoist central state sufficiently monopolized resources to prevent most localities from engaging in anything other than evasive and passive strategies of resistance. There were few opportunities to build independent resource bases or to take positive action, as most allocations still came from the center. Because of the ideological links between economic performance and political loyalty, a minimum of compliance was necessary. Localities could do no more than maneuver within and around the rules set by the central state. The balance of power and control clearly was with the center.[110]

109. CI 23696.
110. Vivienne Shue underestimates this in her *Reach of the State*.

While counties were able to expand their industrial bases, they had little leeway to develop industry because of the tight control the center maintained on agricultural procurements. This control robbed the localities of necessary raw materials. The within-budget funds—and the limited extrabudgetary funds—that were legitimately in the hands of the localities were subject to various upper-level controls; the localities did not have the authority to decide on their expenditures and investments.

A minimum of compliance is still necessary, but the reforms and the increased scale of economic activity have given the localities greater economic independence and capacity for economic investment. This chapter has highlighted the consequences of the rise of local state corporatism on the central state's ability to control the development stemming from economic reform. Central control policies are being implemented, but either they are being manipulated to further local interests or they are proving inadequate to control growing sources of locally owned funds.

The 1994 reforms have mandated some change over the control of extrabudgetary funds. These funds are now called the "second budget" (*dier yusuan*), which reflects an attempt to put them under stricter budgetary control. All extrabudgetary funds must now be under what is called "unified management" by the county finance bureau, and county government approval is required before they can be used. There are examples of county officials not giving approval for a unit's use of these funds. For instance, a county industrial-commercial management bureau applied to use its funds to build a new dormitory. The county refused, saying that the agency already had sufficient space. However, it is still questionable how much more effective the 1994 reforms will be in controlling extrabudgetary spending. In many ways, the arrangements remain much the same as in the past, except that there seem to be more procedures that units must go through to use what is still considered their money. Most important, extrabudgetary funds still remain at the local level.

CHAPTER 7

The Political Basis
for Economic Reform

Concluding Reflections

China's experience suggests that economic reform and growth can occur in a Leninist system if the bureaucracy is given a stake in the process. The fusion of economic and political power does not have to be destroyed; economic change does not necessarily undermine the power of the existing political elite. The issue is not whether the system is Leninist but what incentives exist for implementing reform. While communist officials may well obstruct reforms that threaten their power, the lure of profits and benefits from the reforms can also inspire them to pursue rapid economic development.

No simple correlation exists between economic reform and the power of local officials. The Chinese experience has shown that some local governments have been weakened by the reforms, whereas others have been strengthened. The key is the sources of income that officials have under their control. In most villages, the determining factor is the degree of local industrialization. Local governments that control a primarily agricultural, particularly grain-based, economy have few options other than to levy ad hoc surcharges and various other fees and penalties. The local state corporatism described in this volume is unlikely to exist in such villages. The greater the level of industrialization, the more likely that the local government will act in a corporate manner to intervene, extract, and redistribute income.

Obviously, the reforms have not led all villages to industrialize. Whether a locality succeeds or not depends on concrete circumstances.

My point is that China's rural reforms were crafted in such a way as to allow those who promoted economic development and pursued rural industrialization to strengthen, not weaken, their official power.[1] China's economic reforms took off in many parts of the countryside precisely because the key entrepreneurs leading the charge were those who had the economic and political resources—the cadres themselves. Rooted in the prior existence of collective and central planning, local state corporatism is the path of least resistance in the transition from a Leninist system.

China's reform strategy has been characterized as "groping for stepping stones in crossing the river." The varied and changing patterns of local development strategies over the course of the reform period lend credence to such a characterization. While some may criticize China for the lack of a bold and clear plan to reform its economy quickly, the progress the country has made during the reform period suggests that it is not such a bad idea to pay heed to the constraints and opportunities embedded in the stones already lying in the path. China has trodden carefully either to surmount or to sidestep the stones it cannot remove, and only gradually, after it has passed those stones, has it moved to the next section of the river and implemented a new stage of reform. This is a solution involving slow institutional change within a context of rapid economic growth.

China's experience offers no formula for success. It is unclear whether the same outcome could have occurred in the Soviet Union, where the Leninist system left a legacy very different from the one it left in China.[2] China's reform experience is a story of path dependence—the condition of being bound by the effects of history—but it was altered by institutional change. While the post-Mao state retains key features of the Maoist system, the decision to accommodate mandates of rapid economic development in a market context has resulted in a qualitatively new variety of developmental state and not merely a modified Leninist system. This study underscores Evans's general point that no two examples of state-led growth are the same.[3] The system of local state-led growth that I describe as local state corporatism is a hybrid that utilizes capacities

1. Authors who formerly stressed the tendency of markets to reduce the power of local officials now emphasize the ways in which rural governments act like local corporations. Compare two articles by Nee: "Theory of Market Transition" and "Organizational Dynamics of Market Transition."

2. This point is elaborated in Jean C. Oi, "Role of the Local State," and in Goldstein, "China in Transition."

3. Evans, *Embedded Autonomy.*

inherited from the Maoist state and forms found in capitalist developmental states. Whether others can replicate China's developmental experience depends less on historical legacy than on whether prospective reformers have the political capabilities that characterized the Maoist state—and whether they can craft sufficient incentives to persuade those responsible for implementation that economic development is in their interests. China's reform experience supports Douglass North's assertion that institutions are "the underlying determinant of the long-run performance of economies."[4]

THE SECURITY OF PROPERTY RIGHTS AND ECONOMIC GROWTH

To explain away the contradiction between economic growth and the lack of clear and secure private property rights, some have suggested that such rights have been overemphasized and may not be necessary in all cultural contexts.[5] This study provides no evidence to indicate whether growth can occur without property rights. What it does show is that *individuals* need not have property rights over enterprise profits for economic growth to occur. Growth occurs as long as there are property rights for some organized entity. Local governments, if they have sufficient incentive and resources to pursue growth, can assume an entrepreneurial role.[6]

The point of this study is not that collective property rights—that is, public ownership—are conducive to growth, only that they can be used to achieve growth. While that distinction may seem overly academic, it has significant policy implications. Countries in transition to a market economy need not immediately privatize. Intermediate forms of property rights are capable of engendering economic growth in transitional systems under certain conditions.

In China, local state ownership in the development of rural industry made use of limited resources when individuals lacked sufficient resources to be entrepreneurial themselves. But ownership forms have evolved along with changes in the economic and political contexts. This study

4. Douglass North, *Institutions*, p. 107.
5. See Weitzman and Xu, "Township-Village Enterprises."
6. This study recognizes that there are also distinct interests within local governments. For a discussion of how individual actors within a government act as entrepreneurs, see Duckett, "Market Reform"; and Yi-min Lin and Zhanxin Zhang, "Private Assets of Public Servants."

has shown how original forms of collective ownership have become out-dated. The role of government must also change if growth is to continue. So far, local governments have shown impressive flexibility in adapting local state corporatism to encompass a growing private sector. The question is whether such accommodations will continue.

Those who maintain that individual private property rights provide the best basis for growth may ultimately be proved right. But that misses the point. There is no need to make value judgments about the inherent superiority of one ownership form over another. Different environments are capable of supporting different forms of ownership and property rights. The point is that privatization does not have a monopoly on the capacity to generate growth. China's experience has shown that gradual reform can be an effective alternative route.

The debate needs to move away from the question of whether there should be a "big bang" or "gradual reform." The more important question is, What are the precise mechanisms that will best suit the conditions of a country wanting to make the transition? Those intent on creating economic as well as political change must consider the concrete political and economic contexts in which reforms will take place. Reformers need to start with a realistic picture of what they have and what the root causes of the problems are. The findings of this study beg them to consider the possibility that what they have, rather than be a liability, can be turned into an asset. To reiterate, it is not a radical change of personnel or a rapid dismantling of the established economic structure that accounts for the growth in China, but the creation of effective institutional incentives that provided the existing bureaucracy with a new economic and political context in which to calculate the costs and benefits of supporting reform.

The findings of this study also raise the possibility that "clear and secure," the usual description of the type of property rights deemed necessary for effective growth, need not have a fixed meaning. Although I have argued throughout this study that local governments were assigned property rights to the residual, in actuality these were never secure rights firmly protected by law. The center could take back the rights of the localities at any time—as it partly did with its 1994 tax measures. Even more evident is that secure property rights still elude private business. Yet growth has been pursued by both local governments and the private sector. Perhaps it is enough that each is comfortable in its *expectation* that the rights it has will yield an acceptable return.

This line of argument finds further support in recent research that shows an increasing fuzziness between different forms of ownership as the reforms have progressed in China.[7] In this study, I have taken seriously the difference between collective and private ownership and have used the distinction to explain how rural industry took off in the 1980s and how local government and private business participated in that process. In trying to understand the takeoff, maintaining a clear distinction is essential. But as the reforms have progressed—particularly as new forms of ownership and management have been introduced in the 1990s, as government agencies have started businesses, and as state-owned institutions have taken on a much more complex form—a blurring of the categories "public" and "private" has occurred. Labels such as "private," "collective," and "joint" seem to be adopted for economic or political convenience. What is important is that those who are responsible for the growth of enterprises, those who make the investments, feel that they will be able to enjoy a more or less stable return for their efforts.[8] Studies of the private sector strongly suggest that secure private property rights guaranteed by law may not be essential. All that may be needed is what Wank calls "socially guaranteed, informal property rights."[9] All of this leads me to conclude that in certain contexts, growth can occur as long as there are relatively secure and relatively clear property rights for some organized entity that has an incentive to pursue economic development.

The important analytical question is, What are the conditions under which this system will work? Is it viable only in the short term—that is, in the transitional period when old networks and clientelist ties are still in force? This is a question for future research, but it is quite clear that one should not expect such a system to work in all contexts or even in the same place over time. It is already apparent that as rural industries have begun to trade outside their communities, in areas where they have few social or kinship ties, conducting business on the basis of a handshake no longer works. Local governments and firms alike are beginning to retain lawyers and use the law. But for the time being, within local communities where kinship and clientelist ties still abound, social relationships have enabled private entrepreneurs to maintain stable expectations about the returns from their investments. Just as it may be sufficient for local governments to have a credible commitment from the

---

7. See articles in Oi and Walder, eds., *Property Rights.*
8. Some would even argue that property rights are something that can be subject to bargaining. See Corinna-Barbara Francis, "Bargained Property Rights."
9. Wank, "Social Networks and Property Rights."

central state in regard to the residual, perhaps it is these social ties and the credible expectations embedded within them that have made it possible to have growth without clear and secure property rights in the Western sense of the term.[10]

THE POLITICAL CONSEQUENCES OF ECONOMIC REFORM

Theda Skocpol has noted in another context that policies have the ability to "transform or expand the capacities of the state. They therefore change the administrative possibilities for official initiatives in the future, and affect later prospects for policy implementation." [11] The changes spawned by China's economic reforms go beyond most problems of policy feedback. The consequences of successful economic reform unleashed at the behest of the central state transformed the balance of power between the center and the localities. This transformation not only allows the localities an unprecedented degree of autonomy to pursue their own interests but limits the options that the center can now take to remedy the situation. The agents are gathering more and more resources to act as principals.

The problem that the central Chinese state now faces is common to top-down reform efforts: how to control the reforms once they have been unleashed. Mikhail Gorbachev initiated political reform, but it led not only to the fall of the Communist Party but also to that of the Soviet Union. The Chinese leadership, having successfully initiated economic reform, finds itself in the position of having to deal with that reform's unintended consequences. The irony is that many of the present problems stem from the center's success in inducing its agents to fulfill the terms of the original reform contract. The center gave the green light to the localities to pursue growth by providing substantial latitude to maximize revenues, within certain broad outlines.

The center must now renegotiate with its agents and give them a new set of tasks. Motivated by double-digit inflation, the central authorities have periodically tried to slow down growth rates by recentralizing controls. On a number of levels, the strategy has succeeded; by the second half of the 1990s, inflation was at impressively low rates. The problem

---

10. This is akin to North's ideas about the power of informal institutions. *Institutions.*
11. Theda Skocpol, *Protecting Soldiers and Mothers,* p. 58; quoted in Paul Pierson, "When Effect Becomes Cause," p. 603.

for the center is that these efforts began after market reforms had already changed the character of the economy and the localities had gained control of substantial resources. The findings of chapter 6 suggest that this was already the case in the late 1980s. Agents at the local levels were no longer those who had been on the other end of the central-local relationship at the beginning of the reform process.

The economic reforms have wrought political change. In China the seeds of political reform have been planted and have been germinated by the success of economic reform. The political rights of individuals have yet to be guaranteed, but the success of local state corporatism may force the emergence of a federalism that more clearly recognizes the rights and power of the localities.[12]

In many respects, the reforms have recreated a situation that the Chinese Communist Party tried to eliminate in the mid-1950s: one in which large numbers of actors operate without organization and control. The Maoist-era strategy was to divide and rule, to reduce the costs of monitoring though organization and control.[13] The center reduced the numbers of those it had to regulate directly and tried to gain compliance through administrative means. State monopolies and rationing effectively reduced the alternative channels through which inputs could be secured for production. The same principle underlay the decision to assign different sectors of the economy to different specialized banks when the reforms began.

In practice, the effectiveness of the Maoist regulatory mechanisms was less than that implied in the totalitarian image presented by Schurmann. The state had the capacity to institute strangling control over its population and its agents, but in practice, as long as a facade of compliance was maintained, most agents had a significant amount of operational freedom. The Maoist system of control lacked the manpower to check each and every one of its agents at the local level. It was a system of control that was premised on fear: "killing the chicken to scare the monkey," as the Chinese saying goes. As I note in my earlier work, "The most common forms of regulation were the least effective, while the most effective were the least used. The system of control was one of escalating interaction

12. As Gabriella Montinola, Yingyi Qian, and Barry Weingast stress, this is a very different type of federalism, one that focuses on the division of authority between central and local governments, not on the rights of the individual. "Federalism, Chinese Style."

13. The Chinese made use of the "organizational weapon" to achieve control. The term is from Selznick, *Organizational Weapon*. This idea is central in Schurmann's classic work, *Ideology and Organization*.

predicated on example and deterrence rather than on the comprehensive application of sanctions against each and every possible offender." [14]

The communist planning and control system was always hostage to the information flow in the multilayered bureaucracy. The failure of the system saw its most disastrous consequences in the famine during the Great Leap Forward. [15] The major weakness of the Maoist system of control was that it "depended heavily on the cooperation of local cadres to effectively implement its more routine forms of control. . . . Regardless of who the cadre was, whether local or an outsider, the exercise of authority was personalized, and the degree of enforcement was subject to individual cadre discretion. This personalization of authority formed the center of a clientelist system of politics." [16]

This study has shown that the dependence of the center on local agents has not been reduced. Power is still personalized, and local officials are still engaging in the "facade of compliance." But the situation is now in many ways more critical for the center. It is trying to use a system of regulation crafted during the Maoist period for a centrally planned economy to control what is well on its way to becoming a market economy. The regulatory bureaucracy has been little reformed, while sources of funding and resources have rapidly evolved in the localities that the center is trying to control. The holes in the credit control system during the 1988–1989 retrenchment are a clear illustration of this lag in capacity. Now, more than ever before, the regulatory system is vulnerable to competing interests. An inherently flawed monitoring system becomes even less effective as agents are lured by incentives that flow from their regional administrative leaders rather than from the center. The incentives built into the fiscal reforms have motivated local governments to become more protective and more local in their orientation.

LOCAL STATE CORPORATISM AND CENTRAL CONTROL IN A TRANSITIONAL SYSTEM

Readers should not conclude, however, that the central state has hopelessly lost control. Far from it. In contrast to Eastern Europe and the former Soviet Union, local and central governments in China are parts of the same functioning unitary state and party. There are no opposition par-

---

14. Oi, *State and Peasant*, p. 102.
15. See Bernstein, "Stalinism, Famine and Chinese Peasants."
16. Oi, *State and Peasant*, p. 103.

ties ruling the localities and trying to overthrow those in power at the center. The Chinese state remains vertically integrated. The weaknesses that have been highlighted in this study are weaknesses in comparison with the Maoist period. This must be kept in mind in any discussion of the power of the center. The caveat is particularly needed in the face of theories that predict the emergence of "civil society" or a "societal take-over." Objective analysis should not be mixed with wishful thinking.

When market economies are characterized as examples of state corporatism, the implication is that they are marked by tighter control. But in China, where the system was formerly Leninist, the emergence of corporatism in many ways represents a relaxation of the control system. It is this easing that has led some to look for the re-emergence of civil society, but the findings of this study suggest that such efforts are premature, at least within local rural communities.[17] The operation of local state corporatism, though it suggests a loosening of Leninist central control, in fact contradicts, or at least greatly qualifies, theories of market transition that posit a corrosive effect of markets on the power of local officials.[18] Local state corporatism is similarly difficult to square with the view that market reform is breaking the cellular or "honeycomb" nature of rural Chinese society and allowing for greater penetration by the central state.[19] On the contrary, this study highlights the fact that local public and private enterprises, and local governments, have all been able to thrive independently in the new market economy, which is overseen by a still effective but now weakened central state.

REMAINING QUESTIONS

China may well have managed an industrial takeoff in the countryside, but the initiation of reforms is only the beginning of the process of achieving long-term economic growth and political stability. The experience of other nations suggests that consolidation is in many respects more challenging than the initiation of reform.[20] As the honeymoon period, when reforms are welcomed, draws to a close, policy makers lose their freedom

17. The link between relaxation of control and the re-emergence of civil society is explicit in David Ost's treatment of Solidarity as an example of societal corporatism. "Towards a Corporatist Solution." A similar link to civil society is found in writings on China, although with many more reservations. See, for example, Chan, "Revolution or Corporatism?"; Yang, "Between State and Society"; and Lee, "Chinese Industrial State."
18. Nee, "Theory of Market Transition."
19. Shue, *Reach of the State*.
20. See Joan Nelson, "Politics of Economic Transformation."

to maneuver. Policies that initially were successful begin to lose effectiveness, new wrinkles emerge, problems develop, and the trickle-down theory is increasingly questioned as those who have fallen behind become anxious and those who have failed to benefit lose patience. China entered that stage in the mid-1990s. Some of these issues have already been addressed in the discussion of problems arising from collective ownership of township and village enterprises, a system that seemed to work so well in the 1980s. But many questions remain unanswered and await future research. The following are just a few of the issues that grow directly out of *successful* rural industrialization.

Many problems stem from the regional disparities that exist in rural industrialization. This is the other face of the Chinese countryside, one that this study has not examined. Some areas have failed to industrialize and therefore have been unable to enjoy the benefits of increased revenues and incomes. This study has necessarily focused on the more successful cases because its purpose is to understand how rural industrialization was achieved. Successful development of township- and village-owned enterprises brought relative political stability, and satisfaction with existing authorities. But the situation is dramatically different in the poor areas, where the peasants are getting tired of waiting for the benefits of reform. There the legitimacy of the regime is under threat. Numerous peasant disturbances have occurred since the reforms began.[21] During the Maoist period, peasants engaged in resistance, but it was mostly passive.[22] In the 1990s, some are openly resisting. Officials are beaten, property damaged, orders simply ignored; taxes and fees go unpaid, village coffers stand empty, and sometimes officials pay the price by being dismissed.[23] In extreme cases, there are violent demonstrations and destruction of property, as occurred in Renshou county, Sichuan, in 1993. These problems challenge the regime and threaten to undermine the achievements of more than almost two decades of reform.

The press reveals that officials at both the national and the local levels are sensitive to the destabilizing effects of peasant disturbances. Various leaders have explicitly addressed the importance of this issue to China's reform and stability.[24] Central authorities acknowledge that the reforms have increased inequalities, and they readily admit that decol-

21. See, for example, O'Brien and Li, "Villagers and Popular Resistance."

22. See Oi, *State and Peasant,* especially chap. 5.

23. See O'Brien and Li, "Villagers and Popular Resistance," for a useful summary of different types of resistance.

24. See, for example, Wang Qinglin and Fan Wenke, "Jiaqiang nongcun jiceng."

lectivization left some villages "paralyzed" or "partially paralyzed" because of a lack of economic resources,[25] an aging village leadership, and incompetent successors.[26] The challenge facing the regime is how to maintain its legitimacy. The central leadership has tried to exculpate itself by attributing economic backwardness to poor leadership at the local levels. A call has been issued for new leadership in China's backward villages. But how will this be achieved? One solution involves experimentation with democratic self-governance in villages. This carries political risks and has tremendous ramifications for the future character of rule in China. How far will the regime let such political reform go? What is the relationship between economic development and political change? These are the key questions that face China as it enters into its next phase of reform.[27]

Another set of problems stems from the changing character of rural industry itself. Changes in ownership systems are not simply an economic fact; they also carry social consequences. The dislocations of the transition to a market economy found in Eastern Europe and the former Soviet Union have been attenuated in China by the redistributive socialism that continues to be practiced, at least to a limited degree, under local state corporatism. The collective ownership of township and village enterprises provided local authorities with an economic cushion and structured the relationships between enterprises and local governments. An ethos of redistributive socialism and community obligation gave the local population first chance at available employment in village and township enterprises. Efforts were made to ensure that at least one person from each village family received first rights to jobs in village-owned enterprises. When outsiders were given jobs, some villages discriminated against them by providing locals with better workers' benefits. In some instances village factories kept unprofitable operations open to provide

25. See, for example, the speech by the outgoing National People's Congress chairman, Wan Li, in Lu Yu-sha, "Wan Li Delivers Speech, Expressing Worry about Peasant Rebellion," *Tang-tai*, 15 April 1993, no. 25, pp. 13–14, translated in *FBIS-CHI-93–072*, 16 April 1993, pp. 43–44; Vice premier Tian Jiyun's warnings were reported in *South China Morning Post*, 23 March 1993; Jiang Zemin also addressed the topic in his Fourteenth Party Congress speech in 1992.

26. See, for example, Zhang Guoqing, Fan Zhiyong, and Yan Xinge, "Zhuazhu sange huanjie." Also see an account written by a county party vice secretary, Chen Yuming, "Diaodong cunji ganbu gongzuo jiji xing zhi wojian," on the difficulties of being a cadre.

27. Democratic change may indeed occur, but it will not necessarily be a consequence of China's successful economic reform. Preliminary research on the implementation of the draft Village Organic Law, which gives peasants the right to elect their leaders directly in competitive elections, shows no linear relationship between higher incomes and participatory decision making. Jean C. Oi and Scott Rozelle, "Democracy and Markets."

wage income to village members. What will happen if more than a few of the township- and village-owned enterprises are sold? Who are the entrepreneurs who are buying such factories? Are they locals or outsiders? What will happen to villagers who have been working in such village and township factories? What stipulations for village welfare do local governments make in the sales of these enterprises?

Changes in ownership restructure the resource base of local governments. What will happen to government revenues when township and village governments sell their enterprises and no longer have access to the associated enterprise profits and nontax revenues? The legitimate access of local authorities to revenues of private firms is limited to taxes. Changes of this kind are potentially the most threatening to the continuation of redistributive socialism, particularly at the level of village government, which still has no right to any income from taxes.

Collective ownership of enterprises allowed township and village governments to take considerable nontax revenues out of such firms, but it also allowed them to provide these enterprises with extensive services, which helped the firms grow rapidly in the 1980s. Local officials set limits on managers' salaries to ensure a larger return to the village; this practice also served to maintain a minimum of equality in the transitional economy. Redistribution also took place as the profits of collectively owned enterprises subsidized village welfare and infrastructure costs.

Will privatization force yet further reform of the fiscal system? Will villages finally become a formal level of government allowed to partake in revenue sharing, and thus to have a regular income? Where will the village's share come from? Will the upper level give up a portion of its current share? Or will villagers have to pay an additional set of taxes? How will the already poor respond to such moves?

The effect of privatization goes beyond questions of redistribution; it also raises the issue of the relationship between local governments and the new private entrepreneurs. The possibility that privately owned firms will overshadow collective and state-owned firms raises the question of whether China will go the way of some underdeveloped states of Africa and Latin America as the local state is denied the access to nontax revenues that it currently enjoys in its ownership of township and village enterprises. So far, the symbiotic nature of the relationship between the local state and the private sector has kept such predatory behavior to a minimum.[28] But will the corporatist relationship become in-

28. David Wank, "Bureaucratic Patronage and Private Business."

creasingly asymmetrical, with the local state taking more than it gives? What will happen as private businesspeople become increasingly skilled and well connected, and therefore resentful of payments for services no longer needed or rendered? Will the local state allow the power of private business to grow, as has occurred in other state-led corporatist systems? How long can the local state keep the private sector in a subordinate position? As others have asked, can China move successfully to the next stage of development without the relationship between the state and the private sector becoming more equal?[29]

These all remain questions for future research. Meanwhile, I hope that the findings of this study provide a clearer understanding of how China's rural industrialization process took off and evolved. If this work fulfills its purpose, it will remind future researchers to look at the political underpinnings of economic activity and to respect both the economic and the political logic behind patterns of development. Institutional incentives, resource endowments, and constraints all matter. I hope this study will provide the basis for more informed and precise questions about future reform as China moves to the next stone in the river. There is a long way to go to the other side of the river; the story of reform in China is far from over.

29. Pearson, *China's New Business Elite.*

Research and Documentation

This study draws on published materials in English and in Chinese, official statistics, and interviews conducted in China. The openly available published sources include Chinese press reports, periodicals, and the recently available local gazetteers and national and provincial yearbooks. A list of the periodicals and newspapers is provided at the beginning of the bibliography. In addition to the standard sources, I used county statistical yearbooks and local statistical compilations. The latter were particularly useful for gaining a disaggregated view of China's administrative regions and economy.

While the written materials available for the study of contemporary China have become increasingly rich, my most valuable sources of information were the interviews I conducted in China between 1986 and 1996. Table 9 shows the provinces where I did my interviews, the years in which the interviews were conducted, and the approximate number of interviews conducted in each province. Each interview generally lasted between two and a half to three hours.

Because of the sensitive nature of some of the information that officials and others provided me in the localities where I did my research, I have chosen to protect the identities of those I interviewed. In most cases, I have also withheld the name of the county, township, or village. This causes some awkwardness in my text. I cite these interviews as China Interviews (CI) plus the transcript accession number. I hope readers will understand the necessity of such precautions, as I am anxious to avoid

TABLE 9.   INTERVIEW LOCATIONS, DATES,
AND NUMBERS

Province (and Provincial-level Municipalities)	Year Interviews Conducted	Number of Interviews Conducted
Beijing	1986, 1991, 1994	27
Liaoning	1986	25
Sichuan	1986	12
Tianjin	1986, 1988	26
Shandong	1988, 1990, 1991, 1994, 1996	198
Guangdong	1994	15
Henan	1994	6
Hunan	1994	7
Jiangsu	1994	8
Zhejiang	1994	9
TOTAL		333

jeopardizing any of the generous individuals who helped me understand the process of transition.

THE INTERVIEW SAMPLE

I conducted interviews in ten different provinces and municipalities in various parts of China, some of which are noted for their collective development strategies, others for their private enterprises, and some, such as Guangdong, for substantial foreign investment. However, this is far from a representative sample. As table 9 shows, the provinces in which I did the majority of my interviews are largely those in North China and the coastal provinces; only a few of the central and western provinces are included. These are the provinces that promoted rural enterprises and are among the most developed.

My interview sites were not chosen randomly: few, if any, statistical generalizations can be made based on my findings. Although I spent close to a thousand hours interviewing more than three hundred sources, my concern was not with a large or randomly derived sample. I was concerned with variation, but mine is a purposive sample intended to gain as much detailed information as possible about how and why rural industrialization occurred. My method was to develop a rapport that permitted in-depth interviews with those who had detailed knowledge of the local development process. I explored both their formal and informal modes of achieving their goals. Whenever possible, I made repeated visits to the same site to see change over time and to understand the dynamic of the transition I was observing. As the table shows, I did extensive field-work in two counties of Shandong province, one within two hours by superhighway from Ji'nan and the other within three hours of Qingdao. I made three research trips to one of the counties and five to the other between 1988 and 1996. My stays in each county usually lasted one to three weeks. I also spent over two weeks in a county outside Tianjin in 1988.

Aside from a small number of interviews with central-level officials in Beijing, and researchers there and in the provincial social science academies in Tianjin, Liaoning, and Sichuan, the majority of my interviews were with officials at the county, township, and village levels, with managers of industrial enterprises owned by these local governments, and with private entrepreneurs. A smaller number of interviews were with officials at the prefectural and provincial levels. The government agencies where I interviewed included the finance and tax bureaus, banks, material and supply bureaus, rural industry management bureaus, agricultural bureaus, grain bureaus, science and technology commissions, industrial-commercial management bureaus, and economic and planning commissions. I also interviewed county magistrates and county party secretaries, township and village party secretaries, township heads, village committee chairmen, and accountants, and officials of savings and loan cooperatives, supply and marketing cooperatives, grain stations, private entrepreneurs' associations, and semi-official credit associations.

THE INTERVIEW PROCEDURE

Almost all of the 333 interviews I conducted were done with official approval. These were not so-called guerrilla interviews done on the streets or in taxicabs but pre-arranged sessions. While these were authorized, they were not rehearsed sessions with prepared answers. I never submitted my questions in advance nor was I limited in what I could ask. In most cases, I was able to dispense with the formalized "simple introduction" (*jiandan jieshao*) and move directly to an open-ended session where I was able to ask questions directly on topics of my choice and probe issues as they came up in conversation. To make the interviewees feel less inhibited, I took only handwritten notes; no recordings were made of the conversations.

Local authorities arranged my interviews, usually with authorization from the Chinese Academy of Social Sciences or from higher levels of government, and in some cases with direct approval and instructions from Beijing. The usual procedure was for me to submit to the local authorities a list of the offices and units where I wanted to conduct interviews. While this procedure may seem constraining, I came to realize that it ensured that those whom I wanted to interview would have time to see me. Having a pre-arranged schedule enabled me usually to work at least five days a week, sometimes on Saturday, and on rare occasions even on Sunday. I was able to conduct two full three-hour interviews per day and sometimes one after dinner if my time in a locality was particularly tight.

Almost all my requests were granted, and I was allowed to go to the relevant bureau, factory, township, or village to conduct the interviews. In a few instances, especially if my stay was short and I was a first-time visitor, officials were brought to me and I interviewed them in my guesthouse or hotel. In a couple of instances—the least successful of my interviews and a situation that I have since tried hard to avoid—eager-to-please local officials brought a number of those whom I wanted to interview together for a single session. My preferred and usual method of interviewing was to go directly to the unit and speak only to one or two people from the same organization at a time.

My questions focused on the institutional arrangements in the locality. I began with the economic and political organization of the place and then asked about the processes and procedures and changes in the ways things were organized and done. I probed into the technicalities of their work, the resources they controlled, and how they allocated those resources. I always asked for specific examples, and whenever possible for names, dates, and amounts. I asked about restrictions and how they solved problems that arose in their work. As a check on the accuracy of the answers I was receiving, I asked the same questions everywhere I went and asked similar questions of different officials within the same locality.

Whenever appropriate I asked for statistical information to supplement the interviews, although I was not always given all the numbers that I requested. Sometimes the statistical material followed a few days after my visit, especially if I had asked for a long historical run of material. I was most successful in obtaining detailed information from the bureaus where I had already established a relationship; this was one of the reasons for my repeated visits to a few research sites.

I usually did not pay the individuals whom I interviewed;[1] on the contrary I was sometimes given a meal by those I interviewed. These sessions

---

1. I was assessed a research fee by the local authorities for arranging my interviews in addition to the usual costs for research assistance, lodging, and transportation.

often turned into wonderful opportunities to pursue a variety of topics that were sometimes difficult to broach during the formal sessions.

LIMITATIONS

Interviewing in China allows direct access to those who are currently involved in the issues one is attempting to research, but it also carries some costs. In most cases I had a government-provided assistant with me during my interviews, so that these interviews were not as private as I would have liked. But generally, privacy was not a problem. In one county my assistant was a local bureau vice head who had many years of experience dealing with rural industry and detailed knowledge of each of the units I visited. He provided clarification and additional information when I requested it, but normally he simply waited for me to conduct my work. Sometimes, particularly after I had worked with him for some years, he retired to another room as I continued my questioning. I was able to have some private interviews with higher-ranking officials, such as county party secretaries or powerful village party secretaries.

At bureaus and government agencies, I usually spoke with either the bureau head or the vice head. In factories I interviewed mostly the director or vice directors; in private firms I spoke with the owners. Often these were the individuals most open and willing to discuss problems that their subordinates might have shied away from. They called in assistants or accountants who had specialized knowledge and could provide the statistics on issues I was most concerned about. Among the most useful interviews were those with older bureau heads and factory managers who had been in office for decades and had personally experienced the changes I was asking about.

I was required to live in county guesthouses or sometimes in village or factory guesthouses. The guesthouse served as the base from which I would travel to different townships and villages on day trips. I often stayed in those locations for the noon meal, returning at the end of the afternoon's interviews. This arrangement was not ideal for getting to know a village or township, but the noon meals provided an opportunity for more informal exchange and often led to more open discussions in the afternoon sessions. For most of these trips to outlying townships and villages I was accompanied by a driver and my assistant. Sometimes an additional county official might join us to pave the way because the person had good relations with those in the locality where I was interviewing. Fortunately in most instances the group was still limited to two or three individuals. At times, the size and composition of the group limited the questions I could ask, but I learned to make the most of these situations. In a few instances, the presence of higher-level officials turned out to be helpful in authorizing subordinates to provide information that they might otherwise have been hesitant to disclose.

Research in China still involves limitations, and most interviews are with officials or with those approved by officials. However, for my particular topic, this proclivity provided me with easy access to precisely those individuals who could give me the information that I needed. Moreover, these individuals, many of them government officials, were not without criticism of the policies or developments in their areas. Some used me as a conduit for expressing their concerns and criticism.

Despite the inherent problems of interviewing in China and the biases that are likely to result, I remain convinced that interviews are invaluable for understanding the problems and the process of change that has enveloped China over almost two decades of reform. Regulations and statistics are now more readily available, but those alone cannot fully describe the problems localities face in China's rapidly changing economic and political situation. It is the interviews that have provided me with an understanding of the informal politics and the logic behind the various strategies of development adopted by those charged with the implementation of reform.

Changes in China's Fiscal System

TABLE 10. REVENUE-SHARING SYSTEM, 1980

Central Fixed Revenue

Profit from centrally owned enterprises
Customs duty and industrial-commercial tax collected by customs
Industrial-commercial tax from railroads

Local Fixed Revenue

Profit from locally owned enterprises
Salt tax
Agriculture tax
Business income tax
Industrial-commercial tax

Shared Revenue at Fixed Ratio

In 1980, some locally owned enterprises were taken back by the central
government, and their revenue was shared—80% to the center and the
remaining 20% to the local governments.

Adjusted Revenue*

Industrial-commercial tax

SOURCE: Adapted from Ramgopal Agarwala, *China: Reforming Intergovernmental Fiscal Relations*, p. 66.
*Adjusted revenue is shared between central and local government at various ratios depending on the overall revenue situation of each province.

TABLE 11. REVENUE-SHARING SYSTEM, 1985

Central Fixed Revenue

Income tax and adjustment tax of all central government enterprises
Business tax from railroads, bank and insurance company headquarters
Profit remittances from all centrally owned enterprises
Price subsidies paid to producers of grain, cotton, and oil (treated as a negative revenue of the central government)
Fuel oil special tax
Income tax, sales taxes, and royalties from offshore oil activities of foreign companies and joint ventures*
Treasury bond income
70% of the three sales taxes collected from enterprises owned by the Ministry of Petrochemical Industry, the Ministry of Power, SINOPEC, and the China Nonferrous Metals Company
All customs duty and all VAT and product taxes collected at customs
Tobacco tax and business tax on tobacco*
Product tax on liquor and tobacco*

Local Fixed Revenue

Income tax and adjustment tax of locally owned enterprises
Income tax from collectively owned enterprises (ICIT)
Agriculture tax
Rural market trading tax levied on private-sector traders
Local government grain trading loss (a negative tax)
Fines for delinquent taxes
Urban maintenance and construction tax (UMCT)[a]
Housing tax[b]
Vehicle utilization tax
30% of the sales tax revenues collected from enterprises owned by the Ministry of Petrochemical Industry, the Ministry of Power, SINOPEC, and the China Nonferrous Metals Company
Wage bonus tax from state-owned enterprises
Self-employed entrepreneurs tax
Slaughter tax
Cattle-trading tax
Contract tax

Shared Revenue

Sales taxes (VAT, business, and product) from all enterprises, except those marked above with an asterisk
Natural resources tax
Construction tax
Salt tax
Industrial-commercial tax and income tax levied on foreign and joint venture enterprises
Energy and transportation fund tax
Personal income tax

SOURCE: Adapted from Ramgopal Agarwala, *China: Reforming Intergovernmental Fiscal Relations*, p. 67.

[a] UMCT was set at 7% of total sales tax liability for municipalities, 5% for towns, and 1% for all other localities.

[b] Private, owner-occupied houses and government buildings were exempt, and the Housing Bureau paid at a preferential rate of 12%. Payments by enterprises were deductible from adjustments tax liability. The housing tax levied on foreigners was called the "real estate tax"; it was equal to 18% of rental value or 1.2% of capital value. Land was not taxed, only buildings.

*Excluded from shared revenue sales tax.

TABLE 12. EVOLUTION OF CHINA'S
FINANCIAL MANAGEMENT SYSTEM
(1949–1994)[a]

Year	Policy	Content	Administrative Levels Involved	Link Between Local Revenue and Expenditure	Term of Commitment
1950	Unified Control over Revenue and Expenditure (*tongshou tongzhi*)	Total fiscal centralization of revenue and expenditure, except local taxes	None	No	Not set
1951–1957	Divide Revenue and Expenditure, Management by Administrative Levels (*huafen shouzhi, fenji guanli*)	1. Revenue is divided into state revenue, local revenue, and revenue shared by central and local governments, in proportions determined by the balance between local expenditure and revenue. 2. Local expenditure is first met from local budget revenue; shortfall is subsidized from "shared revenue."	1951–1952: center, large administrative areas, provinces; 1953–1957: center, provinces, counties	Yes	One year
1958	Couple Expenditures to Revenue, No Change for Five Years (*yishou dingzhi, wunian bubian*)	1. Local budget revenue is divided into fixed revenue, enterprise shared revenue (20% of enterprise revenue is allocated to the localities by the center), and adjusted revenue. 2. After balancing of revenue and expenditure, surplus is turned over to the center; shortfall is subsidized by the center through enterprise shared revenue, adjusted revenue, or direct fund appropriation.	Center, provinces, and counties	Yes	Five years (in fact, changed after one year)

(continued)

TABLE 12 (*continued*)

Year	Policy	Content	Administrative Levels Involved	Link Between Local Revenue and Expenditure	Term of Commitment
1959–1970	Share Total Revenue, Change Once a Year (*zong'e fencheng, yinian yibian*)	1. Revenue and expenditure power is given to the localities, which contract according to plans. If revenue exceeds expenditure, surplus is shared with the center. 2. The ratio for revenue and expenditure, as well as amount of subsidies, is ratified by the center annually.	Center, provinces, and counties	Yes	One year
1971–1973	Contract System for Revenue and Expenditures (*caizheng shouzhi baogan*)	The center ratifies local revenue and expenditure, which are contracted. Localities guarantee to turn over contracted amount. If expenditure exceeds revenue, the center subsidizes the shortfall. Surpluses are for local use.	Center, provinces, and counties	Yes	One year
1974–1975	Fixed Ratio for Retained Profits (*guding bili liucheng*)	Localities retain revenue by a fixed ratio; surplus revenue is subject to a different ratio; expenditure is contracted by quota.	Center, provinces, and counties	No	One year

(continued)

TABLE 12 (continued)

1976–1979	Link Revenue and Expenditure, Share Total Revenue; or Link Revenue and Expenditure, Share Surplus Revenue (*shouzhi guagou, zong'e fencheng; shouzhi guagou, zengshou fencheng*)	Similar to 1959–1970 system. The center sets amounts for local revenue and expenditure; local revenue and expenditure are linked. The center and the localities share according to total revenue. After 1978, some provinces and cities experiment with "sharing surplus revenue."	Center, provinces, and counties	Yes	One year
1980–1985	Divide Revenue and Expenditure, Contract by Different Administrative Levels (*huafen shouzhi, fenji baogan* [Guangdong and Fujian adopt a lump-sum contract system (*Guangdong Fujian shixing dabaogan*)]	1. Central and local budget revenue and expenditure are divided. 2. Revenue is divided into fixed revenue, fixed-ratio shared revenue, and adjusted revenue; expenditure is the responsibility of the administrative level that owns the enterprises and nonprofit enterprises. 3. Using 1979 as the base year, the surplus is turned over to the center by a fixed ratio; shortfalls are compensated for by a certain ratio of the adjusted revenue. If shortfalls still exist, the center subsidizes by a fixed amount.	Center, provinces, and counties	Yes	Five years
1985–1988	Divide Tax Types, Bind Revenue and Expenditure, Contract by Different Administrative Levels (*huafen shuizhong, heding shouzhi, fenji baogan*)	1. Fixed central revenue, fixed local revenue, and other revenue are divided. 2. Expenditure is still on the basis of administrative level and ownership of enterprises.	Center, provinces, counties, and townships	Yes	Five years

(continued)

TABLE 12 (continued)

Year	Policy	Content	Administrative Levels Involved	Link Between Local Revenue and Expenditure	Term of Commitment
1988–1994	Progressive Contract System (diceng baoganzhi)	Financial contracting for the thirteen provinces and cities that turn over fairly large amounts of revenue. There are three methods: progressive revenue contract; sharing of total revenue plus revenue increase; and sharing of total revenue.	Center, provinces, counties, and townships (along with special administrative districts)	Yes	Three years
1994–	Tax Division System (Fenshuizhi)	1. Tax revenue is divided into three categories: central, local, and central-local shared taxes. 2. Expenditure is divided according to administrative responsibility of central and local government. 3. Tax collecting agencies divided into national tax and local tax offices.	Center, provinces, counties, and townships	Yes	Indefinite

SOURCES: Caizhengbu zonghe jihuasi, Caizheng zhishi wenda, guojia yusuan fence, guojia yusuan guanlixue, pp. 125–39; Caizhengbu yusuansi, Guojia yusuan guanlixue, pp. 24–40; Zhong Pengrong, Shinian jingji gaige, pp. 161–66; Xiaolin Guo, ed. and trans., "Readjusting Central-Local Relations," pp. 5–13.

NOTE: Before 1980, the center sent down quota plans for revenue and expenditures. Local revenue had to fulfill the quota, and local governments were to strive to exceed it. Expenditure could not surpass the central quota, and local governments were expected to save as much as possible. After 1980, the center sent down a quota plan for revenue only; local expenditure was met from revenue retained by the local governments.

TABLE 13. DIVISION OF TAX
CATEGORIES, 1994

Central Taxes	Local Taxes	Central-Local Shared Taxes
Customs duties	Sales tax	Value-added tax
Value-added tax	from enterprises other than railways and head offices	75% central
Consumption tax	of all banks and insurance companies	25% local
Enterprise income tax	Local enterprise income tax	Natural resources tax
from central enterprises	from enterprises other than local banks	offshore oil tax, central;
from local banks	from foreign banks	all other, local
from foreign banks	from other nonbanking financial enterprises	Stock market trading tax
from other nonbanking financial	Profit turnover	50% each
enterprises	from local enterprises	
Sales tax, income tax, profits and	Personal income tax	
urban maintenance and construction	Urban land-use tax	
tax from the railways and head	Fixed-asset investment orientation regulation tax	
offices of all banks and insurance	Urban maintenance and construction tax	
companies	from enterprises other than railways and head offices	
Profit turnover	of banks and insurance companies	
from central enterprises	House property tax	
Tax refunds	Vehicle and vessel license tax	
to enterprises involving foreign	Stamp tax	
countries	Animal slaughter tax	
	Agriculture-animal husbandry tax	
	Special agricultural product tax	
	Farmland-use tax	
	Contract tax	
	Inheritance tax	
	Land value-added tax	
	Compensatory payment	
	for appropriation of state-owned land	

SOURCE: Adapted from Xiaolin Guo, ed. and trans., "Readjusting Central-Local Relations," p. 7.

Bibliography

All material from translation services such as FBIS and JPRS is cited in full in the footnotes and is not included in the bibliography. Original material from Chinese newspapers is also cited in full in the footnotes and not included in the bibliography. All other sources are listed in the bibliography and cited with a shortened title in the footnotes.

CHINESE NEWSPAPERS AND NEWS AGENCY

Guangming ribao
Jiangxi ribao
Jingji daobao (Hong Kong)
Ming pao (Hong Kong)
Shijie jingji daobao
Wen wei po (Hong Kong)
Xinhua
Zhongguo qingnian bao

CHINESE PERIODICALS

Chiu-shih nien-tai (Hong Kong)
Gaige neican
Hebei nongcun gongzuo
Jingji cankao
Jingji yanjiu

Liaowang zhoukan
Nongye jingji wenti
Tang-tai (Hong Kong)
Xiangzhen jingji yanjiu
Zhongguo jingji wenti
Zhongguo nongcun jingji

TRANSLATION SERVICES

Foreign Broadcast Information Service—China (FBIS)
Joint Publications Research Service—China (JPRS-CHI)
Summary of World Broadcasts—The Far East (SWB FE)

BOOKS AND ARTICLES

"1984–1988 nian liangshi shengchande weiguan tanshi" (A Micro-Analysis of 1984–1988 Grain Production). *Zhongguo nongcun jingji*, 20 March 1990, no. 3, pp. 16–24.

Agarwala, Ramgopal. *China: Reforming Intergovernmental Fiscal Relations.* Discussion Paper no. 178. Washington, D.C.: World Bank, 1992.

Alt, James E., and Kenneth A. Shepsle, eds. *Perspectives on Positive Political Economy.* New York: Cambridge University Press, 1990.

Amsden, Alice. "A Theory of Government Intervention in Late Industrialization." In Louis Putterman and Dietrich Rueschemeyer, eds., *State and Market in Development,* pp. 53–84. Boulder, Colo.: Lynne Rienner, 1992.

Anagnost, Ann. "Prosperity and Counter-Prosperity." Unpublished manuscript, October 1986.

Applebaum, Richard, and Jeffrey Henderson. "Situating the State in the East Asian Development Process." In Richard Applebaum and Jeffrey Henderson, eds., *States and Development in the Asian Pacific Rim,* pp. 1–26. Newbury Park, Calif.: Sage Publications, 1992.

Applebaum, Richard, and Jeffrey Henderson, eds. *States and Development in the Asian Pacific Rim.* Newbury Park, Calif.: Sage Publications, 1992.

Bahl, Roy, and Sally Wallace. "Revenue Sharing in Russia." Paper presented at the Taxation, Resources, and Economic Development Conference, "Local and Intergovernmental Finance in Transitional Economies," Lincoln Institute of Land Policy, Cambridge, Mass., 15–16 October 1993.

Banister, Judith. *China's Changing Population.* Stanford, Calif.: Stanford University Press, 1987.

Barnett, A. Doak, with Ezra Vogel. *Cadres, Bureaucracy, and Political Power in Communist China.* New York: Columbia University Press, 1967.

Barzel, Yoram. *Economic Analysis of Property Rights.* New York: Cambridge University Press, 1989.

Bates, Robert. *Markets and States in Tropical Africa: The Political Basis of Agricultural Policies.* Berkeley: University of California Press, 1981.

———. *Beyond the Miracle of the Market: The Political Economy of Agrarian*

Development in Kenya. Cambridge, England: Cambridge University Press, 1989.

————. "Macropolitical Economy in the Field of Development." In James E. Alt and Kenneth A. Shepsle, eds., *Perspectives on Positive Political Economy,* pp. 31–56. New York: Cambridge University Press, 1990.

Baum, Richard, ed. *Reform and Reaction in Post-Mao China: The Road to Tiananmen.* New York: Routledge, 1991.

Bernstein, Thomas. "Stalinism, Famine, and Chinese Peasants." *Theory and Society,* May 1984, vol. 13, no. 3, pp. 339–77.

————. "Local Political Authorities and Economic Reform: Observations from Two Counties in Shandong and Anhui, 1985." Unpublished manuscript.

Bird, Richard. "Intergovernmental Finance and Local Taxation in Developing Countries: Some Basic Considerations for Reformers." *Public Administration and Development,* July–September 1990, vol. 10, no. 31, pp. 277–88.

Bird, Richard, and Christine Wallich. "Local Finance and Economic Reform in Eastern Europe." Paper presented at the Taxation, Resources, and Economic Development Conference, "Local and Intergovernmental Finance in Transitional Economies," Lincoln Institute of Land Policy, Cambridge, Mass., 15–16 October 1993.

Blass, Anthony, Carl Goldstein, and Lincoln Kaye. "Get off Our Backs." *Far Eastern Economic Review,* 15 July 1993, vol. 156, no. 28, pp. 68–70.

Blecher, Marc, and Vivienne Shue. *Tethered Deer: Government and Economy in a Chinese County.* Stanford, Calif.: Stanford University Press, 1996.

Boycko, Maxim, Andrei Shleifer, and Robert Vishny. *Privatizing Russia.* Cambridge, Mass.: MIT Press, 1995.

Brosseau, Maurice, Suzanne Pepper, and Shu-ki Tsang, eds. *China Review 1996.* Hong Kong: Chinese University Press, 1996.

Byrd, William, and Qingsong Lin. "China's Rural Industry: An Introduction." In William Byrd and Qingsong Lin, eds., *China's Rural Industry: Structure, Development, and Reform,* pp. 3–18. New York: Oxford University Press, 1990.

Byrd, William, and Qingsong Lin, eds. *China's Rural Industry: Structure, Development, and Reform.* New York: Oxford University Press, 1990.

Caizhengbu caishui tizhi gaigesi. *Caishui gaige shinian* (Ten Years of Tax Reform). Beijing: Zhongguo caizheng jingji chubanshe, 1989.

Caizhengbu yusuansi. *Guojia yusuan guanlixue* (Management of the National Budget). Beijing: Zhongguo caizheng jingji chubanshe, 1986.

Caizhengbu zonghe jihuasi. *Caizheng zhishi wenda: guojia yusuan fence* (Questions and Answers on Finance: Volume on the National Budget). Beijing: Zhongguo caizheng jingji chubanshe, 1987.

Calder, Kent. *Strategic Capitalism: Private Business and Public Purpose in Japanese Industrial Finance.* Princeton, N.J.: Princeton University Press, 1993.

Cha Zhenxiang. "Lun woguo nongcun gufen hezuozhi chansheng de beijing" (The Background to the Emergence of Our Country's System of Cooperative Shares). *Nongye jingji wenti,* 1994, no. 7, pp. 30–38.

Chan, Anita. "Revolution or Corporatism? Chinese Workers in Search of a Solution." Paper presented at the conference "Toward the Year 2000: Socio-Economic Trends and Consequences in China," Asia Research Centre, Murdoch University, Western Australia, 29–31 January 1992.

Chan, Anita, Richard Madsen, and Jonathan Unger. *Chen Village Under Mao and Deng: Expanded and Updated Edition.* Berkeley: University of California Press, 1992.

Chaudhry, Kiren Aziz. "The Myth of the Market and the Common History of Late Development." *Politics and Society,* September 1993, vol. 21, no. 3, pp. 245–74.

Chen, Chih-jou Jay. "Local Institutions and Property Rights Transformations in Southern Fujian." In Jean C. Oi and Andrew G. Walder, eds., *Property Rights and China's Economic Reforms.* Stanford, Calif.: Stanford University Press, 1999.

Chen Yuming. "Diaodong cunji ganbu gongzuo jiji xing zhi wojian" (My Opinions on the Shift in the Enthusiasm of Village-Level Cadres). *Xiangzhen jingji yanjiu,* 1995, no. 4, p. 42.

China Agricultural Yearbook, 1988. Beijing: Agricultural Publishing House, 1989.

China Statistical Yearbook, 1989. Chicago: China Statistical Information and Consultancy Service Center and University of Illinois, 1990.

China Statistical Yearbook, 1990. Chicago: China Statistical Information and Consultancy Service Center and University of Illinois, 1991.

Chinese Association of Agriculture Students and Scholars. *First Conference Proceedings.* Ithaca, N.Y.: Cornell University, 1989.

Chun, Jacky Tsang Wai. "The Private Sector in Wenzhou." Unpublished manuscript, Hong Kong University of Science and Technology, 1997.

Chung, Jae Ho. "Beijing Confronting the Provinces: The 1994 Tax-Sharing Reform and Its Implications for Central-Provincial Relations in China." *China Information,* Winter 1995, vol. 9, nos. 2/3, pp. 1–23.

Collier, David, and James E. Mahon, Jr. "Conceptual 'Stretching' Revisited: Adapting Categories in Comparative Analysis." *American Political Science Review,* December 1993, vol. 87, no. 4, pp. 845–55.

Collier, Ruth Berins, and David Collier. "Inducements Versus Constraints: Disaggregating 'Corporatism.'" *American Political Science Review,* December 1979, vol. 73, no. 4, pp. 967–86.

Craig, Jon, and George Kopits. "Intergovernmental Fiscal Relations in Transition: The Case of Russia." Paper presented at the Taxation, Resources, and Economic Development Conference, "Local and Intergovernmental Finance in Transitional Economies," Lincoln Institute of Land Policy, Cambridge, Mass., 15–16 October 1993.

Crook, Frederick. "Current Problems and Future Development of China's Agricultural Sector." In Chinese Association of Agricultural Students and Scholars, *First Conference Proceedings,* pp. 9–19. Ithaca, N.Y.: Cornell University, 1989.

———. *China: Agriculture and Trade Report.* Economic Research Service, no. RS-89-5. Washington, D.C.: U.S. Department of Agriculture, November 1989.

————. "Sources of Rural Instability." *China Business Review,* July–August 1990, vol. 17, no. 4, pp. 12–15.

Cyert, Richard, and James March. *A Behavioral Theory of the Firm.* Englewood Cliffs, N.J.: Prentice-Hall, 1963.

Davis, Deborah, and Ezra Vogel, eds. *Chinese Society on the Eve of Tiananmen: The Impact of Reform.* Cambridge, Mass.: Council on East Asian Studies, Harvard University, 1990.

Delman, Jorgen. "Current Peasant Discontent in China: Backgrounds and Political Implications." *China Information,* autumn 1989, vol. 4, no. 2, pp. 42–64.

Demsetz, Harold. "The Structure of Ownership and the Theory of the Firm." *Journal of Law and Economics,* June 1983, vol. 26, no. 2, pp. 375–90.

Donnithorne, Audrey. *China's Economic System.* London: George Allen and Unwin, 1967.

————. *Centre-Provincial Economic Relations in China.* Canberra: Contemporary China Centre, Research School of Pacific Studies, Australian National University, 1981.

Downs, Anthony. *Inside Bureaucracy.* Boston: Little, Brown, 1967.

Duckett, Jane. "Market Reform and the Emergence of the Entrepreneurial State in China: The Case of State Commercial and Real Estate Departments in Tianjin." Unpublished manuscript, 1997.

Eatwell, J., M. Milgate, and P. Newman, eds. *The New Palgrave: A Dictionary of Economics,* vol. 3. New York: Stockton Press, 1987.

Evans, Peter. *Embedded Autonomy: States and Industrial Transformation.* Princeton, N.J.: Princeton University Press, 1995.

Evans, Peter B., Dietrich Rueschemeyer, and Theda Skocpol. *Bringing the State Back In.* New York: Cambridge University Press, 1985.

Fei Xiaotong. "Nongcun, xiaochengzhen chuyu fazhan" (The Process and Development of Township Villages). *Beijing daxue xuebao,* 1995, no. 2, pp. 4–11.

Fewsmith, Joseph. *Party, State, and Local Elites in Republican China: Merchant Organizations and Politics in Shanghai, 1890–1930.* Honolulu: University of Hawaii Press, 1985.

————. *Dilemmas of Reform in China: Political Conflict and Economic Debate.* Armonk, N.Y.: M. E. Sharpe, 1994.

Financial Structural Reform Department of the People's Bank of China. "Survey of Reform of Financial System in 1990." In Gao Shangquan and Sen Ye, eds., *China Economic Systems Reform Yearbook 1991,* pp. 100–105. Beijing: China Reform Publishing House, 1991.

Francis, Corinna-Barbara. "Bargained Property Rights: China's High Technology Spin-off Firms." In Jean C. Oi and Andrew G. Walder, eds., *Property Rights and China's Economic Reforms.* Stanford, Calif.: Stanford University Press, 1999.

Freeman, Richard. "Labor Markets and Institutions in Economic Development." *American Economic Review,* May 1993, vol. 83, no. 2, pp. 403–8.

Friedman, Debra, and Michael Hechter. "The Contribution of Rational Choice Theory to Macrosociological Research." *Sociological Theory,* fall 1988, vol. 6, no. 2, pp. 201–18.

Gao Shangquan and Sen Ye, eds. *China Economic Systems Reform Yearbook 1991*. Beijing: China Reform Publishing House, 1991.

Gerschenkron, Alexander. *Economic Backwardness in Historical Perspective.* Cambridge, Mass.: Harvard University Press, 1962.

Goldstein, Steven M. "China in Transition: The Political Foundations of Incremental Reform." *China Quarterly,* December 1995, no. 144, pp. 1105–31.

Goodman, David S. G., and Beverley Hooper, eds. *China's Quiet Revolution: New Interactions Between State and Society.* Melbourne, Australia: Longman Cheshire, 1994.

Grindle, Merilee, ed. *Politics and Policy Implementation in the Third World.* Princeton, N.J.: Princeton University Press, 1980.

Grindle, Merilee, and John W. Thomas. *Public Choices and Policy Change: The Political Economy of Reform in Developing Countries.* Baltimore: Johns Hopkins University Press, 1991.

Guo, Xiaolin. "Variation in Local Property Rights: The Role of Local Government Incentives in Northwest Yunnan." In Jean C. Oi and Andrew G. Walder, eds., *Property Rights and China's Economic Reforms.* Stanford, Calif.: Stanford University Press, 1999.

Guo, Xiaolin, ed. and trans. "Readjusting Central-Local Relations in Revenue Distribution: China's 1994 Fiscal Reform." *Chinese Economic Studies,* July–August 1996, vol. 29, no. 4, pp. 5–13.

Guowuyuan, "Guowuyuan guanyu jiaqiang yusuanwai zijin guanli de tongzhi" (Notice on Strengthening the Management of Extrabudgetary Revenues), April 13, 1986. In Guowuyuan Fazhiju, ed., *Zhonghua renmin gongheguo fagui huibian* (Compilation of the Laws of the People's Republic of China), January–December 1986, pp. 339–42. Beijing: Falü chubanshe, 1987.

Guowuyuan Fazhiju, ed. *Zhonghua renmin gongheguo fagui huibian* (Compilation of the Laws of the People's Republic of China) January–December 1986. Beijing: Falü chubanshe, 1987.

Haggard, Stephan, and Robert Kaufman. "The State in the Initiation and Consolidation of Market Oriented Reform." In Louis Putterman and Dietrich Rueschemeyer, eds., *State and Market in Development,* pp. 221–42. Boulder, Colo.: Lynne Rienner, 1992.

He Kang, "Woguo nongcun gaige, nongye shengchande xianzhuang yu qianjing" (The Current Situation and Prospects for Our Country's Rural Reforms and Agricultural Production). Unpublished paper presented at Hong Kong University of Science and Technology. 3 March 1996.

He Xian. "Woguo xiangzhen qiye shouru fenpei wenti" (The Question of Our Country's Rural Enterprise Income Distribution). *Zhongguo nongcun jingji,* 1988, no. 3, p. 34.

Holz, Carsten. *The Role of Central Banking in China's Economic Reforms.* Ithaca, N.Y.: East Asian Program, Cornell University, 1992.

———. "Implementation of Contractionary Macroeconomic Policy in China: A Case Study of Administrative Control over Investment in 1988/89." Working Papers in the Social Sciences, no. 24. Hong Kong: Division of Social Science, Hong Kong University of Science and Technology, July 1997.

Hua, Sheng, Xuejun Zhang, and Xiaopeng Luo. *China: From Revolution to Reform*. London: Macmillan, 1993.

Huang, Yasheng. *Inflation and Investment Controls in China: The Political Economy of Central-Local Relations During the Reform Era*. New York: Cambridge University Press, 1996.

Hughes, Helen, ed. *Achieving Industrialization in East Asia*. New York: Cambridge University Press, 1988.

Jensen, Michael. "Organization Theory and Methodology." *Accounting Review,* April 1983, vol. 58, no. 2, pp. 319–39.

Jensen, Michael, and William Meckling. "Theory of the Firm: Managerial Behavior, Agency Costs, and Ownership Structure." *Journal of Financial Economics,* October 1976, vol. 3, no. 4, pp. 305–60.

Johnson, Chalmers. *MITI and the Japanese Miracle: The Growth of Industrial Policy, 1925–1975*. Stanford, Calif.: Stanford University Press, 1982.

———. "Capitalism: East Asian Style." Panglaykim Memorial Lecture, Jakarta, Indonesia, 15 December 1992.

Johnson, Graham. "The Fate of the Communal Economy." Unpublished manuscript.

Kelliher, Daniel. *Peasant Power in China: The Era of Rural Reform, 1979–1989*. New Haven, Conn.: Yale University Press, 1992.

———. "The Chinese Debate over Village Self-Government." *The China Journal,* January 1997, no. 37, pp. 63–86.

Khan, Azizur Rahman, et al. "Household Income and Its Distribution in China." *China Quarterly,* December 1992, no. 132, pp. 1029–61.

Kornai, János. *The Road to a Free Economy: Shifting from a Socialist System: The Example of Hungary*. New York: Norton, 1990.

———. *The Socialist System: The Political Economy of Communism*. Princeton, N.J.: Princeton University Press, 1992.

Kraus, Willy. *Private Business in China: Revival Between Ideology and Pragmatism*. Honolulu: University of Hawaii Press, 1991.

Krueger, Anne. "The Political Economy of the Rent-Seeking Society." *American Economic Review,* June 1974, vol. 64, no. 3, pp. 291–303.

Krugman, Paul. "The Myth of Asia's Miracle." *Foreign Affairs,* November–December 1994, vol. 73, no. 6, pp. 62–78.

Kung, James Kai-sing. "Property Rights in Chinese Agriculture." Paper presented at the annual meeting of the Association for Asian Studies, Los Angeles, 25–28 March 1993.

———. "The Evolution of Property Rights in Village Enterprises: The Case of Wuxi County." In Jean C. Oi and Andrew G. Walder, eds., *Property Rights and China's Economic Reforms*. Stanford, Calif.: Stanford University Press, 1999.

Latham, Richard. "The Implications of Rural Reform for Grass-Roots Cadres." In Elizabeth Perry and Christine Wong, eds., *The Political Economy of Reform in Post-Mao China*, pp. 157–73. Cambridge, Mass.: Council on East Asian Studies, Harvard University, 1985.

Lee, Hong Yung. *From Revolutionary Cadres to Party Technocrats in Socialist China*. Berkeley: University of California Press, 1991.

Lee, Peter Nan-shong. "The Chinese Industrial State in Historical Perspective: From Totalitarianism to Corporatism." In Brantly Womack, ed., *Contemporary Chinese Politics in Historical Perspective*, pp. 153–79. Cambridge, England: Cambridge University Press, 1991.

Levi, Margaret. *Of Rule and Revenue*. Berkeley: University of California Press, 1988.

Lin, Yi-min, and Zhanxin Zhang. "The Private Assets of Public Servants: Profit-Seeking Entities Sponsored by State Agencies." In Jean C. Oi and Andrew G. Walder, eds., *Property Rights and China's Economic Reforms*. Stanford, Calif.: Stanford University Press, 1999.

Little, Daniel. "Rational-Choice Models and Asian Studies." *Journal of Asian Studies*, February 1991, vol. 50, no. 1, pp. 35–52.

Liu, Yia-Ling. "Reform from Below: The Private Economy and Local Politics in the Rural Industrialization of Wenzhou." *China Quarterly*, June 1992, no. 130, pp. 293–316.

Lu Mai. "Reform of the Incremental Economy." Unpublished manuscript, 1993.

"Lun nongcun xinyongsuode kunjing yu gaige silu" (On the Difficulties Facing Rural Credit Unions and Reform). *Zhongguo nongcun jingji*, 20 June 1990, no. 6, pp. 35–42.

Manion, Melanie. "The Electoral Connection in the Chinese Countryside." *American Political Science Review*, December 1996, vol. 90, no. 4, pp. 736–48.

March, James G., and Johan P. Olsen. *Rediscovering Institutions: The Organizational Basis of Politics*. New York: Free Press, 1989.

March, James G., and Herbert Simon. *Organizations*. New York: Wiley, 1958.

Martinez-Vazquez, Jorge. "Expenditure Assignment in the Russian Federation." Paper presented at the Taxation, Resources, and Economic Development Conference, "Local and Intergovernmental Finance in Transitional Economies," Lincoln Institute of Land Policy, Cambridge, Mass., 15–16 October 1993.

McCormick, Barrett. *Political Reform in Post-Mao China: Democracy and Bureaucracy in a Leninist State*. Berkeley: University of California Press, 1990.

McKinnon, Ronald. *The Order of Economic Liberalism: Financial Control in the Transition to a Market Economy*. Baltimore: Johns Hopkins University Press, 1991.

———. *Gradual Versus Rapid Liberalization in Socialist Economies: Financial Policies in China and Russia Compared*. San Francisco: ICS Press, 1994.

McMillan, John, and Barry Naughton. "How to Reform a Planned Economy: Lessons from China." *Oxford Review of Economic Policy*, spring 1992, vol. 8, no. 1, pp. 130–42.

Migdal, Joel S. *Strong Societies and Weak States: State-Society Relations and State Capabilities in the Third World*. Princeton, N.J.: Princeton University Press, 1988.

Mirrlees, J. "The Optimal Structure of Incentives and Authority within an Organization." *Bell Journal of Economics*, spring 1976, vol. 7, no. 1, pp. 105–31.

Mitchell, Timothy. "The Limits of the State: Beyond Statist Approaches and their Critics." *American Political Science Review*, March 1991, vol. 85, no. 1, pp. 77–96.

Moe, Terry. "The New Economics of Organization." *American Journal of Political Science,* November 1984, vol. 28, no. 4, pp. 739–77.

Montinola, Gabriella, Yingyi Qian, and Barry Weingast. "Federalism, Chinese Style: The Political Basis for Economic Success in China." Unpublished manuscript. Stanford, Calif.: Stanford University and the Hoover Institution, 1993.

Moore, Barrington, Jr. *Social Origins of Dictatorship and Democracy: Lord and Peasant in the Making of the Modern World.* Boston: Beacon Press, 1966.

Munro, J. E. C. "Principal and Agent (i)." In J. Eatwell, M. Milgate, and P. Newman, eds., *The New Palgrave: A Dictionary of Economics,* vol. 3, p. 966. New York: Stockton Press, 1987.

Murrell, Peter, and Mancur Olson. "The Devolution of Centrally Planned Economies." *Journal of Comparative Economics,* June 1991, vol. 15, no. 2, pp. 239–65.

Naughton, Barry. "The Decline of Central Control over Investment in Post-Mao China." In David M. Lampton, ed., *Policy Implementation in Post-Mao China,* pp. 51–80. Berkeley: University of California Press, 1987.

———. "Implications of the State Monopoly over Industry and Its Relaxation." *Modern China,* January 1992, vol. 18, no. 1, pp. 14–41.

Nee, Victor. "A Theory of Market Transition: From Redistribution to Markets in State Socialism." *American Sociological Review,* October 1989, vol. 54, no. 5, pp. 663–72.

———. "Organizational Dynamics of Market Transition: Hybrid Forms, Property Rights, and Mixed Economy in China." *Administrative Science Quarterly,* March 1992, vol. 37, no. 1, pp. 1–28.

Nee, Victor, and Sijin Su. "Institutional Change and Economic Growth in China: The View from the Village." *Journal of Asian Studies,* January 1990, vol. 49, no. 1, pp. 3–25.

Nelson, Joan. "The Politics of Economic Transformation: Is Third World Experience Relevant in Eastern Europe?" *World Politics,* April 1993, vol. 45, no. 3, pp. 433–63.

Niskanen, William. "Bureaucrats and Politicians." *Journal of Law and Economics,* December 1975, vol. 18, no. 3, pp. 617–43.

Nongyebu xiangzhen qiyeju jihua caiwuchu. *Quanguo xiangzhen qiye jiben qingkuang ji jingji yunxing fenxi, 1996 nian* (Analysis of Basic Conditions and Economic Balance of Township Village Enterprises in the Entire Country, 1996). Beijing: Nongyebu xiangzhen qiyeju jihua caiwuchu, 1997.

Nongyebu xiangzhen qiyesi jihua caiwuchu. *1995 nian quanguo xiangzhen qiye jiben qingkuang ji jingji yunxing fenxi* (Analysis of Basic Conditions and Economic Balance of Township Village Enterprises in the Entire Country, 1995). Beijing: Nongyebu xiangzhen qiyesi jihua caiwuchu, 1996.

Nordlinger, Eric. *On the Autonomy of the Democratic State.* Cambridge, Mass.: Harvard University Press, 1981.

Nordlinger, Eric, Theodore Lowi, and Sergio Fabbrini. "The Return to the State: Critiques." *American Political Science Review,* September 1988, vol. 82, no. 3, pp. 875–901.

North, Douglass. *Structure and Change in Economic History.* New York: Norton, 1981.

————. *Institutions, Institutional Change and Economic Performance.* Cambridge, England: Cambridge University Press, 1990.

North, Douglass, and Barry R. Weingast. "Constitutions and Commitment: The Evolution of Institutions Governing Public Choice in Seventeenth-Century England." *Journal of Economic History,* December 1989, vol. 49, no. 4, pp. 803–32.

O'Brien, Kevin. "Implementing Political Reform in China's Villages." *Australian Journal of Chinese Affairs,* July 1994, no. 32, pp. 33–60.

O'Brien, Kevin, and Lianjiang Li. "Villagers and Popular Resistance in Contemporary China." *Modern China,* January 1996, vol. 22, no. 11, pp. 28–61.

Odgaard, Ole. *Private Enterprises in Rural China: Impact on Agricultural and Social Stratification.* Brookfield, Vt.: Ashgate, 1992.

Ody, Anthony J. *Rural Enterprise Development in China, 1986–90.* Discussion Paper no. 162. Washington, D.C.: World Bank, 1992.

Oi, Jean C. "Communism and Clientelism: Rural Politics in China." *World Politics,* January 1985, vol. 37, no. 2, pp. 238–66.

————. "Peasant Grain Marketing and State Procurements: China's Grain Contracting System." *China Quarterly,* June 1986, no. 106, pp. 272–90.

————. "Commercializing China's Rural Cadres." *Problems of Communism,* September–October 1986, vol. 35, no. 5, pp. 1–15.

————. "The Chinese Village, Inc." In Bruce Reynolds, ed., *Chinese Economic Policy: Economic Reform at Midstream,* pp. 67–87. New York: Paragon House, for Professors World Peace Academy, 1988.

————. *State and Peasant in Contemporary China: The Political Economy of Village Government.* Berkeley: University of California Press, 1989.

————. "The Fate of the Collective After the Commune." In Deborah Davis and Ezra Vogel, eds., *Chinese Society on the Eve of Tiananmen: The Impact of Reform,* pp. 15–36. Cambridge, Mass.: Council on East Asian Studies, Harvard University, 1990.

————. "Fiscal Reform, Central Directives, and Local Autonomy in Rural China." Paper presented at the annual meeting of the American Political Science Association, Washington, D.C., 29 August–1 September 1991.

————. "Private and Local State Entrepreneurship: The Shandong Case." Paper presented at the annual meeting of the Association for Asian Studies, Washington, D.C., 2–5 April 1992.

————. "Fiscal Reform and the Economic Foundations of Local State Corporatism in China." *World Politics,* October 1992, vol. 45, no. 1, pp. 99–126.

————. "Reform and Urban Bias in China." *Journal of Development Studies,* July 1993, vol. 29, no. 4, pp. 129–48.

————. "Rational Choices and the Attainment of Wealth and Power in the Countryside." In David S. G. Goodman and Beverley Hooper, eds., *China's Quiet Revolution: New Interactions Between State and Society,* pp. 64–79. Melbourne, Australia: Longman Cheshire, 1994.

————. "The Role of the Local State in China's Transitional Economy." *China Quarterly,* December 1995, no. 144, pp. 1132–49.

————. "Cadre Networks, Information Diffusion, and Market Production in

Coastal China." Private Sector Development Department, Occasional Paper no. 20. Washington, D.C.: World Bank, December 1995.

———. "Economic Development, Stability and Democratic Village Self-Governance." In Maurice Brosseau, Suzanne Pepper, and Shu-ki Tsang, eds., *China Review 1996,* pp. 125–44. Hong Kong: Chinese University Press, 1996.

———. "The Evolution of Local State Corporatism." In Andrew Walder, ed., *Zouping in Transition: The Process of Reform in Rural North China,* pp. 35–61. Cambridge, Mass.: Harvard University Press, 1998.

Oi, Jean C., and Scott Rozelle. "Democracy and Markets: The Link Between Participatory Decision-Making and Development in China's Rural Reforms." Paper presented at the annual meeting of the Association for Asian Studies, Chicago, 13–16 March 1997.

Oi, Jean C., and Andrew G. Walder, eds. *Property Rights and China's Economic Reforms.* Stanford, Calif.: Stanford University Press, 1999.

Okimoto, Daniel. *Between MITI and the Market: Japanese Industrial Policy for High Technology.* Stanford, Calif.: Stanford University Press, 1989.

Oksenberg, Michel, and James Tong. "The Evolution of Central-Provincial Fiscal Relations in China, 1971–1984: The Formal System." *China Quarterly,* March 1991, no. 125, pp. 1–32.

Ost, David. "Towards a Corporatist Solution in Eastern Europe: The Case of Poland." *Eastern European Politics and Societies,* winter 1989, vol. 3, no. 1, pp. 152–74.

Parish, William, and Martin Whyte. *Village and Family in Contemporary China.* Chicago: University of Chicago Press, 1978.

Park, Albert, Scott Rozelle, Christine Wong, and Changqing Ren. "Distributional Consequences of Reforming Local Public Finance in China." *China Quarterly,* September 1996, no. 147, pp. 751–78.

Parris, Kristen. "Local Initiative and National Reform: The Wenzhou Model of Development." *China Quarterly,* June 1993, no. 134, pp. 242–63.

Pearson, Margaret. *China's New Business Elite: The Political Consequences of Economic Reform.* Berkeley: University of California Press, 1997.

Peck, Merton, and Thomas Richardson, eds. *What Is to Be Done? Proposals for the Soviet Transition to the Market.* New Haven, Conn.: Yale University Press, 1991.

Pei, Minxin. *From Reform to Revolution: The Demise of Communism in China and the Soviet Union.* Cambridge, Mass.: Harvard University Press, 1994.

Pierson, Paul. "When Effect Becomes Cause: Policy Feedback and Political Change." *World Politics,* July 1993, vol. 45, no. 4, pp. 595–628.

Pike, Frederick B., and Thomas Stritch, eds. *The New Corporatism: Social-Political Structures in the Iberian World.* Notre Dame, Ind.: University of Notre Dame Press, 1974.

Pitt, Mark, and Louis Putterman. "Employment and Wages in Township, Village and Other Enterprises." Unpublished manuscript, Department of Economics, Brown University, 1992.

Pratt, John W., and Richard J. Zeckhauser, eds. *Principals and Agents: The Structure of Business.* Boston: Harvard Business School Press, 1985.

Prime, Penelope. "Taxation Reform in China's Public Finance." In U.S. Congress Joint Economic Committee, *China's Economic Dilemmas in the 1990s: The Problems of Reforms, Modernization, and Interdependence,* vol. 1, pp. 167–85. Washington, D.C.: U.S. Government Printing Office, 1991.

Putterman, Louis, and Dietrich Rueschemeyer, eds. *State and Market in Development.* Boulder, Colo.: Lynne Rienner, 1992.

Qian, Yingyi, and Chenggang Xu. "Why China's Economic Reforms Differ: The M-Form Hierarchy and Entry/Expansion of the Non-State Sector." *Economics of Transition,* 1993, vol. 1, no. 2, pp. 135–70.

Reynolds, Bruce, ed. *Chinese Economic Policy: Economic Reform at Midstream.* New York: Paragon House, for Professors World Peace Academy, 1988.

Riskin, Carl. "China's Rural Industries: Self-Reliant Systems or Independent Kingdoms?" *China Quarterly,* March 1978, no. 73, pp. 77–98.

Ross, Stephen. "The Economic Theory of Agency: The Principal's Problem." *American Economic Review,* May 1973, vol. 63, no. 2, pp. 134–39.

Rozelle, Scott. "The Economic Behavior of Village Leaders in China's Reform Economy." Ph.D. dissertation, Cornell University, 1991.

———. "Principals and Agents in China's Rural Economy: A Decision Making Framework of Township Officials, Village Leaders and Farm Households." Unpublished manuscript, 1991.

———. "Decision-Making in China's Rural Economy: The Linkages Between Village Leaders and Farm Households." *China Quarterly,* March 1994, no. 137, pp. 99–125.

———. "Rural Industrialization and Increasing Inequality: Emerging Patterns in China's Reforming Economy." *Journal of Comparative Economics,* December 1994, vol. 19, no. 3, pp. 362–92.

Rueschemeyer, Dietrich, and Peter B. Evans. "The State and Economic Transformation: Toward an Analysis of the Conditions Underlying Effective Intervention." In Peter B. Evans, Dietrich Rueschemeyer, and Theda Skocpöl, *Bringing the State Back In,* pp. 44–76. New York: Cambridge University Press, 1985.

Ruf, Gregory. "Collective Enterprise and Property Rights in a Sichuan Village: The Rise and Decline of Managerial Corporatism." In Jean C. Oi and Andrew G. Walder, eds., *Property Rights and China's Economic Reforms.* Stanford, Calif.: Stanford University Press, 1999.

Sachs, Jeffrey. *Poland's Jump to the Market Economy.* Cambridge, Mass.: MIT Press, 1993.

Sartori, Giovanni. "Concept Misformation in Comparative Politics." *American Political Science Review,* December 1970, vol. 64, no. 4, pp. 1033–53.

Schmitter, Philippe. "Still the Century of Corporatism?" In Frederick B. Pike and Thomas Stritch, eds., *The New Corporatism: Social-Political Structures in the Iberian World,* pp. 85–131. Notre Dame, Ind.: University of Notre Dame Press, 1974.

Schurmann, Franz. *Ideology and Organization in Communist China.* Berkeley: University of California Press, 1968.

Scott, James C. *The Moral Economy of the Peasant: Rebellion and Subsistence in Southeast Asia.* New Haven, Conn.: Yale University Press, 1976.

Selznick, Philip. *The Organizational Weapon: A Study of Bolshevik Strategy and Tactics.* New York: McGraw-Hill, 1952.

Shandong tongjiju. *Huihuang chengjiu: nongcun gaige shinan* (The Achievements of Ten Years of Agricultural Reform). Ji'nan, China: Shandongsheng tongjiju, 1989.

Shandong Zouping. Beijing: Zhongguo zhanwang chubanshe, 1990.

Shirk, Susan. *The Political Logic of Economic Reform in China.* Berkeley: University of California Press, 1993.

Shue, Vivienne. "Beyond the Budget: Finance Organization and Reform in a Chinese County." *Modern China*, April 1984, vol. 10, no. 2, pp. 147–86.

———. *The Reach of the State: Sketches of the Chinese Body Politic.* Stanford, Calif.: Stanford University Press, 1988.

Sicular, Terry. "China's Agricultural Policy During the Reform Period." In U.S. Congress Joint Economic Committee, *China's Economic Dilemmas in the 1990s: The Problems of Reforms, Modernization, and Interdependence,* vol. 1, pp. 340–64. Washington, D.C.: U.S. Government Printing Office, 1991.

Simon, Herbert. *Administrative Behavior: A Study of Decision-Making Processes in Administrative Organization.* New York: Macmillan, 1947.

Siu, Helen. *Agents and Victims in South China: Accomplices in Rural Revolution.* New Haven, Conn.: Yale University Press, 1989.

Skocpol, Theda. *Protecting Soldiers and Mothers: The Political Origins of Social Policy in the United States.* Cambridge, Mass.: Belknap Press, 1992.

Solinger, Dorothy J. *Chinese Business Under Socialism: The Politics of Domestic Commerce, 1949–1980.* Berkeley: University of California Press, 1984.

———. "Urban Reform and Relational Contracting in Post-Mao China." In Richard Baum, ed., *Reform and Reaction in Post-Mao China: The Road to Tiananmen,* pp. 104–23. New York: Routledge, 1991.

Spence, Michael, and Richard Zeckhauser. "Insurance, Information, and Individual Action." *American Economic Review,* May 1971, vol. 61, no. 2, pp. 380–87.

Steinfeld, Edward. *Forging Reform in China: The Fate of State-Owned Industry.* New York: Cambridge University Press, 1998.

Stepan, Alfred. *The State and Society: Peru in Comparative Perspective.* Princeton, N.J.: Princeton University Press, 1978.

Stiglitz, Joseph. "Principal and Agent (ii)." In J. Eatwell, M. Milgate, and P. Newman, eds., *The New Palgrave: A Dictionary of Economics,* vol. 3, p. 966. New York: Stockton Press, 1987.

Streeten, Paul. "Markets and States: Against Minimalism." *World Development,* August 1993, vol. 21, no. 8, pp. 1281–98.

Tam On Kit. "Fiscal Policy Issues in China." Unpublished manuscript, University of New South Wales, Canberra, Australia, 1990.

———. "Prospects for Reforming China's Financial System." Paper presented at "Conference on China's Reforms and Economic Growth," Australian National University, 1991.

Taylor, Jeffrey. "Rural Employment Trends and the Legacy of Surplus Labour, 1978–1986." *China Quarterly,* December 1988, no. 116, pp. 736–66.

Tong, James. "Fiscal Reform, Elite Turnover and Central-Provincial Relations in Post-Mao China." *Australian Journal of Chinese Affairs,* July 1989, no. 22, pp. 1–28.

———. "Central-Provincial Fiscal Relations in Post-Mao China." Unpublished manuscript.

Tyson, James L., "China to Boost Loans to Rural Enterprises." *Christian Science Monitor,* 26 March 1990.

Unger, Jonathan. "The Struggle to Dictate China's Administration: The Conflict of Branches vs. Areas vs. Reform." *Australian Journal of Chinese Affairs,* July 1987, no. 18, pp. 15–45.

Unger, Jonathan, and Anita Chan. "China, Corporatism, and the East Asian Model." *Australian Journal of Chinese Affairs,* January 1995, no. 33, pp. 29–53.

U.S. Congress Joint Economic Committee. *China's Economic Dilemmas in the 1990s: The Problems of Reforms, Modernization, and Interdependence.* Washington, D.C.: U.S. Government Printing Office, 1991.

Vermeer, Eduard. "The Development of the Shareholding Cooperative System: A Property Rights Analysis." In Jean C. Oi and Andrew G. Walder, eds., *Property Rights and China's Economic Reforms.* Stanford, Calif.: Stanford University Press, 1999.

Vogel, Ezra. *One Step Ahead in China: Guangdong Under Reform.* Cambridge, Mass.: Harvard University Press, 1989.

Wade, Robert. "The Role of Government in Overcoming Market Failure: Taiwan, Republic of Korea, and Japan." In Helen Hughes, ed., *Achieving Industrialization in East Asia,* pp. 129–63. New York: Cambridge University Press, 1988.

———. *Governing the Market: Economic Theory and the Role of Government in East Asian Industrialization.* Princeton, N.J.: Princeton University Press, 1990.

Walder, Andrew G. *Communist Neo-Traditionalism: Work and Authority in Chinese Industry.* Berkeley: University of California Press, 1986.

———. "Local Governments as Industrial Firms: An Organizational Analysis of China's Transitional Economy." *American Journal of Sociology,* September 1995, vol. 101, no. 2, pp. 263–301.

———. "The County Government as an Industrial Corporation." In Andrew G. Walder, ed., *Zouping in Transition: The Process of Reform in Rural North China.* Cambridge, Mass.: Harvard University Press, 1998.

Walder, Andrew G., ed. *The Waning of the Communist State: Economic Origins of Political Decline in China and Hungary.* Berkeley: University of California Press, 1995.

Wang Qiang. "2000 nian zhongxibu nongcun shixin xiaokang de chengdu you duoda" (Prospects for Villages in China's Central and Western Regions to Attain a Basically Comfortable Standard of Living by the Year 2000). *Gaige neican,* 1995, no. 9, pp. 33–35.

Wang Qinglin, and Wenke Fan. "Jiaqiang nongcun jiceng dang zuzhi jianshe shi dangwu zhi ji" (Strengthening Basic-Level Party Organization Is a Party Task). *Hebei nongcun gongzuo,* 1994, no. 12, pp. 7–8.

Wang, Shaoguang. "The Rise of the Regions: Fiscal Reform and the Decline of Central State Capacity in China." In Andrew G. Walder, ed., *The Waning of the Communist State,* pp. 87–113. Berkeley: University of California Press, 1995.

Wang Xiaoxu, ed. *Nashui shiyong shouce* (Tax Handbook). Beijing: Zhongguo zhanwang chubanshe, 1988.

Wank, David. "From State Socialism to Community Capitalism: State Power, Social Structure, and Private Enterprise in a Chinese City." Ph.D. dissertation, Harvard University, 1993.

———. "Bureaucratic Patronage and Private Business: Changing Networks of Power in Urban China." In Andrew G. Walder, ed., *The Waning of the Communist State,* pp. 153–83. Berkeley: University of California Press, 1995.

———. "Social Networks and Property Rights: Enforcement, Expectations, and Efficiency in the Urban Nonstate Economy." In Jean C. Oi and Andrew G. Walder, eds., *Property Rights and China's Economic Reforms.* Stanford, Calif.: Stanford University Press, 1999.

Watson, Andrew, ed. *Economic Reform and Social Change in China.* New York: Routledge, 1992.

Weitzman, Martin, and Chenggang Xu. "Chinese Township-Village Enterprises as Vaguely Defined Cooperatives." *Journal of Comparative Economics,* April 1994, vol. 18, no. 2, pp. 121–45.

White, Harrison C. "Agency as Control." In John W. Pratt and Richard J. Zeckhauser, eds., *Principals and Agents: The Structure of Business,* pp. 187–212. Boston: Harvard Business School Press, 1985.

White, Lynn T., III. *Shanghai Shanghaied? Uneven Taxes in Reform China.* Occasional Papers and Monographs, no. 84. Hong Kong: Centre of Asian Studies, University of Hong Kong, 1989.

White, Tyrene. "Political Reform and Rural Government." In Deborah Davis and Ezra Vogel, eds., *Chinese Society on the Eve of Tiananmen,* pp. 37–60. Cambridge, Mass.: Council on East Asian Studies, Harvard University, 1990.

———. "Below Bureaucracy: The Burden of Being a Village Under the Local State." Paper presented at the annual meeting of the Association for Asian Studies, Chicago, 5–8 April 1990.

———. "Postrevolutionary Mobilization in China: The One-Child Policy Reconsidered." *World Politics,* October 1990, vol. 43, no. 1, pp. 53–77.

———. "Reforming the Countryside." *Current History,* September 1992, vol. 91, no. 566, pp. 273–77.

Whiting, Susan. "The Micro-Foundation of Institutional Change in Reform China: Property Rights and Revenue Extraction in the Rural Industrial Sector." Ph.D. dissertation, University of Michigan, 1995.

———. "The Regional Evolution of Ownership Forms: Shareholding Cooperatives and Rural Industry in Songjiang and Wenzhou." In Jean C. Oi and Andrew G. Walder, eds., *Property Rights and China's Economic Reforms.* Stanford, Calif.: Stanford University Press, 1999.

Whyte, Martin, and William Parish. *Urban Life in Contemporary China.* Chicago: University of Chicago Press, 1984.

Winiecki, Jan. "Are Soviet-Type Economies Entering an Era of Long-Term Decline?" *Soviet Studies,* July 1986, vol. 38, no. 3, pp. 325–48.

Wong, Christine. "Interpreting Rural Industrial Growth in the Post-Mao Period." *Modern China,* January 1988, vol. 14, no. 1, pp. 3–30.

———. "Maoism and Development: A Reconsideration of Local Self-Reliance in Financing Rural Industrialization." Working Paper no. 201. Santa Cruz: Department of Economics, University of California, 1989.

———. "Central-Local Relations in an Era of Fiscal Decline: The Paradox of Fiscal Decentralization in Post-Mao China." *China Quarterly,* December 1991, no. 128, pp. 691–715.

———. "Fiscal Reform and Local Industrialization: The Problematic Sequencing of Reform in Post-Mao China." *Modern China,* April 1992, vol. 18, no. 2, pp. 197–227.

Wong, Christine, Christopher Heady, and Wing T. Woo. *Fiscal Management and Economic Reform in the People's Republic of China.* Hong Kong: Oxford University Press, for the Asian Development Bank, 1995.

Wong, John, Rong Ma, and Mu Yang, eds. *China's Rural Entrepreneurs: Ten Case Studies.* Singapore: Times Academic Press, 1995.

World Bank. *China: Revenue Mobilization and Tax Policy.* Washington, D.C.: World Bank, 1990.

Xiang Huaicheng, ed. *Jiushiniandai caizheng fazhan zhanlüe* (The Strategy for the Development of Finance in the 1990s). Beijing: Zhongguo caizheng jingji chubanshe, 1991.

Yan, Yunxiang. *The Flow of Gifts: Reciprocity and Social Networks in a Chinese Village.* Stanford, Calif.: Stanford University Press, 1996.

Yang, Dali. *Calamity and Reform in China: State, Rural Society, and Institutional Change Since the Great Leap Famine.* Stanford, Calif.: Stanford University Press, 1996.

Yang, Mayfair. "Between State and Society: The Construction of Corporateness in a Chinese Socialist Factory." *Australian Journal of Chinese Affairs,* July 1989, no. 22, pp. 31–60.

"Yindao nongcun zijin zengjia nongye touru" (Let Village Funds Increase Agricultural Investment). *Nongye jingji wenti,* 23 April 1990, no. 4, pp. 20–25.

You, Ji. "Zhao Ziyang and the Politics of Inflation." *Australian Journal of Chinese Affairs,* January 1991, no. 25, pp. 69–91.

Young, Susan. "Policy, Practice and the Private Sector in China." *Australian Journal of Chinese Affairs,* January 1989, no. 21, pp. 57–80.

———. "Wealth but Not Security: Attitudes Towards Private Business in the 1980s." In Andrew Watson, ed., *Economic Reform and Social Change in China,* pp. 63–87. New York: Routledge, 1992.

Zhang Guoqing, Zhiyong Fan, and Xinge Yan. "Zhuazhu sange huanjie, gaohao cunji ganbu guifanhua guanli" (Seize the Three Links, Manage the Standards of Village-Level Cadres Well). *Hebei nongcun gongzuo,* 1994, no. 5, pp. 40–41.

Zhang Renshou, and Hong Li. *Wenzhou moshi yanjiu* (Research on the Wenzhou Model). Beijing: Zhongguo shehui kexue chubanshe, 1990.

Zhong Pengrong. *Shinian jingji gaige: licheng, xianzhuang, wenti, chulu* (Ten Years of Economic Reform: Course, Conditions, Problems, Solutions). Zhengzhou, China: Henan renmin chubanshe, 1990.

Zhongguo nongcun jinrong tongji, 1979–1989 (China Rural Financial Statistics, 1979–1989). Beijing: Zhongguo tongji chubanshe, 1991.

Zhongguo nongcun jinrong tongji nianjian, 1995 (China Rural Financial Statistical Yearbook, 1995). Beijing: Zhongguo tongji chubanshe, 1996.

Zhongguo nongye nianjian, 1989 (China Agricultural Yearbook, 1989). Beijing: Nongye chubanshe, 1989.

Zhongguo tongji nianjian, 1987 (China Statistical Yearbook, 1987). Beijing: Zhongguo tongji chubanshe, 1987.

Zhongguo tongji nianjian, 1988 (China Statistical Yearbook, 1988). Beijing: Zhongguo tongji chubanshe, 1988.

Zhongguo tongji nianjian, 1989 (China Statistical Yearbook, 1989). Beijing: Zhongguo tongji chubanshe, 1989.

Zhongguo tongji nianjian, 1990 (China Statistical Yearbook, 1990). Beijing: Zhongguo tongji chubanshe, 1990.

Zhongguo tongji nianjian, 1991 (China Statistical Yearbook, 1991). Beijing. Zhongguo tongji chubanshe, 1991.

Zhongguo tongji nianjian, 1993 (China Statistical Yearbook, 1993). Beijing: Zhongguo tongji chubanshe, 1993.

Zhongguo tongji nianjian, 1996 (China Statistical Yearbook, 1996). Beijing: Zhongguo tongji chubanshe, 1996.

Zhongguo xiangzhen qiye nianjian, 1978–1987 (Township and Village Enterprise Yearbook, 1978–1987). Beijing: Nongye chubanshe, 1989.

Zhongguo xiangzhen qiye nianjian, 1991 (Township and Village Enterprise Yearbook, 1991). Beijing: Nongye chubanshe, 1992.

Zhongguo xiangzhen qiye nianjian, 1992 (Township and Village Enterprise Yearbook, 1992). Beijing: Nongye chubanshe, 1993.

Zhou, Kate Xiao. *How the Farmers Changed China: Power of the People.* Boulder, Colo.: Westview Press, 1996.

Zweig, David. "Opposition to Change in Rural China: The System of Responsibility and People's Communes." *Asian Survey,* July 1983, vol. 23, no. 7, pp. 879–900.

———. "Rural Industry: Constraining the Leading Growth Sector in China's Economy." In U.S. Congress Joint Economic Committee, *China's Economic Dilemmas in the 1990s: The Problems of Reforms, Modernization, and Interdependence,* vol. 1, pp. 418–36. Washington, D.C.: U.S. Government Printing Office, 1991.

———. "Internationalizing China's Countryside: The Political Economy of Exports from Rural Industry." *China Quarterly,* December 1991, no. 128, pp. 716–41.

———. "Export-Led Growth, Local Autonomy, and U.S.-China Relations." *In Depth: A Journal for Values and Public Policy,* fall 1993, vol. 3, no. 3, pp. 19–36.

————. "Rural People, the Politicians, and Power." *China Journal,* July 1997, no. 38, pp. 153–68.

Zweig, David, Kathleen Hartford, James Feinerman, and Jianxu Deng. "Law, Contracts, and Economic Modernization: Lessons from the Recent Chinese Rural Reforms." *Stanford Journal of International Law,* summer 1987, vol. 23, no. 2, pp. 319–64.

Zysman, John. *Governments, Markets, and Growth: Financial Systems and the Politics of Industrial Change.* Ithaca, N.Y.: Cornell University Press, 1983.

Index

accounting: creative, 101–02, for extra
   budgetary funds, 163–64
Administration for Industry and Commerce: county, 43; state, 130–31
administrative controls: in local state corporatism, 128–31. *See also* bureaucracy; licensing; regulation
"administrative guidance," Japan, 24,
   118, 119
Africa: government intervention in markets, 66; late-industrializing, 96
agents: becoming principals, 161–90,
   196–97; bureaucracy as, 6–10, 17–18,
   107, 109, 139–60; different types, 107,
   109, 153; local regulatory, 15, 143–
   59. *See also* principal-agent theory
Agricultural Bank (*nongye yinhang*),
   120–22, 173, 176, 177, 178; audited,
   150–51; corruption case, 158–59;
   diversion of funds, 180–81; fund
   sources, 175; loans, 107, 114, 115,
   120–22, 167, 172n, 174; and nonbank
   funds, 183; officials, 120; township
   branches, 109, 120–21, 122
agriculture, 190; agriculture-animal husbandry tax, 55; cash crops, 61, 67, 78;
   decollectivization of, 8, 18, 19–27, 67,
   78; development of commercial, 56;
   investment in, 21–23, 22fig1, 25, 78–
   79; land/harvest ownership, 18–20;
   loan repayment rate, 186n; peasant
   skills in, 67; peasants left in, 61, 78–
   79; production teams, 18–20, 67, 79,
   179; rural industry supporting (*yigong*

bunong), 21–23, 78–79; rural industry
   surpassing income in, 1, 77–78; special
   agricultural products tax, 55, 56; subsidies for, 21–23, 78–79; taxes, 20,
   41, 45, 55–56, 75n, 78–79, 144n; tax
   exemptions, 36; tax revenue (1952–
   1994), 41fig3; village officials in charge
   of, 113. *See also* grain
Agriculture Ministry, 88n, 90, 167–68
All-China Federation of Industry and
   Commerce (*quanguo gongshang lianhui*), 129n
Amsden, Alice, 57
Applebaum, Richard, 7n
associations: credit, 131–32. *See also*
   Chinese Communist Party; connections; cooperatives; interest groups;
   networks; trade associations
auction (*paimai*), of collectively owned
   firms, 88, 89, 91, 92
audit bureau (*shenjiju*), 100 table 4, 144–
   57; announced audits, 148–49; officials, 145; suboffices (*shenjisuo*), 145;
   team, 148–49; uncovering misconduct, 149–57. *See also* investigations
authority: federalism and, 197n; intersecting lines of, 141–52; personalization of, 66, 198. *See also* government;
   leadership; power; regulation; state

bankrupt (*pochan*) firms, 88, 89, 90–91
banks: assignment to, 176; audited, 150–
   51; autonomy gains, 175; bad debt
   held by, 90–91; basic account (*jiben*

banks (*continued*)
  zhanghu)/secondary or supplementary
    account (*fuzhu zhanghu*), 178n; and
    central quotas, 75n; commercialization
    of, 173–76; competition between,
    176–77, 178; Construction, 173,
    176–77, 178, 179; county, 100 table
    4, 104, 106–7, 114, 120–22, 131–32,
    150–51, 158–59, 173–83 passim;
    credit from, 47, 67, 87, 107, 114–15,
    119–22, 131–32, 172–77; credit plan,
    174–75; deposits, 174–75, 176–77,
    180; finance bureau extrabudgetary
    account (*caizheng zhuanhu chucun*),
    163–64; Industrial Commercial (*gong-
    shang yinhang*), 173, 176, 177, 178;
    licensing verifications, 129; loans, 67,
    71, 87, 90–91, 106–7, 114, 120–22,
    158, 166–82 passim; local officials'
    power, 178–81; manipulation of funds
    (*nuoyong*), 179–81, 182; in Maoist
    period, 119–20, 173, 182; "money
    market" (*zijin shichang*), 176; People's
    Bank of China, 120n, 144, 167, 173–
    75, 178, 180; private, 119, 177, 184;
    profits from, 54; reserve requirements,
    174; retrenchment (1988–89) and,
    166–67, 169, 172–77, 179–84. *See
    also* Agricultural Bank; World Bank
Barnett, A. Doak, 120n, 141
Bates, Robert, 8n, 60, 66
Beijing: county officials' trips to, 106;
    interviews in, 207; State Planning
    Commission, 116n. *See also* central
    government
biaoxian (political attitude), 6, 154–55
"big bang" approach, 2, 194
bonuses: cadre, 48–50, 75, 77n, 159;
    labor, 25; management, 26; regulation
    of, 151; retained enterprise, 43; tax
    (*jiangjin shui*), 53
brigades, 18–19; central regulation and,
    139; fees levied on, 45; income paid to,
    20. *See also* villages
budget: fixed calculations, 30–34; "mini-
    mum essential," 30. *See also* budget
    allocations to local governments; pay-
    ments; revenues
budget allocations to local governments,
    20, 28, 119–22; and bank diversion of
    funds, 180–81; constraints in, 14, 15,
    28, 56, 108, 112, 168; county to town-
    ship, 29n, 108, 144; Maoist period, 6,
    18, 19, 34–35; preferential, 118–19.
    See also expenditures; subsidies
bureaucracy: in Africa and Latin Amer-
    ica, 96; as agents, 6–10, 17–18, 107,
    109, 139–60; collective ownership in,
    74–80; compliance with state direc-
    tives, 3–10, 14, 17–18, 139–60, 162,
    170–72, 189–90, 197–98; fixed subsi-
    dies paying for, 34; as information and
    technology source, 123–27; interview-
    ing, 207, 209; maturity of, 96n; net-
    works, 123–27; organizational capac-
    ity, 96, 99, 100–101 table 4; strategy
    for survival, 28; vertical (*tiao*) integra-
    tion, 11–12, 28, 141, 199; "well-
    bounded" system, 9. *See also* Chinese
    Communist Party; government; incen-
    tives; regulation; state
Byrd, William, 79

capital: agricultural, 22–23; changes in
    access, 87, 119–22, 182–89; fixed
    investment, 86–87; growth of regis-
    tered, 86; local corporate, 70–73; non-
    bank sources, 109, 182–89, 185 tables
    7&8; private sector, 67–68, 86–87.
    See also credit; investment; loans
capitalism, 193; "capitalist revolution,"
    63; "capitalist roaders," 59n; laissez-
    faire, 99; "plan rational," 7. *See also*
    market economy; newly industrializing
    countries (NICs), East Asian
central government: bureaucratic compli-
    ance with, 3–10, 14, 17–18, 139–60,
    162, 170–72, 189–90, 197–98; con-
    trol consequences in local state cor-
    poratism, 161–90, 196–99; credible
    commitment, 10–11, 47–52, 195–96;
    and extrabudgetary revenues, 38–42,
    40 fig. 2, 48–49, 52–56, 140, 162–
    66, 190; grain production constraints
    by, 59–60; infrastructural investment
    shifted to localities from, 21–23, 78;
    from limited indirect extractions to
    direct taxation, 52–56; limits of con-
    trol, 189–90, 196; local appropriation
    of controls of, 159–90, 196–99; and
    local power, 15, 139–90, 196–99;
    nomenklatura system, 143–44, 153,
    160; and peasant disturbances, 200–
    201; as principal, 7, 17–18, 139–60;
    and private sector, 73–80; and prod-
    uct preference lists, 116n; quotas, 18,
    53, 75n; retrenchment (1988–89),
    162, 166–90; revenues shared with,
    29, 31n, 32–33 table 1, 54–56. *See
    also* Beijing; budget allocations to local
    governments; central planning; Maoist
    period; policies; political elites; regula-
    tion; state
central planning, 3–4, 19; and bank

funds, 175n; egalitarian, 7, 77, 117–
19; gradually jettisoned, 2, 75; ideological, 7, 115–17; and selective allocation, 118–22. *See also* plans
Changzhou method, 163n
Chen, Chih-jou Jay, 67–68
Chinese Academy of Social Sciences, 207
Chinese Communist Party, 2–5, 130n,
197; lines of authority, 141, 142–43;
local state corporatism and, 97, 102,
112–13; village party cell (*dangzhibu*),
129. *See also* party secretaries; state
"civil society," 199
clientelism, 66, 136n, 198
collective ownership (*jiti suoyou*), 2, 18,
23–47, 58–80, 195; agricultural
investment, 21–23; auction (*paimai*) of
firms, 88, 89, 91, 92; belief in superiority of, 5; and cadre power, 11, 74–
80, 91–92, 98; contracting, 23–24,
26, 74, 80; costs and benefits vs. private ownership, 88–93; county, 58,
74–76, 133, 147, 148, 177; *cunban
qiye*, 112; "fake," 63, 133; "finance
support fund" (*caizheng fuchi zijin*)
for, 184–85; "horizontal linkage"
(*hengxiang lianhe*), 134; local services
underwritten by profits of, 25, 78,
79–80, 98; logic of development by,
65–80; new management structures
(1990s), 81–85, 128; number of enterprises (1980s), 67n; outdated, 193–94;
preferential treatment, 60; of property, 20; and ratings of enterprises,
121; "red umbrella" and, 64, 85,
133; reserves (*gonggongjilei*), 146;
resources, 67, 70–73, 187–89;
retrenchment (1988–89) and, 80,
166–72, 187–89; symbiotic relationship with private sector, 133–37,
202–3; taxes, 35–47; and technological advances, 81; township, 27–47,
58–80, 88–93, 170–72, 176, 181,
201, 202; village, 50, 58–80, 88–93,
112, 170–72, 176, 200, 201–2; weaknesses, 89; *xiangzhen qiye*, 62. *See also*
cooperatives; decollectivization; local
government
Collier, David, 12n, 13
Collier, Ruth Berins, 13
commercialization: of agriculture, 56; of
banks, 173–76. *See also* decollectivization; industry; market
communes, 45; brigades in system of, 19;
central regulation and, 139; disbanded,
23; income paid to, 20; ownership by,
18. *See also* township

communism: and economics, 2, 3–4, 10,
11, 191; and local officials' power
retention, 3, 74, 89, 191; "plan ideological" governments, 7; statist view
and, 9. *See also* Chinese Communist
Party; Leninist systems
community services. *See* services, local
competition: bank, 176–77, 178; contract bidding, 25; and corporate good,
118; local cadre networks assisting,
123; "plan rational" capitalism/Chi-
nese "industrial policy" and, 7; rising
challenges (1990s), 80, 81, 89, 92;
state-owned vs. rural industry, 166
conglomerates (*jituan*), forming (1990s),
81, 85, 88n, 93
connections, 115, 135–36; *guanxi* for
resources, 117, 123–27; "horizontal
linkage" (*hengxiang lianhe*), 117, 134;
in symbiotic private-collective-state
relationship, 133–37, 202–3. *See also*
associations; contracting
consignment selling (*daixiao*), 137
construction: banks assigned to, 176;
extrabudgetary funds for, 163, 165;
investigations of, 150; nonbank loans
for, 183; taxes, 21, 55
Construction Bank, 173, 176–77, 178,
179
consumption tax (*xiaofei shui*), 54
contracting (*chengbao*), 17, 23–34, 46–
54 passim, 74, 80; fees, 24, 46–47;
leasing vs., 81, 82; legalities, 27, 156–
57; new structures instead of (1990s),
81; responsibility systems, 79, 155;
revenue-sharing, 29–34, 32–33 table 1;
in state-private symbiosis, 134–37;
weaknesses, 89, 91–92
controls. *See* administrative controls;
investigations; regulation
cooperatives: credit, 109, 115, 120–21,
132, 166–84 passim; sales and marketing, 176; savings and loan, 122,
183, 188; shareholding (*gufenzhi*), 73,
81, 84–85, 93, 188
corporate good, 118
corporations (*gongzi*): forming, 81, 85,
88n, 93, 202–3; local corporate state
like large multilevel, 102
corporatism, 11–13, 97; corporate good,
118; of local control, 152–59, 162–
90; redistributive, 79–80, 97–98,
201–3. *See also* collective ownership;
local state corporatism
corruption: bank, 179; individual
(*tanwu*), 151–52, 154; in licensing,
128; and local cadres' attitude toward

corruption (*continued*)
  economic reforms, 3–4, 6; misappropriation of public funds (*nuoyong
  gongkuan*), 151–52; village, 157–59.
  See also crime
costs: collective vs. private ownership,
  88–93; debts written off as, 181; factory closure, 171; production, 80–81,
  169. *See also* interest rates; prices
county: audited, 150–51; banks, 100
  table 4, 104, 106–7, 114, 120–22,
  131–32, 150–51, 158–59, 173–83
  passim; budget allocations to townships, 29n, 108, 144; cadre evaluation
  offices (*ganbu kaohe bangongsi*), 49;
  cadre power, 74–76; and central regulation in Maoist period, 139, 190; collective ownership, 58, 74–76, 133,
  147, 148, 177; coordination (*xietiao*)
  role/corporate headquarters, 103–7;
  economic commission, 100 table 4,
  165; economic reform committee
  (*jingji tizhi gaige weiyuan hui*), 157;
  and extrabudgetary revenues, 42–
  43, 53, 55, 144, 164–66, 184, 190;
  finance investment companies (*caizheng touzi gongsi*), 131; foreign trade
  companies, 101 table 4, 104; industrial-commercial management bureau,
  88n, 100 table 4, 129, 190; investment
  at level of, 75–76, 90, 103, 131; land
  management bureau (*tudi guanli ju*),
  101 table 4, 178; leadership, 103–4;
  local state corporatism, 99–115, 100–
  101 table 4, 153; magistrate (*xian
  zhang*), 100 table 4, 103–4, 142;
  "major investigation office" (*dajiancha
  bangongsi*), 147; meetings, 124–25;
  nonbank support funds from, 184–87,
  185 tables 7&8; party secretary (*xian
  dangwei shuji*), 100 table 4, 103–4,
  142, 153, 209; planning commission,
  100 table 4, 165; poor, 38; price
  bureau, 147; as principals, 153; property rights relations, 73, 75–76, 87–
  91, 133; and rapid development, 96;
  residual, 42–45, 53; resources, 104–7,
  110–11 table 6; revenues, 27–47, 55,
  75, 90; science and technology commissions, 101 table 4, 186–87; successfully industrializing, 58, 124; tax
  bureau, 100 table 4, 106–7, 144–48,
  153, 185–86; village representation,
  112. *See also* audit bureau; finance
  bureaus; rural enterprise management
  bureau, county

credible commitment, 10–11, 47–52,
  195–96
credit: associations, 131–32; bank, 47,
  67, 87, 107, 114–15, 119–22, 131–32,
  172–77; cadre power and, 114, 120;
  cooperatives, 109, 115, 120–21, 132,
  166–84 passim; erosion of central control over, 172–82; limit, 121–22; nonbank, 182–84; plan, 174–75; preferential treatment, 133, 156; ratings for,
  121–22, 156, 159, 168–69; retrenchment (1988–89) and, 80, 166–67,
  172–89, 198; state-allocated, 119–22;
  tight, 80; township vs. village, 114–15.
  See also debt; interest rates; loans
crime: economic, 145–59. *See also* corruption; law
Cultural Revolution, 142

Daqiuzhuang, 46n; factory manager
  income, 27; grain production constraints, 60; specialized agricultural
  teams, 79; Yu Zuomin, 50, 114
debt: bad, 90–91, 120, 166n, 169–70,
  181–82; erasing, 181–82; local redistribution of, 70, 71, 98; "triangular,"
  169–70. *See also* credit
decollectivization, 56, 58; agriculture, 8,
  18, 19–27, 67, 78; cadre power after,
  76, 89, 91, 113–14; fiscal flows altered
  by, 14, 18, 19–27; labor after, 77–78;
  peasant disturbances after, 200–201;
  townships as communes before, 45.
  See also commercialization; private
  ownership
democratization, 112, 201
Deng Xiaoping, 8
development: bureaucratic compliance in,
  3–10, 14, 17–18, 139–60, 162, 170–
  72, 189–90, 197–98; commercial agriculture, 56; and extrabudgetary revenues, 40, 53; incentives as key factor
  in, 56–57; in local fixed expenditures,
  30; logic of collectively owned, 65–
  80; NIC, 3, 4, 57, 96, 102, 113, 135;
  political constraints on, 59–61; and
  retrenchment (1988–89), 167–68; and
  revenue-sharing terms, 29–30, 51;
  state-led, 3–10, 14–15, 89, 93–99,
  113, 115, 137–38, 192–93; strategies
  of, 28, 58–94, 133, 192, 210; village
  profits for, 27n. *See also* growth, economic; industry

East Asian NICs. *See* newly industrializing countries (NICs), East Asian

Eastern Europe, 2, 57, 198, 201; depoliticization of enterprises, 56; lack of institutional support, 4; privatization, 10;
Solidarity, 199n
economic commissions: county, 100
table 4, 165; township, 46–47, 72,
75, 90, 97n, 100 table 4, 108–9, 112n,
116, 121, 125, 147, 158, 181
economic elite: collective ownership and,
74–75; private ownership and, 99,
128, 134
"economic miracle," 1–2
economic results: and lines of authority,
143; local officials' political promotion
tied to, 104; successful growth, 58, 76,
78, 80, 91–93, 113–15, 117, 200.
See also growth, economic; output;
production
economic retrenchment (1988–89), 80,
129, 162, 166–90, 198
economic retrenchment (1993), 172n
egalitarianism, 7, 77, 117–19
elections, village, 112, 201n
enterprise management committee, village, 26n, 100 table 4, 102, 113, 142.
See also rural enterprise management
bureau, county
enterprises: on agricultural schedule, 78;
bankrupt (*pochan*), 88, 89, 90–91;
banks as, 173–76; as "cash registers"
of local authorities, 47; changes (1985–
1995), 82–83 table 3, 89; corporatization of, 81, 85, 88n, 93, 202–3; depoliticized, 56; family, 67; in information
hierarchy, 124; key-point, 147, 156;
large-scale, 86–87, 90, 133; local
cadre power over, 74, 97–98; losses
(*kuisun*), 89–90; merged (*jianbing*)/
closed (*daobi*), 170–71; number of
collective/private township/village
(1980s), 67n; number of commune/
township, 67n, 108n; "prefectural
advanced enterprise," 156; punishment
of economic infractions in, 153–59;
ratings of, 121–22, 156, 159, 168–69;
reinvestment of profits in, 25, 97–98;
retained enterprise funds, 43, 54; retrenchment (1988–89) and, 80, 166–
90; self-raised funds, 71–72, 183, 187–
89; sold, 88, 89, 91, 92, 128; targets,
49, 75, 115, 116–17, 168; taxes on,
34–47, 55, 76, 89, 151, 181. *See also*
contracting; development; entrepreneurs; industry; ownership; plans;
technology
entrepreneurs, 10; associations, 43, 129–

31, 132, 137; "entrepreneur" (*qiyejia*)
title for successful officials, 78, 114;
individual (*geti*), 86n, 170; local governments as, 2–3, 50, 78, 114, 123–
27, 193; management fee (*geti guanli
fei*), 50; political interest group, 13–
14; small, 66, 67, 133; as "underground snakes," 74. *See also* enterprises; licensing; private ownership
Evans, Peter, 4, 192
expenditures: commune factory, 45;
extrabudgetary revenue, 163–66, 184,
190; fixed, 30–34; illegal distribution,
151; monitoring, 140, 149, 151; tax
reforms (1994) and, 55–56. *See also*
budget allocations to local governments; income; subsidies; taxes
exports, from rural industry, 1, 80, 167n,
169n
extrabudgetary revenues (*yusuanwai
zijin*), 38–43, 163n, 182, 189–90;
ballooning, 57; central government
(1982–1994), 40 fig. 2; central government levies on local, 52–53, 140, 162;
county and, 42–43, 53, 55, 144, 164–
66, 184, 190; expenditure of, 163–66,
184, 190; finance of administrative
institutional units (*xingzheng shiye
danwei caizheng*), 164; local finance
(*difang caizheng*), 164; local government (1982–1994), 38–42, 40 fig. 2,
162–66, 190; Maoist period, 38–39,
48–49; regulation of, 162–66, 190;
"second budget" (*dier yusuan*), 190;
sources (1981–1990), 44 fig. 4; state
enterprise finance (*guoying caizheng*),
164; tax reforms (1994) and, 54–56,
140, 162, 190; township, 45–46, 53,
108

factories. *See* enterprises; industry
family: enterprises with, 67; extraordinary resources from, 67–69; local
government as, 154, 157. *See also*
households
federalism, 197
fees, 38; *bunong bufu jijin*, 46n; collectors of, 50; contract, 24, 46–47; on
county bureau loans, 107; Individual
Entrepreneurs Association, 43; management, 43, 46–47, 50, 79, 121n;
research, 208n; during retrenchment
(1988–89), 171; *tiliu*, 21, 23n, 45, 79,
146, 151n; *tongchou*, 45; township,
45, 46–47; village, 45, 112n, 133. *See
also* rent; surcharges

Fewsmith, Joseph, 11n
finance bureaus, 43, 100 table 4, 104,
    109, 144–55, 163–65, 167; budget
    section (*yusuan gu*), 164, 165; "con-
    solidated planning office" (*zonghe
    jihuachu*), 164; "develop agriculture"
    fund (*nongye fazhan zijin*), 184; extra-
    budgetary expenditures records
    (*yusuanwai shouzhibiao*), 164; extra-
    budgetary fund control, 163–66, 184,
    190; "extrabudgetary fund manage-
    ment office" (*yusuanwai zijin guan-
    lichu*), 164; extrabudgetary section
    (*yusuanwai gu*), 164–65; "finance sup-
    port fund" (*caizheng fuchi zijin*), 184–
    85; nonbank capital sources, 107,
    184–87; North China County loans,
    185 table 7; revenue plans from, 75,
    116; "support agriculture" fund (*zhi-
    nong zhouzhuanjin*), 184–85; technol-
    ogy development fund (*keji fazhan
    jijin*), 186n; township, 50, 100 table 4,
    109, 147
Finance Ministry, 29n, 31n, 163, 173
fiscal reforms, 2–3, 14, 18–58, 159–60,
    198, 211–17; commercialization of
    banks, 173–76; contracting, 23–34,
    32–33 table 1, 46–54 passim; corpo-
    rate financing, 97–98; "eat in separate
    kitchens" reform, 28; evolution of
    financial management system, 213–16
    table 12; local state corporatism, 102,
    160; residual rights and fiscal flows,
    27–47, 51–52; retrenchment (1988–
    1989), 80, 129, 162, 166–90; revenue
    sharing, 29–56, 32–33 table 1, 211
    table 10, 212 table 11; tax reforms
    (1994), 54–56, 140, 162–63, 190,
    194. *See also* banks; credit; expendi-
    tures; income; resources; revenues; sub-
    sidies; surplus; taxes
Fujian: "fake collectives," 63, 133; lump-
    sum system revenues, 52n; private
    enterprise, 58, 63–64, 67–70, 85, 133;
    resources, 87

General Auditing Administration, 150n
Gerschenkron, Alexander, 65–66
Gorbachev, Mikhail, 196
government: property rights protected
    from expropriation by, 10. *See also*
    bureaucracy; central government;
    intervention, government; Leninist sys-
    tems; local government; Maoist period;
    policies; state
grain: and contracting, 24; after decollec-
    tivization, 20, 78; Maoist period, 6, 18,
    179; political constraints on, 59–60,
    78; production, 6, 18, 21, 59–60, 78,
    179; urban/rural households registra-
    tion and, 107–8n, 112n
Great Leap Forward, famine during, 6,
    198
growth, economic, 1–10, 81, 191; corpo-
    ratism and, 12; depoliticization of
    enterprises for, 56; evolutionary, 93–
    94, 137–38; Japan (1960s & 1970s),
    24; politics and, 2–11, 50, 56–60,
    66–68, 74–80, 104, 113, 161, 191–
    203; private enterprise (1990s), 85–
    87, 98–99; without privatization, 10,
    56, 62–65, 194; and property rights,
    10–11, 17–57, 193–96; rapid, 2–3, 5,
    11, 15, 19, 52n, 94, 95–138, 191, 192;
    retrenchment (1988–89) and, 168–
    70; rural industry (1980s), 61–65, 80;
    state-allocated credit targeting, 119–
    22; successful, 58, 76, 78, 80, 91–93,
    113–15, 117, 200. *See also* develop-
    ment; incentives
Guangdong: Engineering and Equipment
    Supply Company, 127; job bonding,
    72n; lump-sum system revenues, 52n;
    officials and special visas, 127; private
    enterprises, 86n; tax cuts, 37
guanxi: for resources, 117, 123–27. *See
    also* connections
guarantors, loan, 121, 122–23n, 158,
    177n
guesthouses, 209–10
Guizhou, local taxes, 21
Guo Xiaolin, 34n, 55n

Hebei, private enterprises, 86n
Heilongjiang, cadres powerless, 76n
He Kang, 167–68
Henderson, Jeffrey, 7n
Holz, Carsten, 175n
Hong Kong, product copying near, 127
horizontal (*kuai*) rule, 28, 141
"horizontal linkage" (*hengxiang lianhe*),
    industrial, 117, 134
households: five-guaranteed, 25n; house-
    hold production, 14, 19, 20, 137; spe-
    cialized farm, 79; urban/rural registra-
    tion, 107, 108n, 112n, 133; worker
    per, 77. *See also* family
Huang, Yasheng, 143n, 150n, 160, 167
Hunan, private enterprise, 58n

incentives, 6, 7–8, 11, 14–15, 137–38;
    for agricultural work, 78–79; and cen-
    tral control, 166; contracting system
    and, 23–34, 46–54n, 74; intervening,

59–61; key factor in development, 56–57; in local state corporatism, 153, 159–60; property rights as, 10, 17–57; residuals' potency as, 44–45, 47–58; village vs. other levels, 112. *See also* decollectivization; fiscal reforms

income: agricultural vs. nonagricultural, 1, 77–78; agriculture, 1, 14, 19–20, 77–78; brigade, 19; categories, 48; commune factory, 45; contracting, 25–27; decollectivization and loss of, 19–27; factory manager, 26–27, 92n, 202; factory manager vs. worker, 26; head of Association of Individual Entrepreneurs, 130n; higher in areas with rural industry, 61; increases in wages (1990s), 90; investigation target, 147; local cadres, 48–50, 77n, 78, 107; local officials' power and sources of, 191; local payroll budget, 30; local redistribution of, 70, 191, 202; national (*guomin shouru*), 39n; "nested principal-agent model" and, 153; production team members, 67; property rights to, 18, 19–20; during retrenchment (1988–89), 171; socialist egalitarian distribution of, 7; state cadres working at local level, 30; surplus, 18, 20; and tax cuts, 38; tax on enterprise, 34–47, 55, 76, 149, 151, 167, 172, 181; tax on individual (*geren suode shui*), 55; tax reforms (1994) and, 55; unreported funds/"small treasure chests" (*xiaojin ku*), 152; village officials, 109–12. *See also* bonuses; profits; residual; revenues

Individual Entrepreneurs Association (*geti xiehui*), 43, 129–31, 137

Individual Entrepreneurs and Private Business Economic Fund (*geti siying jingji jijin hui*), 132

Industrial Commercial Bank (*gongshang yinhang*), 173, 176, 177, 178

industrial policies: China (*chanye zhengce*), 7, 115–22; Japan, 7, 24, 116, 118, 119; NIC, 7, 116n, 118, 119

industry: Maoist period, 7; tax revenue (1952–1994), 41 fig. 3. *See also* enterprises; industrial policies; rural industry

inflation, 7, 166–67, 196–97

information: bureaucratic sources, 123–27, 132–34; and communist planning and control, 198; local internal, 155–56; market, 132–34; technical, 123–27, 132–34. *See also* investigations; networks

infrastructural investment: local, 21–23, 78–80. *See also* agriculture; services, local

inputs, 4, 117–22, 133–34; and cadre power, 113, 115; production, 80, 106, 118–19; retrenchment (1988–89) and, 80, 168, 169, 172–77. *See also* budget allocations to local governments; capital; credit; labor; resources; subsidies

institutions, 2–3, 14–15, 123; changes, 8–9, 56–57, 94, 161, 192, 194; interviews focused on, 208; Maoist period, 95–99, 115–27; North on, 9n, 193, 196n. *See also* decollectivization; fiscal reforms; incentives; local state corporatism

interest groups, 13–14, 129–31. *See also* associations

interest rates: bank vs. credit cooperative, 120, 121; for bank depositors, 177; on county bureau loans, 107, 186n; on enterprise funds, 72, 73; on nonbank credit, 183; retrenchment (1988–89) and, 166–67, 168, 173, 177

intervention, government: credit allocation, 119–22; in local state corporatism, 102, 112–13, 134–38; Maoist period, 7; in market economies, 4; in "plan rational" economy, 7; and state-private symbiosis, 134–37, 202–3; and successful economic development, 3–10, 65–66, 91–93, 113–14. *See also* incentives; ownership; reforms, economic; regulation

interviewing, 205–10; guerrilla, 207; limitations, 209–10; locations/dates/numbers, 206 table 9; procedure, 207–9; sample, 206–7

investigations, 144–54, 160; ad hoc, 146–48; announced audits, 148–49; contested decisions, 149n; county "major investigation office" (*dajiancha bangongsi*), 147; county tax office investigative team (*jicha dui*), 144–45; "high-level supervision" (*gaozeng jiandu*), 145; "major investigation on taxes, finances, and prices" (*shuiwu caizheng wujia dajiancha*), 147; misconduct uncovered by, 149–57; "propaganda" stage, 146; and punishment, 153–57; scheduled, 146–47; self-examination (*sicha*) stage, 150; township tax office "investigative group" (*jicha zu*), 145. *See also* audit bureau; finance bureaus; regulation; tax bureaus

investment: in agriculture, 21–23, 22fig1,
    25, 78–79; county-level, 75–76, 90,
    103, 131; fixed capital, 86–87; *guanxi*
    for, 117; investigations of, 150; local
    infrastructural, 21–23, 78–80; pro-
    tecting, 157–59; reinvestment of
    profits, 25, 97–98; retrenchment
    (1988–89) decreasing, 167; by state
    (1949–1978), 69n. *See also* capital;
    credit; loans; resources; shareholding
"IOU problem," 180
"iron rice bowl," 31, 171

Japan: "administrative guidance," 24,
    118, 119; industrial policy, 7, 24, 116,
    118, 119; "plan rational" capitalism,
    7; state-led development, 3, 113
Jiangsu: collective enterprise selling, 88n;
    experimental model, 52; fixed-rate
    responsibility system (1977-1980),
    48n; private enterprise resisted, 74.
    See also Wuxi
job bonding system, 72, 188. *See also*
    labor
Johnson, Chalmers, 3n, 7, 24

kinship network: extraordinary resources
    from, 67–69. *See also* family

labor: benefits (*fuli*), 25, 76; bonuses, 25;
    collective vs. private, 92; and corporate
    good, 118; corvée (*yiwu gong*), 23,
    133; costs (1990s), 80; after decollec-
    tivization, 77–78; disciplining, 92;
    enterprise funds borrowed from, 71–
    72, 188; food rations for workers, 45;
    individual (*geti*) and private enter-
    prises, 86n; job bonding system, 72,
    188; in large-scale private enterprises,
    86–87; levy on enterprise workers,
    46n; lump sum (*daizi ruchang*) funds
    from, 71–72; migrant, 69; peasants
    in rural enterprise, 66; population
    of rural, 77; private hiring bans, 73;
    regional differences, 62; during re-
    trenchment (1988–89), 171; rural
    enterprise (1978–1990), 1–2; rural
    industrial employee numbers by owner-
    ship type, 62, 64 fig. 6; state-owned
    enterprises (1952–1986), 1–2; surplus,
    4; unskilled, 67, 77–78
land: contracting of, 24; easy acquisition
    of, 133n; finance bureau control, 144n;
    ownership, 18–20. *See also* agricul-
    ture; property
land management bureau (*tudi guanli ju*),
    county, 101 table 4, 178

Latin America, late-industrializing coun-
    tries, 96
law: contract, 27; property rights, 10,
    194, 195; Village Organic, 201n; vio-
    lating (*weifa*), 145–59. *See also* crime;
    punishment; regulation
leadership: local, 103–4, 108–9, 112–
    15, 147, 201. *See also* authority;
    bureaucracy; political elites; power;
    state
leasing (*zulin*), 81–84, 88n, 89, 93
Leninist systems, 2, 4, 18–19, 191; local
    state corporatism and, 13, 14, 97, 192,
    199; and officials' power, 3, 74, 89,
    191. *See also* communism; Eastern
    Europe; Maoist period; Russia
Liaoning: interviews in, 207; private
    enterprises, 86n
licensing, 86, 109, 128–29, 130; assis-
    tance with, 115, 133; certification
    (*zhengming*) for, 129; management fee
    (*geti gongshang yehu guanli fei*) for, 43
loans: bank, 67, 71, 87, 90–91, 106–7,
    114, 120–22, 158, 166–82 passim;
    cadre power and, 114; center from
    localities, 53; circulation fund, 167n,
    169n, 181, 188; from collective mem-
    bers, 72–73; county-level, 107, 109,
    114, 120–22; credit cooperative, 115,
    120–21, 172n; deposits and, 174–75;
    guarantors, 121, 122–23n, 158, 177n;
    localities from collective enterprises,
    71; nonbank, 182–89, 185 tables 7&8;
    payoffs before tax assessment (*shuiqian
    huankuan*), 106–7; renamed as con-
    tributions, 53; retrenchment (1988–
    1989) and, 80, 166–69, 172, 179–89;
    village self-reliance and, 115. *See also*
    credit; debt; interest rates
local government, 5, 8–10; agents
    becoming principals, 161–90, 196–
    97; appropriation of central controls,
    159–90, 196–99; cadre income and
    bonuses, 48–50, 75, 77n, 78, 107,
    159; cadre power, 3, 11, 74–80, 89,
    91–93, 97–98, 112–15, 178–79, 191–
    92, 199; central government levies on
    extrabudgetary revenues of, 52–53,
    140, 162; and central regulation, 15,
    139–90, 196–99; contracting, 23–27,
    50–51, 74; corporate control by, 152–
    59, 162–90; de facto ownership by,
    18–19; entrepreneurship of, 2–3, 50,
    78, 114, 123–27, 193; extrabudgetary
    revenues (1982–1994), 38–42, 40
    table 2, 162–66, 190; "facade of com-
    pliance," 139–40, 197–98; as family,

154, 157; horizontal (*kuai*) rule, 28,
141; interviewing, 207–8, 209; leadership, 103–4, 108–9, 112–15, 147,
201; lines of authority, 141–52; Maoist period, 5, 6, 18–19, 48, 66, 182,
189, 198; minimal compliance, 140,
141, 159–60, 162, 189–90; *nomenklatura* system, 143–44, 153, 160; privatization promoted by, 11, 85–89,
91, 99, 128–37, 202–3; privatization
resisted by, 73–76, 91; quasi-corporate
organization, 97; and rapid development, 5, 96, 191; rational actors/
bounded rationality, 7, 59; recogni-
tions for industrially successful officials, 78, 102, 114; redistribution, 70,
71, 79–80, 97–98, 187–89, 201–2;
regulatory agents in, 15, 143–59; residual rights, 14, 19, 23–57, 89, 98, 112,
153, 194; resources at disposal of,
10, 66–73, 76, 104–7, 109, 110–11
table 6, 161–90; response to economic
reforms, 3–10, 11, 14–15, 74–80,
113–14, 191–99; and retrenchment
(1988–89), 80, 167–68, 170–72,
179–90; revenue sharing, 29–56, 32–
33 table 1; selective compliance, 170–
72; tax break generosity, 36–47; technological challenges, 81; *xiangzhen
qiye* ownership by, 62. *See also* budget allocations to local governments;
bureaucracy; county; infrastructural
investment; local state corporatism;
township; villages
local state corporatism, 11–14, 95–138,
191–203; adapting to private enterprise, 128–37, 194; and central control in transitional system, 198–99;
and central-local relations, 139–90,
196–99; consequences for central control, 161–90, 196–98; defined, 11–13,
97; economic duties, 105 table 5; interests and collusion, 178–82; local control, 152–59, 162–90, 196–99; three
levels, 99–102, 100–101 table 4
Lowi, Theodore, 9

magistrate (*xian zhang*), county, 100
table 4, 103–4, 142
Mahon, James E., 12n
management: bonuses, 26; citizen management board (*minguanhui*) over
credit cooperatives, 120n; credit cooperative ratio management (*bili guanli*),
174; decentralized, 74–75; enterprise
funds from, 72; evolution of China's
financial management system, 213–16

table 12; of extrabudgetary funds,
163–66, 190; factory manager
income, 26–27, 92n, 202; factory
manager responsibility system (*changzhang ziren zhi*), 25, 26; fees, 43, 46–
47, 50, 79, 121n; financial service center management committee (*jinrong
fuwu suo guanli weiyuan hui*), 183;
forms (1990s), 80–93; local governments' restricted rights to, 19; local
officials intervening in, 92–93, 102,
113; new structures (1990s), 81–85,
128; private entrepreneurs' fee (*geti
guanli fei*), 50; residual rights separated from rights of, 24–25; unified
(*tongyi guanli*), 174, 190. *See also*
bureaucracy; contracting; regulation
Maoist period, 59, 95–99, 199; attitude
(*biaoxian*) in, 6, 154–55; banks, 119–
20, 173, 182; central regulation in,
139, 140, 162, 189–90, 197–98; collective production (three decades), 67;
and credible commitment, 48; Daqiu
Zhuang in, 114; divide and rule strategy, 197; "eating from one kitchen" in,
28; economic efficiency undermined by
ideology of, 6–7; Fujian and Wenzhou
financially neglected, 69; illegal practices, 179; infrastructural investment
in, 21–22; institutions as foundation of
local state corporatism, 95–99, 115–
27, 138, 192; intersecting lines of
authority, 141, 143; local cadres in, 5,
6, 18–20, 48, 66, 182, 189, 198; number of township-level enterprises, 108n;
passive resistance in, 18, 161, 189,
200; personalization of authority, 66,
198; principal-agent theory and, 17–
18; reporting system, 75; residuals in,
47–49; rural industrial precariousness
in, 166n; state-owned industries, 34–
35; successful economies and political
status in, 113; township industrial
base, 108; within-budget vs. extrabudgetary funds in, 38–39
March, James G., 159; "satisficing," 60,
89
market: information, 132–34; "money
market" (*zijin shichang*), 176; reintroduced, 2; during retrenchment (1988–
89), 169–70; success of rural industry
as result of, 4. *See also* competition;
exports; prices; production; profits;
sales
market economy: corporatist vs. free
market system, 13, 199; government
intervention in, 4; Maoist closure

market economy (*continued*)
  (1957), 7; Maoist institutions adapted
  to, 115–27; "plan rational" systems
  and, 7; privatization and transition to,
  193; property rights in, 10; social dislocations in transition to, 201–2; state
  symbiosis with, 134–37, 202–3. *See
  also* capitalism; competition; market;
  private ownership
"market ideological" systems, 7
marketing cooperatives, 176
market planning, 115–17
"market rational" systems, 7
market transition theories, 13–14, 199
Marx, Karl, 178
meetings, official, 124–25, 149
mobilization system, China as, 5–6
model status, 114, 126–27
Moe, Terry, 56
monitoring. *See* investigations; regulation
Montinola, Gabriella, 197n
Murrell, Peter, 5

National Association of Individual Entrepreneurs, 130n
National Union of Associations of Independents, 130–31
neoclassical economic theories, 135
networks: cadre, 123–27; kinship, 67–
  69; patron-client, 66, 136n, 198. *See
  also* connections; interest groups
newly industrializing countries (NICs),
  East Asian: development, 3, 4, 57, 96,
  102, 113, 135; industrial policies, 7,
  116n, 118, 119; private ownership, 135
nomenklatura system, 143–44, 153, 160
Nordlinger, Eric, 9n
North, Douglass C., 9n, 10, 193, 196n

Oksenberg, Michel, 51n, 52n
Olsen, Johan P., 159
Olson, Mancur, 5
organization: bureaucratic, 96, 99, 100–
  101 table 4; local government quasi-
  corporate, 97; local state corporate,
  99, 100–101 table 4; Maoist, 162;
  "slack" in, 56. *See also* associations;
  authority; corporatism
Ost, David, 199n
output: China's growth in, 1–3; by ownership type (1978–1990), 65 fig. 7;
  rural industry, 1, 65 fig. 7, 78n, 167–
  68; total national product (*chanzhi*),
  39n. *See also* expenditures; growth,
  economic; production
overseas Chinese, resources from, 68, 69
ownership, 18–20; and economic growth,

10, 56, 58, 80, 91–93, 193–96; forms
  (1978–1990), 62–65, 63 fig. 5; forms
  (1990s), 80–94, 98–99; fuzzy differences in, 195; and information hierarchy, 124; joint, 195; local government
  de facto, 18–19; and number of employees (1978–1990), 64 fig. 6; output
  by (1978–1990), 65 fig. 7; politics dictating, 60; semiprivate, 24, 98–99, 109,
  131–32, 184; social consequences of
  changes in, 201–2. *See also* collective
  ownership; private ownership; property rights; state ownership

Park, Albert, 23n, 31n, 38n
party secretaries, 142–43; county, 100
  table 4, 103–4, 142, 153, 209; township, 100 table 4, 108, 114; village,
  100 table 4, 102, 112–14, 142, 157–
  58, 187–88, 209
patron-client relations, 66, 136n, 198
payments: fixed, 30–34. *See also* budget
  allocations to local governments;
  expenditures; income; rent; subsidies;
  surcharges; taxes
Pearson, Margaret, 136n
peasants: left in agriculture, 61, 78–79;
  agricultural skills limited, 67; banks
  serving, 120–21, 180; "burdens," 21,
  23, 98; collective borrowing from, 72–
  73, 183, 188; and contracting, 24;
  entrepreneurship, 66, 67; focus of
  inquiry shifted from, 8; grain production quotas, 59; income paid to, 20; in
  industrial labor force, 66; "IOU problem," 180; licensing, 129; and local
  cadre power after decollectivization,
  76; management and residual rights,
  19, 24; poor, 21, 61, 200; resisting, 18,
  21, 200; savings (1979–1994), 4, 67,
  68 fig. 8, 87; *tiliu* levied on, 21, 79;
  "unorganized power of," 4. *See also*
  villages
Pei, Minxin, 4n
People's Bank of China, 120n, 144, 167,
  173–75, 178, 180
People's Congress, 113, 151n, 154n
personal relations: importance of, 135–
  36. *See also* connections
"plan ideological" systems, 7, 115–17
"plan rational" systems, 7
plans, 75, 115, 116–17; credit, 174–75;
  for extrabudgetary revenues, 162–63,
  165; guidance (*zhidaoxing jihua*),
  116–17; mandatory (*zhilingxing
  jihua*), 116–17, 136; retrenchment
  (1988–89) and, 168; symbiosis with

market development, 135–36, 138.
See also central planning
Poland: privatization, 10; Solidarity,
199n
policies, 8–9, 51–52, 196; agriculture
supported by industry (*yigong bunong*),
21–23, 78–79; radical shifts in Maoist, 59; retrenchment (1988–1989), 80,
129, 162, 166–90, 198. *See also* industrial policies; institutions; preferential
treatment; reforms, economic
political elites, 8–9, 60, 141, 191. *See
also* bureaucracy; Chinese Communist
Party; leadership; power; state
politics: collective ownership serving
interests of, 74–80; constraints based
on, 59–61, 73–80; and economic
growth, 2–11, 50, 56–60, 66–68,
74–80, 104, 113, 161, 191–203; economic reforms based on, 191–203;
informal, 210; monetary skills linked
to advancement in, 50; reform consequences in, 161, 196–98; shareholding
serving interests of, 83. *See also* communism; government; political elites;
power; state
population: in poverty, 61; rural labor
force, 77; shareholding cooperatives,
84
poverty: agricultural regions, 23; county,
38; peasant, 21, 61, 200; population
living in, 61
power, 8–9; central regulatory/local control, 139–90, 196, 198–99; decentralized, 96; local cadre, 3, 11, 74–80, 89,
91–93, 97–98, 112–15, 178–79, 191–
92, 199; peasants' "unorganized," 4;
and state-private symbiosis, 134–35;
village committee, 112. *See also* authority; leadership; political elites
preferential treatment: for bank depositors, 177; credit, 133, 156; from equal
allocation to, 117–19; retrenchment
(1988–1989) and, 167; tax breaks,
36–47, 118, 133, 167n, 180; toward
collective ownership, 60; toward private sector, 87, 91, 133; toward successful villages, 114, 115
prices: agricultural procurement, 20;
inflation, 7, 166–67, 196–97; refusal
to free, 2; resource allocation at market, 118–19; during retrenchment
(1988–1989), 169–70; sales taxes
depending on, 186; setting, 7. *See also*
costs
principal-agent theory, 6–10, 17–18,
139–60; from agents to principals,

161–90, 196–97; "nested principal-
agent model," 153. *See also* agents
private ownership, 2, 4, 10–11, 58, 62–
80, 85–87, 98–99, 195; associations,
43, 129–31, 132, 137; banks, 119,
177, 184; and cadre power, 89, 91–93;
collective ownership dominating, 60,
66; corporatization and, 85, 93, 202–
3; costs and benefits of collective ownership vs., 88–93; gradual movement
toward growth of, 60, 62–65, 93–94,
128, 138, 194; growth possible without, 10, 56, 62–65, 194; individual
(*geti*), 86n, 170; inducements for, 131–
34; interviewing, 209; investigations of,
147, 148, 149, 150; large-scale, 86–87,
133; local government promoting, 11,
85–89, 91, 99, 128–37, 202–3; local
state corporatism adapting to, 128–
37, 194; new management structures
approximating (1990s), 81, 128; NIC,
135; number of enterprises (1980s),
67n; political constraints, 73–80; preferential treatment toward, 87, 91, 133;
rapid growth, 11, 99; reconsidered
(1990s), 85–87; under "red umbrella,"
64, 84–85, 133; resource allocation
changes (1990s), 87; resource limitations (1980s), 67–70; during retrenchment (1988–89), 170; semiprivate, 24,
98–99, 109, 131–32, 184; shareholding, 84–85; state-sponsored, 88, 134;
symbiotic relationship with collective
and state, 133–37, 202–3; taxes, 45,
74, 89, 133, 144n, 148, 186; and technological advances, 81, 132–34. *See
also* decollectivization; entrepreneurs;
licensing
product copying, 127
production: costs, 80–81, 169; grain, 6,
18, 21, 59–60, 78, 179; household,
14, 19, 20, 137; inputs, 80, 106, 118–
19; Maoist period, 6, 7, 18, 67; quotas, 59, 72, 75n. *See also* industry;
market; output; plans
production teams, agricultural, 18–20,
67, 79, 179
product preference lists, 116n
product taxes (*chanpin shui*), 35, 156–
57, 171
profits: after-tax, 46, 47; agriculture supported by industrial, 21–23, 78–79;
collective funds from, 71; commune
factory, 45; contracting remuneration
from, 25–27; and corporate good,
118; illegal, 149n; illegal distribution
of, 151; local cadre power over, 74, 78,

profits (*continued*)
79, 97–98; local services funded by,
25, 78, 79–80, 98; Maoist period, 34–
35; and nonbank funds, 189; over-
quota, 26, 47; overreporting, 150, 156;
redistribution and, 202; reinvestment
of, 25, 97–98; residual rights and, 24–
25; retained enterprise, 43, 54; retention (*liuli*), 43; retrenchment (1988–
89) and, 168, 169, 171–72; "tax for
profit" (*ligaishui*), 34–35, 43; technology and, 80–81; underreporting
(*shaobao*), 150, 151. *See also* residual;
surplus
property: destruction of public (*langfei
sunshi*), 152; right to sell, 18, 19, 24n;
tax on (*fangchan shui*), 55; village rent
from collectively owned, 20. *See also*
land
property rights, 18–19, 79, 89, 97; credible commitment/security of, 10–
11, 47–52, 193–96; and economic
growth, 10–11, 17–57, 193–96; law,
10, 194, 195; private, 7, 10–11, 193–
96; reassigning, 2–3, 17–57; over revenue, 10, 17–57, 182; right to sell
(right of alienation), 18, 19, 24n; shareholding clarifying, 85; "socially guaranteed, informal," 195; tax reforms
(1994) and, 54, 194. *See also* entrepreneurs; ownership; residual rights;
revenues
punishment: and attitude (*biaoxian*),
154–55; of economic infractions,
153–59

Qian, Yingyi, 102n, 197n

ratings, of enterprises, 121–22, 156, 159,
168–69
rational actors/bounded rationality, 7, 59
receipts: fixed, 30–34. *See also* revenues
redistribution, local, 70, 71, 79–80, 97–
98, 187–89, 191, 201–2
reforms, economic, 191; central state setting in motion, 12, 96; consolidation
more challenging than initiation of,
199–200; gradual, 2, 60, 62–65, 75,
93–94, 128, 137–38, 192, 194; "groping for stepping stones in crossing the
river," 192; interviewing and, 210; and
lines of authority, 141, 143; local officials' response to, 3–10, 11, 14–15,
74–80, 113–14, 191–99; political
basis for, 191–203; political consequences of, 161, 196–98; privatization
not sole path of, 10, 56; profit reten-

tion (*liuli*), 43; redistributive corporatism and, 79–80, 97–98; resource
access, 66–73, 87, 117–22, 182–89;
successful, 2–10, 58, 76, 78, 80, 91–
93, 113–15, 200; tax (1994), 54–
56, 140, 162–63, 190, 194; "tax for
profit" (*ligaishui*), 34–35, 43. *See
also* decollectivization; fiscal reforms;
incentives; institutions; local state
corporatism
regulation, 198, 210; center's elite regulators, 155; central-local, 15, 139–90,
196–99; corporate nature of local,
152–59, 178–82; credit, 172–77; of
extrabudgetary funds, 162–66, 190;
limits of central control, 189–90, 196;
local appropriation of central controls,
159–90, 196–99; Maoist, 139, 140,
162, 189–90, 197–98; nonbank capital avoiding, 183, 187; test of central
control, 166–72; violating (*weiji*),
145–59. *See also* investigations; law;
management; punishment
Renshou, peasant resistance, 200
rent: contract fee, 24, 46–47; contractor's remuneration and, 25–27; fixed,
25–26; floating, 25, 26; new management structures (1990s) and, 81–84;
during retrenchment (1988–89), 171;
underreporting profits and, 151; villages collecting, 20. *See also* fees
rent seeking, 97–98
research and documentation, 205–10.
See also interviewing
residual, 27, 160; county, 42–45, 53;
creating, 27–28, 47; defining, 29–36;
maximizing, 36–47, 55–56, 57; new
management structures (1990s) and,
81–84; "slack," 28, 56; township, 45–
47, 53. *See also* profits; residual rights;
surplus
residual rights, 23–58; fiscal flows and,
27–47, 51–52; of local government,
14, 19, 23–57, 89, 98, 112, 153,
194; and management rights, 24–25;
potency as incentive, 44–45, 47–58;
and principal-agent model, 153; strategy for getting ahead, 28; tax reforms
(1994) and, 55–56
resources: bureaucracy as channel for,
123–27; change in access to, 66–73,
87, 117–22, 182–89; collective, 67,
70–73, 187–89; configuration (1980s),
66–73; connections for, 117, 123–27,
136–37; corporate expanding, 70–73;
county, 104–7, 110–11 table 6; egalitarian distribution of, 7, 117–19; enter-

prise self-raised funds, 71–72, 183, 187–89; and guidance plans, 117; at local government disposal, 10, 66–73, 76, 104–7, 109, 110–11 table 6, 161–90; local state corporatism and, 99–102, 104–7, 109, 110–11 table 6, 118–19, 123–27, 133–37; Maoist period, 162; ownership changes restructuring base of, 202; preferential allocation, 118–19, 133; private, 67–70, 87; township, 67, 69, 70–73, 109, 110–11 table 6, 114–15, 182–83, 187–89; village, 67, 69, 70–73, 110–11 table 6, 113, 114–15, 187–89. *See also* banks; budget; capital; income; information; investment; loans; revenues; savings; subsidies; technology

responsibility systems, 43; contract, 79, 155; factory manager (*changzhang ziren zhi*), 25, 26; Jiangsu fixed-rate (1977–1980), 48n

retrenchment (1988–89), 80, 129, 162, 166–90, 198

retrenchment (1993), 172n

revenues, 51–52n; from agriculture and industry (1952–1994), 41 fig. 3; county, 27–47, 55, 75, 90; divided, 48, 51, 54–56; from factories in short-term difficulty, 171–72; fixed rate system, 52n; illegal retention of, 140; local government rights over, 10, 14, 19, 24–25, 27–57; local governments accused of rent seeking, 97–98; local governments not reporting to upper levels, 21n, 34n; local governments turning over to upper levels, 6, 19, 29–35; lump-sum system, 52, 188; minimum base, 55, 57; monitoring, 140; national within-budget, 39n; nontax, 38, 46–47, 52n, 55, 78, 171–72; over-quota, 29–30; ownership changes restructuring base of, 202; plans, 116; political constraints and, 59, 60; in poor agricultural regions, 23; production team ownership of, 19–20; property rights over, 10, 17–57, 182; responsibility contract payment (*chengbao renwu*), 155; "safety net," 30–31; sharing, 29–56, 32–33 table 1, 211 table 10, 212 table 11; state-owned enterprises, 34–35; state quotas, 18, 53; surplus, 6, 10, 14, 19, 25, 28–52; *tiliu* (retained funds), 21, 23n, 45, 79, 146, 151n; total-revenue-sharing system, 35n, 52; township, 23, 27–53, 98, 108; village after decollectivization, 20–21; *zhuanxiang jizi* (special funds),

21n. *See also* extrabudgetary revenues; fees; receipts; rent; residual; surcharges; taxes; within-budget funds

rural enterprise management bureau, county, 100 table 4, 104, 109, 125, 126, 158; on after-tax profits, 97n; on difficulties of collective ownership, 81n; planning, 116; and ratings of enterprises, 121n; technical assistance, 132

rural industry, 8, 9, 199–203; agriculture supported by (*yigong bunong* policy), 21–23, 78–79; changes (1985–1995), 82–83 table 3, 89; competition with state-owned enterprises, 166; evolutionary, 93–94, 137–38; exports from, 1, 80, 167n, 169n; grain production vs., 59–60; growth (1980s), 61–65, 80; "horizontal linkage" (*hengxiang lianhe*), 117, 134; incentives for developing, 17–57, 137–38; income surpassing agricultural, 1, 77–78; local government entrepreneurship in, 2–3, 50, 78, 114, 123–27, 193; local officials' power strengthened by, 191–203; Maoist period precariousness of, 166n; meetings to develop, 124–25; output, 1, 65 fig. 7, 78n, 167–68; ownership forms (1978–1990), 62–65, 63 fig. 5; ownership forms (1990s), 80–94, 98–99; plans and targets, 49, 75, 115, 116–17, 135–36, 138; political constraints, 59–61, 73–80; rapid growth, 2–3, 5, 15, 19, 95–138, 191, 192; regional differences, 61–62; retrenchment (1988–89), 80, 129, 162, 166–90, 198; successful, 58, 76, 78, 80, 91–93, 113–15, 117, 200; variation and evolution in, 58–94. *See also* collective ownership; contracting; enterprises; labor; management; private ownership; profits

Russia, 2, 57, 192, 198, 201; depoliticization of enterprises, 56; Gorbachev reforms, 196; lack of institutional support, 4; privatization, 10; and revenue sharing, 30, 51; strong ministerial system, 96

sales: consignment selling (*daixiao*), 137; cooperatives, 176; of enterprises, 88, 89, 91, 92, 128; management fee based on, 46; right to sell property, 18, 19, 24n

sales taxes, 35–36, 55, 171; circulation taxes (*liuzhuan shui*), 35–36, 76, 171; house, 144n; temporary traders,' 186

Sartori, Giovanni, 12n

"satisficing," 60, 89

savings: bank deposits of, 174, 175, 177, 180; bonds, 73; credit cooperative funds from, 121; finance bureau extra-budgetary funds, 165; nonbank capital raised from, 188–89; peasant (1979–1994), 4, 67, 68 fig. 8, 87

savings and loan cooperatives, 122, 183, 188

Schmitter, Philippe, 11, 13

schools, village-funded, 79–80

Schurmann, Franz, 197

science and technology commissions, county, 101 table 4, 186–87

Scott, James, 18

self-examination (sicha), 150

Selznick, Philip, 197n

services, local: collective profits underwriting, 25, 78, 79–80, 98, 202; county, 104; in local fixed expenditures, 30, 34; local government to enterprises, 97; retained enterprise funds, 43

Shaanxi: fiscal reform impacts, 23n; increased revenue growth, 31n, 38n

Shandong: auctioning of enterprises, 88; diverse revenue arrangements, 31; interviewing in, 207; job bonding, 72n, 188; leasing, 84; management fee, 46n; number of township-level enterprises, 108n; party secretary term, 103–4; private sector, 74, 85–86, 130n, 186n; retirement pay, 76n; during retrenchment (1988–89), 169–70, 172; savings plans, 73n; village factory manager's salary, 26

Shanghai: levies, 46n; technical assistance in, 132; township/village enterprise assets, 69–70n

shareholding (gufenzhi), 73, 81, 84–85, 93; cooperatives, 73, 81, 84–85, 93, 188; in credit cooperatives, 120n

Shenyang: specialized farm households, 79; village-funded education, 80

Sichuan: industrial cooperative relationships, 117; interviews in, 207; management fee, 46n; peasant resistance, 200; private enterprise, 58n

Simon, Herbert, 60n; "satisficing," 60, 89

Skocpol, Theda, 196

"slack," 28, 56. See also residual

socialism: fiscal reform opposition, 30; gradual transition from, 94; grain as "key link," 59n; "plan ideological" systems, 7, 115–17; redistributive, 201–2; relational contracting in reforming,

136. See also central planning; collective ownership; communism

society: "civil," 199; "honeycomb" nature of rural, 199; reforms' success attributed to, 4; "societal takeover," 4, 199; statist view, 4, 9

Solinger, Dorothy, 135–36

Songjiang, township/village enterprise assets, 69–70n

Soviet Union. See Russia

spending. See expenditures

Stalin, Joseph, 5

standards of living: rural industry affecting, 61. See also income; poverty

state: credit allocations targeting growth, 119–22; credit cooperatives, 132; development led by, 3–10, 14–15, 89, 93–99, 113, 115, 137–38, 192–93; investment (1949–1978), 69n; monopoly, 7; privatization sponsored by, 88, 134; revenue quotas, 18, 53; "strong," 9; taxes paid to, 23–24, 27, 36–47; vertically integrated, 11–12, 28, 141, 199. See also bureaucracy; Chinese Communist Party; government; institutions; Leninist systems; Maoist period; state corporatism; state ownership

State Administration for Industry and Commerce, 130–31

state corporatism: defined, 13. See also local state corporatism

State Council (Guowuyuan), 29n, 121, 147, 157, 163, 164n

state ownership (quanmin suoyou), 2, 4, 18, 195; audited, 147; and bank choices, 177; and budget constraints, 168; competing with rural industry, 166; labor (1952–1986), 1–2; revenues, 34–35; symbiotic relationship with private sector, 133–37, 202–3; and underpayment of taxes, 155

State Planning Commission, 116n

State Statistical Bureau, 77n

"statist" view, 4, 9

Stepan, Alfred, 13n

stockpiling, during retrenchment (1988–89), 169–70

subsidies: for agriculture, 21–23, 78–79; from collective profits, 78, 79–80, 98; fixed, 30–34; selectively targeted, 118–19; tax reforms (1994) and, 54, 55; to townships, 108; village officials not receiving, 109; village profits for, 27n, 79–80. See also budget allocations to local governments; payments

surcharges, 23, 38; ad hoc, 21, 46, 47,

71; on residual, 53; *tiliu,* 21, 23n, 45, 79, 146, 151n. *See also* fees; taxes
surplus, 27; income, 18, 20; labor, 4; revenue, 6, 10, 14, 19, 25, 28–52. *See also* profits; residual
symbiotic relationship, private-collective-state, 133–37, 202–3

tax bureaus, 101n, 144–51, 155, 167; county, 100 table 4, 106–7, 144–48, 153, 185–86; North China County loans, 185 table 8; township, 100 table 4, 144–45, 147, 150
taxes: agricultural, 20, 41, 45, 55–56, 75n, 78–79, 144n; agriculture and industry revenue (1952–1994), 41 fig. 3; bonus (*jiangjin shui*), 53; categories, 217 table 13; circulation (*liuzhuan shui*), 35–36, 76, 171; on collective ownership, 35–47; construction, 21, 55; consumption (*xiaofei shui*), 54; contractor paying, 23–24; county, 55, 75–76, 89, 106; direct, 52–56; enterprise income (*qiye suode shui*), 35–47, 55, 76, 149, 151, 167, 172, 181; exemptions, 36–37, 133; failure to pay (*loushui*)/evasion/fraud, 140, 148, 154; individual income (*geren suode shui*), 55; industrial commercial (*gongshang shui*), 34, 35–36, 37, 38, 41, 76, 144n, 171–72; intentional underpayment (*loushui*), 154; investigating/monitoring, 140, 146–48; limited indirect, 52–56; loan payoffs before tax assessment (*shuiqian huankuan*), 106–7; local, 38, 44–45; minimal compliance, 140, 160; orchard and forest products, 144n; overreporting, 156; preferential breaks, 36–47, 118, 133, 167n, 180; on private enterprises, 45, 74, 89, 133, 144n, 186; product (*chanpin*), 35, 156–57, 171; property (*fangchan shui*), 55; reforms (1994), 54–56, 140, 162–63, 190, 194; during retrenchment (1988–89), 167, 171–72; self-finance basic construction fund (*zichou jiben jianshe jijin*), 53; slaughter, 55; state, 23–24, 27, 36–47; state energy transport key projects fund (*guojia nengyuan jiaotong zhongdian jianshe jijin*), 53; "tax for profit" (*ligaishui*), 34–35, 43; township, 35–36, 54, 74, 107; turnover/business (*yingye*), 35; underpayment, 150, 151, 154, 155; urban maintenance and construction (*chengshi jianshe shui*), 55; value-added (*zengzhi shui*), 35–36, 54; village, 20, 21, 27, 35–36, 42, 112; wage adjustment (*gongzi tiaojie shui*), 53. *See also* revenues; sales taxes
technology: assistance with, 115, 126, 127, 132–34; bureaucracy as source of, 123–27, 132–34; county science and technology commissions, 101 table 4, 186–87; county technology development fund (*keji fazhan jijin*), 186n; extrabudgetary funds for, 163; information, 123–27, 132–34; standards rising, 80–81
Tiananmen, 169n
Tianjin: factory tours for customers and investors, 117; interviews in/outside, 207; Planning Commission, 116n; tax cuts in county outside, 37, 38
tiliu, 21, 23n, 45, 79, 146, 151n
Tong, James, 51n, 52n
totalitarianism, 197
tours, enterprise, for customers and investors, 117
township, 45; as agent for county, 107; auctioning of enterprises, 88, 91, bad debt, 90; banks, 109, 120–21, 122; cadre power, 76; collective funds, 70–71, 187–89; collective ownership, 27–47, 58–80, 88–93, 170–72, 176, 181, 201, 202; contracting, 74; credit associations (*jijinhui*), 131–32; credit/savings and loan cooperatives, 109, 120–21, 122, 132, 182–84; dominance of publicly owned vs. private enterprises, 4; economic commission, 46–47, 72, 75, 90, 97n, 100 table 4, 108–9, 112n, 116, 121, 125, 147, 158, 181; economic work, 105 table 5, 108–9; extrabudgetary revenues, 45–46, 53, 108; finance bureau, 50, 100 table 4, 109, 147; financial service center (*jinrong fuwu suo*), 182–83; financial service center management committee (*jinrong fuwu suo guanli weiyuan hui*), 183; independence, 102n; industrial-commercial management office, 49–50, 100 table 4, 129, 147; industrial profits paid to, 25n; leadership, 108–9; leasing, 84; local state corporatism, 96–115, 100–101 table 4; meetings, 124–25; number of enterprises, 67n, 108n; party secretary, 100 table 4, 108, 114; vs. private enterprises, 74; private enterprise suborganizations, 130; and rapid development, 23, 96, 108; as regional headquarters, 107–9; residual, 45–47, 53; resources, 67, 69, 70–73, 109, 110–11 table 6, 114–

township (*continued*)
  15, 182–83, 187–89; retrenchment
  (1988–89) and, 168, 169–72, 182–
  84, 187–89; revenues, 23, 27–53, 98,
  108; successfully industrializing, 58,
  80; taxes, 35–36, 54, 74, 107; tax
  office, 100 table 4, 144–45, 147, 150;
  township head (*xiang [zhen] zhang*),
  100 table 4, 108, 120–21n, 125;
  "township leading group" (*xiang lingdao xiaozu*), 147; *xiangzhen qiye* ownership by, 62; *zhen* qualification, 108n.
  See also communes
trade associations, 134; All-China Federation of Industry and Commerce
  (*quanguo gongshang lianhui*), 129n;
  Individual Entrepreneurs Association
  (*geti xiehui*), 43, 129–31, 137; professional trade groups (*hangye xiaozu*),
  130

United States: Internal Revenue Service
  employees, 144; security checks on
  government employees, 143n
use rights, 48–50

value-added taxes (*zengzhi shui*), 35–36,
  54
vertical (*tiao*) integration, 11–12, 28,
  141, 199
Village Organic Law, 201n
villages: as agents for county and township, 109; auctioning of enterprises,
  88, 91, 92; bad debt, 90, 169–70; as
  brigades, 19; cadre power, 76, 112–
  15; collective funds, 70–71, 187–89;
  collective ownership, 50, 58–80, 88–
  93, 112, 170–72, 176, 200, 201–2;
  committee (*cunmin weiyuan hui*), 100
  table 4, 112; as companies, 109–15;
  contracting, 23–27, 74; corporatization of enterprises, 85, 93; corruption,
  157–59; *cunban qiye* ownership by,
  112; decollectivization and loss of
  income to governments of, 19–27;
  dominance of publicly owned vs. private enterprises, 4; elections, 112,
  201n; enterprise management committee, 26n, 100 table 4, 102, 113, 142;
  fees, 45, 112n, 133; grain production
  constraints on, 59–60; group head (*zu
  zhang*), 137; leadership, 112–15, 201;
  leasing, 84; local state corporatism,
  96–115, 100–101 table 4; management rights, 24–25; meetings, 124–25;
  model status, 114, 126–27; number

of enterprises (1980s), 67n; officials'
  salaries, 50; party cell (*dangzhibu*),
  129; party secretary, 100 table 4, 102,
  112–14, 142, 157–58, 187–88, 209;
  profits funding community services,
  25, 79–80; and rapid development, 5,
  96, 108, 112; residual rights, 23–27,
  98, 112; resources, 67, 69, 70–73,
  110–11 table 6, 113, 114–15, 187–
  89; retrenchment (1988–89) and,
  168, 169–72, 182–84, 187–89; self-
  reliance of, 102n, 114–15; successfully
  industrializing, 58, 76, 78, 80, 91–93,
  113–15, 124, 200; taxes, 20, 21, 27,
  35–36, 42, 112; *tiliu* (retained funds),
  21, 23n, 45, 79, 146, 151n; village
  committee chairman (*cunmin weiyuan
  hui zhuren*), 100 table 4, 112; village
  head (*cun zhang*), 112, 113; *xiangzhen
  qiye* ownership by, 62. *See also* brigades; local government; peasants
Vogel, Ezra, 120n, 141n

wages. *See* income
Wank, David, 195
Weingast, Barry, 10, 197n
welfare. *See* services, local
Wenzhou: "fake collectives," 63, 133;
  nonbank capital sources, 183–84; private enterprise, 58, 63–64, 67–70, 85,
  133, 134; resources, 87; township/
  village enterprise assets, 70n
Whiting, Susan, 69–70n
Williamson, Oliver, 136
within-budget funds (*yusuannei zijin*),
  38–42, 39 table 2, 45, 54, 144, 190.
  See also sales taxes
Wong, Christine, 31n, 77n
workers. *See* labor
World Bank: on closures of "high polluters," 170n; on extrabudgetary revenues, 43n; on nonagricultural rural
  labor force, 2n; and redistributive corporatism, 79; on revenue from profits
  from state-owned enterprises, 34n; on
  tax rates, 37; on village self-raised
  funds, 187
Wuxi: labor force discipline, 92; Light
  Industrial Research Institute, 126;
  private enterprise, 85; rural industry
  supporting farming, 21–22; worker
  benefits, 76n

xiangzhen qiye, 62. *See also* rural industry
Xu, Chenggang, 102n

Yang, Dali, 172n
Yan Yunxiang, 76n
Yueqing, township/village enterprise
    assets, 70n
Yunnan, local officials hiding enterprises,
    34n
Yu Zuomin, 50, 114

Zhejiang: overseas resources, 69; private
    enterprises, 86n; tax cuts, 37
Zhu Rongji, 155, 172n
Zouping, number of township-level enter-
    prises, 108n
Zweig, David, 5n, 88n
Zysman, John, 14

Compositor: G&S Typesetters, Inc.
      Text: 10/13 Sabon
   Display: Sabon
   Printer: Haddon Craftsmen
    Binder: Haddon Craftsmen